Just Glow

A Memoir

Augusto C. Cespedes, Jr.

Copyright © 2024 by Augusto C. Cespedes, Jr.

All rights reserved.

eBook ISBN: 979-8-9907804-0-8

Paperback ISBN: 979-8-9907804-1-5

Hardcover ISBN: 979-8-9907804-2-2

This memoir is a work of non-fiction based on the author's experiences. However, certain names, identifying characteristics, and locations have been changed to protect the privacy of individuals. Additionally, some scenes have been dramatized or exaggerated for literary effect and to emphasize the themes of the narrative.

No part of this book may be reproduced in any form or by any electronic or mechanical means, including information storage and retrieval systems, without written permission from the author or publisher, except for the use of brief quotations in a book review.

If you would like to use material from this book, prior written permission must be obtained by contacting the publisher at:

justglowamemoir@gmail.com

First edition: August 2024

Formatting by Laura Martinez, owner of The Indie Author's Advocate, LLC.

Cover Design by Tracey C. Witter and The Indie Author's Advocate, LLC

Contents

Remembrance Page	vii
Preface	ix
Prologue	1
1. IF I ONLY KNEW	3
2. ROOTS	11
3. UNDER THE INFLUENCE	21
4. WAKE UP!	31
5. IRONING IN THE DARK	43
6. 808	57
February 2004	57
May 2004	60
FMSS Graduation, November, 2004	67
Paradise	72
Welcome	79
7. DOLLY	85
Lucky Enough	93
April 2005	105
8. HOTTER THAN HELL	111
Afghanistan 2005	121
Operation Red Wings	127
Day One, The Climb	130
July 4th, 2005	141
Day Two	143
The Drop	151
The Descent	156
The DVD	159
Operation فيل (Pil)	175
Flying in the Dark	187
First	212
The Last Days	218

9. THE PRESENCE OF GOD	223
NYE, 1994	227
2001	231
February 2006, Six months before Iraq	237
Baptized	239
August 2006, Thirty days before Iraq	242
10. JUST KIDS	247
March 2006	247
Daily Routines	260
To the Bone	262
Perfect Vision	268
Coffee	279
November 21st, 2006	300
The Hawaiian Night	318
11. VALENTINE'S DAY	335
The One from Ohio	340
Day One	345
12. SHATTERED	355
Day Two	363
Aloha	366
The Room	367
Fire Eyes	370
Frocks	380
13. THE HOUSE ON LITTLE CYPRESS	385
14. A HUI HOU	397
15. IN REVERIE	409
16. KNOWING	415
Epilogue	419
Acknowledgments	427

For the boys who never made it home.

Remembrance Page

"I lift up my eyes to the mountains." Psalm 121

Jacy, graphite sketch, 2020

Preface

Just Glow is a profoundly impactful memoir that provides readers with an unfiltered look at the turmoil and devastation of war, even long after the immediate aftermath has faded.

Augusto has crafted a narrative that reveals some of the most heartrending experiences in human existence. Through the perspective of a young Navy corpsman, he takes us back to the Middle Eastern conflicts, allowing us to witness the tragedy of war and to explore the complex emotions tied to the loss of life.

This memoir also delves into the enduring grief that accompanies the loss of comrades and how that sorrow permeates the lives of those who still remain.

While many stories about Afghanistan and Iraq have been shared, few come from someone who experienced it firsthand. Augusto intricately details the struggles and heartbreak that contributed to the loss of countless lives, while also shedding light on the hope for a deeper understanding of what was ultimately sacrificed.

Preface

Within these pages, you'll discover a testament to the resilience and strength of the human spirit in the face of unimaginable challenges.

Just Glow, A Memoir is an essential read for anyone seeking insight into the realities of the protracted conflicts in the Middle East.

His narrative places you in the midst of the chaos, allowing you to experience the world through his eyes.

Prologue

I hate the fact that you took the photo.

That you were the one who volunteered.

You started to walk towards the middle of the courtyard, where the trucks usually parked.

"Let's find someone to take the picture," someone suggested. But no one was around.

"It's fiiiiine," you'd sarcastically replied, "we've gotta step off soon." You already had your backpack on and your headset in place.

But you were the one who always took the pictures.

"Memories, guys! Memories!" You'd always say, and we'd all just roll our eyes.

I hate that you didn't listen to any of us but... that was you. You were undeniably selfless, cared too much about us and only wanted all of us to be happy.

Augusto C. Cespedes, Jr.

"Move," a Senior had said jokingly but with a straight face, "that's my spot."

"Man, I've literally been sitting here for the past two minutes!"

It took forever to get everyone to sit but I still noticed you, patiently standing there in the middle of the courtyard with the camera in your hand.

You just kept smiling at us, head tilted to the side because the sun was in your eyes and probably laughing in your head at how we were so much like a dysfunctional family.

"Will everyone just face forward so we can step off?!!" Corporal yelled out, leaning his head out so everyone can hear him.

I remember thinking, "Only a few more weeks until we're home."

And just like that, you took the picture.

I hate the fact that you were the one who took it.

Chapter 1
If I Only Knew

"What do you want to do with this?" my mom asked, pointing to the left side of my closet.

Plastic hangers that wore old clothes strung across a white metal pole in the small space. Cardboard boxes that were written on with poor penmanship and milk crates of what accumulated over the years piled high up against its walls. Over the years, my mom had always attempted to organize my closet.

And this time, behind the drapes of clothes that drew over the pile of boxes, she pointed to Matt's med pack. A dusty, black bag that had been untouched since 2007.

My closet was filled with things from when I was a kid to the day I left for Iraq. Thick books with sleeves of sports cards. Or old textbooks my sister and I had forgotten to turn in. Or banners and posters that were held up for when I returned from bootcamp or Afghanistan.

And there were some things that I kept more exposed

than others, ones that I was proud of. Ones that, when I opened the closet, I was glad to see.

A gigantic, clear, plastic cheese curl container that was only stuffed with notes from friends that were shared in between classes. Or my favorite gold-plated trophy, when we won the Labor Day Cup in 1998 in penalty kicks and with pure joy, piled on each other while the photographers from the local newspaper snapped pictures of us.

But what's kind of funny is, well, my mom always asked the same question every time I was home.

"What do you want to do with your stuff?"

And I always said the same thing.

"Ya, I'll look through it."

Over the years, it became so difficult to rummage through it all and sort out what I didn't want. And honestly, I wish I could just keep it all. In the closet. It was comforting to know that every item was at a standstill. Not moving. Not collecting dust. With it all neatly packed, I felt like it was safe.

But every time I came home, I had to open the closet and look at the med pack. Like pushing through heavy vines in a jungle, I would push aside the hangers of clothes and just stare at it. Its imperfections still in existence. The dust of the Haditha Triad remained lingering on its surface, even after all of those years. And every time I opened my closet and turned on the light, I couldn't help but look at it, and it always brought me back to that night.

Just Glow

I can see for miles from where I am, turning back every now and then to see how far I've gone, a long path of sand pressed footprints. The sun was radiating off of my back and the sound of the seagulls were still heard even through the crashing of waves. There was a distinct rhythm of how the ocean hit the sand at my feet, as if I could tell when the next time it'd hit. The summer air, crisp and inviting, had brushed a cool breeze across my face. The sound of waves drowned out the crowd on the beach and for once, I felt at peace. I thought I was alone but suddenly felt a tap on my shoulder.

I knew I didn't walk that far. I didn't turn around but as the tapping continued, I finally did.

"Hey Cespedes, are you awake?" he whispered. It was HM1 Smith, another Corpsman in the company. Dreaming was a privilege while on deployment. When you're in a living Hell, and you're able to dream, it's comforting to know you can still have good nights.

"Hey," I said, rubbing my eyes. "What's up…?" I was barely awake.

"I don't know how to say this, but I wanted to tell you as soon as I heard because I know you and him were very close…" even with the snoring of the Marines, I could hear his voice start to crack.

My heart stopped but my mind suddenly started to race.

No.

Augusto C. Cespedes, Jr.

No.

Can't be.

I was awake now, and I was trying to figure out who he was talking about.

"Conte died this morning," he finally said. "His unit was hit by a roadside bomb." He put his hand on my shoulder, repositioning himself as he knelt in the dark. "From the report, it sounded like it was instant."

My world stopped. I took a deep breath and didn't let it out, causing a memory to come into full view.

Conte used to drive us through Kamehameha Highway, and he usually did it on Sundays. Just to drive. There was something about driving aimlessly in Hawaii, especially when it was raining. It was an absolute privilege to have a vehicle while in the military and being in Hawaii at that.

Every time we drove down the highway, I felt free. I felt like nothing else mattered. Every sorrow, pain and worry was on hold for those few minutes. The highway was surrounded by vast mountains and once in a while, you'd catch glimpses of just how small you were. When it rained, the mountains produced natural waterfalls that could be seen from the highway. It reminded us how fragile and precious our life was.

I'd never experience those moments with Matt ever again and that hurt — it cut deep.

"Cespedes… say something," HM1 said.

Just Glow

"Just need to take a minute," I replied. I felt myself clearing my throat, trying to act "cool" about it. Like it was something that could just be cleared out. But as I took a few more breaths, I knew it was more than I would've been able to handle just lying there.

I walked outside so the Marines didn't see me bothered. I tried to catch my breath, but I couldn't stop. I couldn't focus on one memory of Conte, and then I started to imagine what he was thinking before he died.

All of a sudden, I let it all out.

I covered my mouth as the emotions just completely engulfed me. I couldn't catch my breath as I started to weep, tasting the salt of my tears. At that moment, I realized what hurt the most.

"Doc," *a Junior Marine said to me, placing his hand on my shoulder. He stopped me from walking outside to the trucks.*

"I saw your buddy Conte in one of the shops," he continued to say, munching on a stick of strawberry licorice like a child at a Halloween party.

I already had one foot out the door, eager to go back to our base in Haqlaniyah.

Waving my hand, I just said, "It's fine, I'll see him when we're back in Hawaii." I didn't think anything of it.

The thought of it stabbed into me and twisted, turning its rusty blade into the deep layers of my emotional flesh.

I missed the opportunity to see him. I took for granted

that moment thinking I'd see him in a few months. That we'd be back to what we always did during the weekends. Like going to our favorite skate spot on Ala Moana Boulevard to work on the tricks that we could never get right.

The sounds of dogs barking in the distance echoed as I started walking towards the barrier fence.

I couldn't focus on one thing and felt in complete denial. I couldn't stop moving. I felt restless, shaking. I wanted to go to Conte and hold him. I wanted to take him out on the Kamehameha and just drive forever. The pain I was feeling didn't feel real. I was hoping HM1 was going to tell me "Hey, bad joke, I was kidding," but he never came back.

I stood there in the dark in complete silence but could feel the blood in my head increase, pounding.

Suddenly, a muffled voice began to speak that increased in clarity.

"Jay…"

"Jay…?"

It was my mom.

I opened my eyes, and I noticed my tears had dripped on the med pack, exposing the black material under the caked-on dust.

"Ya," I said, clearing my throat as I wiped my eyes. "I will look through this stuff."

Just Glow

I looked up and saw my old Navy Peacoat and a poster reading "Welcome Home, Hero!" next to it. I noticed a small box labeled "Early Days." I smiled and opened it. The pictures quickly created an instant nostalgia, and I immediately noticed the top picture. It was of me in front of the white truck that I used to drive, and I was standing on my old driveway. The expression on my face in the picture made me chuckle, but a sadness waved over me. I was in my dress whites, a term for one of the Navy uniforms.

As I looked at the picture, I remember feeling unsure.

"Cheeeeese!" my sister said as she was taking a picture with the disposable camera. Bootcamp was an experience. And I'm not talking about the physical aspect of it. For someone who never went away to camp as a kid, it was an eye opener, to say the least. If I was sad, I couldn't call my friends to vent to them. If I was having a bad dream, I couldn't just walk over to my sister's room and sleep on her floor. For the first time in my life, I experienced everything alone. And that was big for me. I smirked at the camera, but it wasn't for intentions of being silly. "Really dude?" my sister said.

I held the picture in my hands and just slowly shook my head.

If I only knew.

Augusto C. Cespedes, Jr.

Chapter 2
Roots

I wouldn't say I wasn't a troubled kid. I wasn't into drugs or anything crazy, but I have no legitimate reason to tell you why I was other than I had let music take over my life. It was 2001 and I had let it engulf me. It was all about the bands we had listened to; The Get Up Kids, The Early November, New Found Glory, The Starting Line. And I loved it so much that I wasn't interested in anything else. Sounds stupid, but it's true. It distracted me from the important things. Applying to colleges. Studying for the SATs. Ya know, basically my future. And it's not that I was hanging out with the wrong group, no, not at all. They were actually the ones who applied to college.

Anytime I heard about their progress of applying or even talking about colleges, I'd rationalize my thought. "I'll just go to community college. Nothing wrong with that."

In our small group of friends, we felt invincible. Whenever we went out, we always had the best music that started the night. Something that made us laugh, made us feel invincible, even if it was just for a few seconds.

Augusto C. Cespedes, Jr.

Saves the Day's "Shoulder to the Wheel."

It started with the microphone giving off major feedback, and suddenly, a guitar wailed with the snare kicking in hot.

The singer began to sing about a "Dave," which was David's cue to do whatever he felt to make us laugh.

He scrunched his face in odd ways but somehow kept his eyes on the road or pointed back to himself like it was the first time he ever heard the song.

We had the best nights, and it was mostly because of our choice in music. The lyrics of the songs we listened to spoke to us. All of us.

David's car was a beat up, tan colored 92' Explorer with the passenger internal door handle hanging on for dear life and only came off if you didn't have your hand in an awkward position.

And once the school bell sounded off at 2:30PM, the time was ours.

During one summer, we created a pop punk band on the fly and, sure, our first "show" was in David's living room playing the same song over and over in front of 20 people but hey, ya have to start somewhere. And surely, we loved it. I loved making music from nothing, sitting in Riley's room for hours on end writing songs for our upcoming shows knowing we had class the next day. At that time, the pop punk and emo scene was HUGE. Crowds of kids from different schools would come together to listen to bands at a place called Java Jazz, a coffee shop in the daytime and a live music venue at night. No alcohol, no drugs, no violence; just sweaty kids, music and coffee.

Just Glow

. . .

It was closing in on the end of our last summer together and we were all trying to hang out on the last days of everyone in town before college. But of course, I was the only one sticking around. We were browsing in Hollister at good ol' Woodlands Mall. Ahh, the smell of fresh cut wood and cologne. But it was the store's lack of light in its attempt to mimic an island in the setting sun that just wasn't doing it for me.

"Dang, they spray waaaaay too much cologne in this place," I laughed to myself. I was seventeen. Self-absorbed. Naive. I started to walk out and then heard a voice.

"How are you doing, Young Man?" The tone was deep, stern, like he knew me, and he meant business.

I looked up and it was an African American man, six feet tall, bald and with a chiseled face, dressed in a military uniform with his badge saying "Gerald, Army Recruiter."

"Uhh, good? How are you?" I asked, following along. I started to touch the apparel at the front of the store, to look like I wasn't done browsing so maybe he'd go away.

"Good, good, can't complain. Thanks for asking. What brings you into this store? Are you looking for new clothes? Summer is almost over, you know." His voice didn't change. It was low, very proper, almost like those radio commercials for lawyers.

"Umm, ya, just lookin'. My friends are the ones who are looking. I'm just tagging along."

"Right, of course. Say, did you just graduate high school?"

I stopped touching the apparel.

"Yes…"

"What's the future looking like for you?"

A part of me knew where this was going. So, I lied. At first, I was offended. His question hit the mark. It's almost as if he knew exactly how I was feeling, grabbed the question out of my own head and put it out on the table for me to hear it from someone else. What was the future looking like for me? I had no idea.

"Haha, just trying to enjoy the summer before going away to college," I wasn't sure what the future was holding for me. I just wanted to be looked at as a normal high

Just Glow

school graduate going away to college, but I was far from normal.

"Ahhh, yes. Good for you, and congratulations. If you can't tell, I work for the Army and we are looking for young men just like you. We have incredible benefits, could pay for your tuition and give you a career you would never forget."

"Say," he continued. "Do you work out? You look muscular."

Is this dude serious?

I haven't worked out in months. I definitely wasn't watching what I was eating. My mom had to go to a couple different stores to find pants big enough for me for prom.

"Haha, yeah…" I lied again.

"Yea, you look like you do. We could definitely use strong guys like you," he continued to say.

Man, this guy is good, I thought. I probably couldn't bench 110 lbs. at that point, but I stood a little taller, feeling myself flex mid conversation.

"Haha, oh ya?"

"Here's my card, Young Man. Name's Gerald Thomas, Sergeant of the Army. Think about it. I'd love to speak with you."

His handshake was firm, almost crushing mine. The gleam in his eye and smile was intimidating but almost robotic, like he'd done it a million times.

"Ok, thanks." He walked away and coincidentally, one of my friends came up to me.

"Who was that?" They asked.

"Some recruiter is trying to get me to go into the Army," I said. Not true at all, but I wanted to feel important. I had no future plans so it was the most I could do to make it seem like I had something in line.

"Damn dude," one of them said. They all started to leave the store and I turned to see where the recruiter went. He was faced towards a shop window, eyes forward and fixing his uniform.

My friends and I all started walking, cracking the usual inside jokes we all knew and commenting on things as we all walked as a group. As for me, I was thinking about what the recruiter had said.

"...and give you a career you'd never forget."

When I got home, I immediately had the urge to tell my parents.

"So you'll never guess what happened to me at the mall," I started to say, rushing in as my parents were sitting at the kitchen table. My mom was working on a Sudoku puzzle and my dad was watching tv.

My parents and I were not close. And when I say not close, I mean I couldn't go up to them and tell them how I was feeling or else they'd cast judgment or just say, "you'll be fine." That's how Filipino parents were, or at least that's how

Just Glow

I felt about mine. They truly meant well, but they definitely did not have an ear for listening. I was also in my own world so I can't imagine how my parents dealt with me.

"This recruiter was asking me if I wanted to join the Army," I said. They stopped what they were doing. I remembered about the business card, so I reached into my pocket and placed the card on the table.

"Army?" My mom questioned, sliding the card to herself. "...Dad?" my mom looked at him.

My Dad was in the Navy, and retired when I was 15. He and his brother joined when they got out of high school, and ultimately that's how he met my mom. When I was growing up, I of course admired my dad being in the Navy, but as I got older and was asked if I'd ever join, I always had the same answer.

"NOPE! Not for me," I'd say, not hesitant in my response. And that went on for years.

We used to travel with him when he'd have temporary assignments in the country, like California and South Carolina, and as a kid, I thought it was fun because it was a different pace from being at home.

"Alright guys, let's go get dinner," my parents would say, driving to the local Piggly Wiggly in South Carolina. We would walk up and down the aisles and eventually pick out the Kids Cuisines we wanted (the decision was based on what the treat was). I thought it was great. We stayed at the Navy Lodge, which was a hotel for service members, and my sister and I easily found things to do. We'd find the closest playground, run around the hotel floors playing tag, and try to meet other kids. Looking back now, I probably would've hated my parents for making us stay in and near the hotel day after day. Oh, and one other thing... we DROVE there.

Spotify and Google Maps weren't created for another, oh, 10-15 years. We used ridiculously big maps that took over two seats and had cassette tapes for music that had to be switched over for the next tracks; AND HAD TO BE REWOUND. Mind blown.

Imagine driving from Houston to Charleston in an SUV packed for four for a week or two, and your sister's current obsession of Ace of Base's "I Saw the Sign." Torture....rewinding Torture.

My sister and I did enjoy it when my dad took us on the Navy ships to show us what it was like to live like a sailor. If you've never been on a Navy ship, the smell is something you will never forget, and the older the ship, the worse the smell. It's basically salt water, rust, grease, and oil that lingers in the stagnant air.

"Wow, that is pretty cool," I'd say.

Times were different back then. I was a small kid and as

Just Glow

I grew older, the idea of going into the military grew further from me. I don't have an exact reason, but I think it's because I was into so much music at the age of 11, I knew the military wasn't for me. I felt like I was going to be limited in the life that I thought I'd want to live.

But there was something rather odd that occurred that day in Hollister. When the recruiter looked me in the eyes and asked me if I had a future, it made me ask myself, "Do I?" I'm not quite sure if I had an answer.

"Jay," my dad shook his head. "Just go to school. Don't go into the Army. You'll end up going to war."

I thought about that for a second and all it took was a second for me to shake it off. I couldn't imagine myself on a battlefield. Ever.

Chapter 3
Under the Influence

When my sister and I were in grade school, my mom's coworker would sometimes take us to school, and she had two grown kids who were looking to get rid of some books. We would race each other up the wooden stairs to the attic and be amazed by the boxes of books they had. I, of course, was interested in Encyclopedia Brown, but we also found books called "Choose Your Own Adventure." It was a series of books that had choices for the reader and different outcomes based on that choice. My sister had to help me with some of the bigger words.

"Oh man, I died!" My sister would yell out, slamming the book shut. She'd throw it over her shoulder and then rummage for the next book.

When my group of friends left for college, I didn't have trouble finding a few friends to hang out with, but it definitely wasn't the same. It wasn't the wholesome, heartwarming feeling when all of us were in high school. There were no more hot tub nights, hangouts that lasted all hours of the night or volleyball games after school. And because of that, we partied. Hard.

Every weekend, there was somewhere to go have fun and we all knew the good spots. People's houses, basements, open fields. You name it, we were there. And because we were underage, it had to be those places. Houses were packed with unfamiliar people but hey, it was free booze, and it was the weekend.

"Man, you gotta come out to this house tonight," my friend would say. "Parents are away, keg's in the tub and free food."

"Definitely! I'll try and be there," I'd reply. Sure, it sounded fun (who turns down free food?) and it was fun for some time, but weekend after weekend, it got old... quick. I wasn't used to it. It was October 2003, and I was partying for two full months. Something had to give.

One night at a house party, people were everywhere; from the lawn to the back of the house. I could barely walk in, and the stench was a mix of marijuana and booze. I had opened the door, and I could barely see two feet in front of me.

"What's up, Bro???!!!" Stumbling over to me, one of my friends greeted me with glazed over eyes and a smile that looked tired. Trash was everywhere, people stood in every space of the rooms and the sound of the music was deafening.

"Hey man, great party!" I yelled. I had to shout because the pulsating bass of the song was rattling the walls.

I got myself a drink in the kitchen and found a spot to

stand in the living room. There were two people sitting on the couch, lighting up a bong to get high.

"What up dude? You ever try this?" they asked. They spoke slow, sounding like they were affected by the drug.

"Oh yea, plenty of times," I lied. I'd had a few hits of a joint, but not from a bong.

"Well, you're up bro!" they both shouted.

Damnit. Not this early in the night. People started rooting for me to take a hit.

I put the bong up to my mouth, inhaled the smoke, waited several seconds and - GONE. I was in such a trance that things felt like they were upside down. I couldn't speak. I was so affected by the drug, I had no control over my voice.

"Dude, are you okay???" one guy asked, coughing from the smoke.

I just mumbled. I couldn't get the words out. I needed to sit down so I sat on the edge of the couch that was free.

It seemed like I was on the couch for hours. I started to focus on the ceiling fan and tried to count how many times the blades spun around. I lost count at 20 so I just stared blankly across the room.

I couldn't move but I noticed a girl laying on the couch, too high or drunk to get up. She tried to use her arms to prop herself up, but it was like her head was weighing her down. She was talking to herself, fighting the effects of whatever she was on. No one even seemed to notice but me.

Is this what I want to be?

I sat there and watched her struggle. Now, I can't explain exactly why I asked myself that question in that exact moment, but I think deep down, I was concerned for her. And thinking about her forced me to reevaluate my current situation; high but starving for something else. Something better. Hopeful that something will change my situation.

As the weeks continued, my life was purely at a standstill. I was barely home, and when I was home, I was asleep. I worked as an overnight shelf stocker at a local grocery store and the hours were difficult to adapt to; 10 p.m. to 6 a.m. I tried to take a few college courses just to get myself started but nope—didn't work out. I would actually skip school because I was either too tired or didn't care. My friend would actually let me sleep in his room at the top bunk during the day after my shift because I wanted my parents to think I was in class. Some days I'd wake up and it would be 5-6 p.m. at his house.

I'd been asleep since 9 a.m., and he'd already ate dinner with his family, and he'd be playing video games in his room. His parents either didn't care that I was sleeping all day in his room, or they had no clue.

"Oh, COME ON!!" he'd yell out, while his fingers were crunching on the game controller, the sound of Socom quietly played through the tv. Him pressing on the buttons was actually louder than the tv.

Just Glow

Rolling over, I checked my watch. 5:58 p.m.

"Geezus, I was asleep that long??" I said, turning over in the bed. I was still in my work clothes from my overnight shift.

"Hahaha, dude that's three days in a row. Work that crappy, huh?" He laughed. Easy for him to say; he had an easy job. He worked at the local Walmart as a cashier, and very seldom.

We spent our days doing useless things to just pass the time. On my days off, I couldn't get my schedule to normalize so I'd sleep all day and go out at night. Sometimes I'd stop by my work and my "of age" coworkers would buy me beer. I would then drive to pick my friend up and we'd drink in a field and talk about the future we could have, which ended up just making fun of each other.

"Maybe I should just kill myself," I would say, taking a swig of beer.

"Ok," he'd start to say, "then… can I have all your stuff?"

And we'd just start to laugh.

I mostly would go to places because people would just say, "Hey what are you doing? Come chill." *Got nothing better to do, sure.*

But there was one particular day that was the start of something. A spark.

I had found myself in the parking lot of the community

college. It wasn't my day to go to class, but my friends were getting out of class.

"Here ya go, but hold it in longer this time," another friend would say, handing me a joint. We were in his car, specks of ash, boxes of fast-food trash and other paraphernalia scattered on the floor.

As I let go of the smoke I held in for 20 seconds, it hit me almost immediately. The timeline of my day went through my head in rapid succession. Up. Breakfast, TV, chores, lunch, nap, argument with my parents, and now here. Repeat. I started to think about things the previous week that didn't matter in the present.

5:30 p.m. my watch said.

I then noticed myself outside, leaning against the back of his car. I felt myself swaying as I started to think about that girl at the party. How helpless she was. How there were so many people surrounding her, but no one even noticed how lifeless she was. I started to imagine myself going to college, my parents proud of me, getting a career and having a family; just how every parent would want their kids to be. As I just stood there in the parking lot, I wondered about the students passing by. *Did they have their life set? What struggles did they have? What was their goal?* This is what marijuana did to me. It made me think of things, and it dug deeper and deeper.

I looked at my watch again. 6:20 p.m. The sun was setting now, and hardly anyone was walking by.

"Alright dude, I gotta get goin'," I'd say, lying but just really worried about driving home when I was as baked as I

Just Glow

was. My knees were buckling from standing in the same spot for almost an hour, so it felt good to move.

I got into my truck and like muscle memory, I got myself out of the parking lot and on the road home.

As I was driving, I wasn't in control, but I was able to still do what I had to do to not kill myself. My mind was outside of my body. I felt like I wasn't driving. I looked up at the sunroof, and it was the passing of trees and a sky turning to dusk. How could I have looked up at the sunroof and not crash? My radio was hooked up to my MP3 player, shuffled on random and playing the most coincidental lyrics…

We don't know which way we're goin'

Don't know where we are,

Find a way out, find a way…

I was able to get home and lock myself in the bathroom. I looked at myself in the mirror, my ears pierced with plastic black earrings, and I saw myself smile, but I could feel that I wasn't happy. I tried to make it seem like I was, but I was too high to really know. I felt like I couldn't get myself out of what I dug myself in. I was stuck in a pit too deep to climb out of.

My thoughts went back to the girl struggling to get off the couch. I didn't want to end up that way. To be honest, it scared the living shit out of me. As I looked at myself in the mirror, I looked directly into my own eyes.

I need out.

Augusto C. Cespedes, Jr.

I was made to do more than what I was doing but I didn't know what.

Maybe the universe listened to me.

The phone on the wall rang on a weekday late afternoon. I was the only one home, with no plans and about to take a nap before my overnight shift.

"Three in a row. Let's go," I said, encouraging myself with whatever motivation I had in me for my shift. I walked over to pick up the phone.

"Hello?"

"Dude. It's me, Ant. Let's join the Navy."

I was completely taken aback by what he even said. "Is this a joke??" I asked. I was preparing myself for a nap, but now fully awake.

"What are you saying? You really going?"

"No, WE'RE going," he corrected.

"We?" I wanted to make sure I was hearing him right.

"Yup. We can go together," he said. He sounded determined, like he already made his decision for the both of us.

The thought of leaving what I only knew was scary. Frightening, actually. Leaving everything behind. Into a future of the unknown. I hadn't even flown by myself anywhere, let alone leave the state by myself.

My thoughts flashed back to those moments reading

Just Glow

"Choose Your Own Adventure." I would read the book only if the cover was appealing. "You're the Star of the Story!" it'd say on the cover, and my imagination would run wild as I thought about every possible scenario that would happen to me.

I couldn't rummage through the box for another book for an adventure. What would be my next choice if I chose to join? It wasn't like I could go back a page if I died.

This was it. What did I have to lose?

"Flight 6247 to O'Hare, now boarding..." the blaring of the intercom spoke as we stood in the main hall.

"Ok, that's you," one friend said, clearing her throat in an attempt to hold back her tears.

"You'll be fine, JR," the other reassured. She patted me on the shoulder, and then crossed her arms.

"Ya, no, I'm good." I looked up at the sign with the gate numbers and began to crumple my boarding pass. I tried to notice anyone else traveling alone, but I couldn't.

"Woah what are you doing? You need that ticket to get on board," she said, wiping her nose with an already used piece of tissue. I was nervous. If she hadn't stopped me, it would've probably been in pieces. I put it back in my pocket.

"Alright guys, it's not good…"

"Bye, it's see you later, we know," they both said

together, looking at each other to make sure they were both okay.

"Call when you can. I'm gonna turn around now," she stated as she was already walking the opposite direction with her arms crossed. The other waved and started walking to catch up.

With one strap over my shoulder, I walked. I looked at my reflection in the window and saw myself with my first luggage.

I was eleven years old when my family and I were at the airport heading to the Philippines in 1996. My sister and I would play tag or sing a song while my parents took care of the tickets or which bags needed to be checked. My parents bought us our first luggage to bring on the plane and we both were so excited because we felt important. And on a new adventure together.

"Just you today, Sir?" the staff asked, grabbing my ticket as I raised it to him. I was staring out the window as the sun lowered for its final moments for the day, casting a subtle glow on the runway.

I smiled, nodded and looked at the family by the window as I started to walk onto the bridge. "You're it!" one of the kids said to her sibling, running around their brightly colored luggage.

Chapter 4
Wake Up!

"IF YOU'RE WALKING, YOU. ARE. WRONG... MOVE!!"

March 2004, Great Lakes, Illinois. Flurries started to fall from the evening sky as dozens of recruits exited the long line of buses. The spotlights from the brick building illuminated the condensation from everyone's mouth. In an unintentional rhythm, the breath of cold air all pointed towards the building as we all stood at attention, hands at our sides, back straight, thousand-yard stare. I could hear sniffling, clearing of throats but they didn't tolerate it.

"DID I SAY YOU COULD MAKE NOISE? DROP. TWENTY. NOW…." The Petty Officer was roughly 6'2, 250 lbs. and African American. Four rows of ribbons on his left chest showed his career history. His voice sounded like he had been yelling that phrase for weeks. Hoarse, raspy, deep. The way he said "now" was something he must have perfected. With both hands behind his back, he laid his chin on the recruit's shoulder, pushing down on it, causing him to lean down towards the ground. The sound of shoes on the gravel as he started to do push-ups was the only thing that could be heard. We stood there as he counted, panting. *What a greeting.*

Once we stepped inside the building, the amount of yelling and crying that occurred was something you'd only find in a movie. Two recruits were being yelled at by one Petty Officer, some recruits were on the ground doing sit-ups, and a few were doing jumping jacks by the wall while two Petty Officers were screaming at them, telling them to count louder. I looked at the clock, and the hour hand was directed at 9, minute hand close to 7.

Long night ahead. And I wasn't wrong. For the next few hours, it was nothing but processing. Getting our uniforms, standing in line.

The horrid stench of feet and body odor overtook the musty air of the outdated building. The floor was covered with sweat while miscellaneous things like belts, hair ties, and socks laid out in the hallway.

"Nut to butt, scumbags!! How hard is that???!!" one Petty Officer yelled out. I smirked at the comment because I'd never heard of it and a third of the recruits were female.

The inside of the building was outdated, walls mounted with plaques, portraits of Government leaders, famous Navy sailors and the phrase "Honor, Courage and Commitment" strewn across one of the walls.

"THE CLOTHES THAT YOU ARE WEARING ARE NOW OF THE PAST," the Chief yelled out. "YOU WILL NOW BE CALLED A RECRUIT AS YOU ARE TO EARN THE TITLE OF SAILOR…"

Just Glow

There was a pause so quiet that you could hear a pin drop.

"GET DRESSED."

Everyone scurried and moved to take off their clothes, while the chief stood there with his arms crossed. The jingling of belts and dog tags rang through the hall. No one spoke, just the sound of coughing.

We were rushed into a large line and were herded into the Infirmary.

"Are you ready for this? Looks like a gauntlet," someone had said under their breath. I peered over someone's shoulder to take a peek, and I couldn't believe what I was seeing. Gauntlet was probably the most accurate description for what was happening.

Shuffling slowly, our sleeves were rolled up by the nurses as we made our way through an assembly line. Every five feet down the long hallway was a staff member on each side, armed with a syringe. Some recruits were whimpering because, well, they were scared. How could you not be? The stainless-steel syringe appeared to be as big as a meat baster. And the sound of it, an automatic injector that's comparable to a paintball gun, still rings in my ear. As we shuffled, they pressed the needles into our arms like we were items on a conveyor belt being assembled. They were making jokes as they pressed into our arms, mocking us and saying, "Enjoy that one, Recruit," or "Oooh, that'll sting later!" The RDCs, Recruit Division Commanders, loved it as they laughed and joined in on the conversation. The quick hiss of the syringe reloaded itself and injected into the next recruit. And the next. And the next. As the whimpering continued, they'd say, "THE NAVY DOES NOT ACCEPT BABIES. YOUR CRYING IS NOT WELCOME HERE." No one made a sound.

The mocking continued and we were dispersed in fives so that we could cover the length of an exam table.

"Side by side, Knuckleheads," he said, as he motioned with his hands but kept his fingers straight as an arrow, a term one would call a "knife hand."

He backed up and said, "Now….Drop. Trou."

Puzzled, I glanced at the guy next to me, and before we could understand each other, someone was dropping our shorts for us. The mocking increased and I heard, "Peanut Butter Shot."

You may be thinking, "I mean, I love peanut butter…" No. They didn't call it that because it was delicious. They called it that because of how THICK the medicine was. So thick, that once it was injected into the muscle, it didn't absorb for days. I mean DAYS. So viscous that you felt like you were sitting on a rock.

There was one person injecting this solution into us, and the needle was at least three inches long, and as thick as a meat thermometer. It had to be, as the substance appeared thick, the solution barely moving in the cylindrical-type syringe.

As they injected, the assistant held a metal tray and clink, the metal syringe was dropped on the tray. One after

Just Glow

the next. Then the next. And then next. And then it was me. I tried to clinch but the needle had already pierced.

The pinch was like an angry yellow jacket stinging you on a hot summer day. The after effect; a nasty sunburn. I took my hands off of the table and tried to straighten out. And the sensation stuck. Peanut butter.

"Get back in line! You're running!!" It was the most awkward run of my life, but I got behind another recruit who was rubbing his cheek.

Once we were divided into rooms by gender, we were led into a room full of bunk beds. I quickly glanced at what seemed like a clock because I was scared of what the RDC would say if they caught me. 1:07a.m.

"Recruits, this is your temporary quarters. Do not, I repeat, do not get comfortable here. If I see anyone trashing this space, you will be doing push-ups out in the cold." I've never experienced complete silence with roughly 50 people in one place. Everyone appeared exhausted, their eyes closing intermittently but blinking and bulging to stay awake. The foul musty smell of the room was of feet, sweat, and body odor. Some were sweating from the calisthenics the RDCs made them do.

"Now that I have your full attention, I want to introduce to you to your Chief RDC." His hand motioned to his left side. The Chief stepped forward.

Standing at five-foot one-inch, red hair tightly secured in a bun, she stood with arms crossed. Her uniform hugged her lean body, and I could see on everyone's faces what they were thinking but no one wanted to look at anything else but her eyes as she spoke.

"Good evening, Recruits," she started to say. Her voice was crisp and soft but high pitched and had a small southern twang to it.

This isn't going to be so bad. The thought of a female RDC put me at ease, reminding me of when I was in grade school with teachers who were nurturing and who comforted us.

"Welcome to Bootcamp!" From sleepy eyes, to now bright eyed and smiling, everyone perked up, mostly because of the voice of a woman.

"For the next eight weeks, you will train to earn the title, Sailor. It will not be easy, but we will get there together." Her voice was so soothing, it made me relax a bit. Too much, maybe. My eyes gazed over to someone who was continuously dozing off and that was when my perception for our Chief changed.

"WAAAKE UUUUP!" Her scream pierced through the air like a bullet to a target. It was loud, sudden, and directed to someone behind me.

In an instant, a horrific screech erupted that broke through an awkward silence.

But everyone just stared.

Exhausted. Yearning for sleep.

Afraid we would get yelled at.

Just Glow

I looked to my right and noticed that a recruit was violently convulsing. He was foaming at the mouth, shaking uncontrollably.

"Back up, back up, Recruits." Calm and composed, Chief took control of the situation. She ran over, squatted down, and turned him to the side.

"Davidson, call the Duty Corpsman and get the cart. We need oxygen, suction, and an NPA." Her movements were swift but fluid. Intentional. Her voice was stern, confident, but not at all rushed. Cradling his head, she rubbed his back and started to try and soothe him. She turned into someone we had never seen before.

"Shh," she lightly said, "it's ok, Bud. Hang in there. We've got you. You're safe."

He was still grunting, but his breathing started to slow down. Using a pillowcase, she gently wiped the saliva from his face, its sticky texture on her wrists. But she didn't seem to mind.

We didn't move.

No one made a sound. Not one.

His eyes started to open, and he looked at her like he'd heard her.

"There you are," she softly said, smiling. "You're safe now." She started to caress his head. "Breathe. Breathe…"

Augusto C. Cespedes, Jr.

She seemed so comfortable. Relaxed. She held him as we all sat there in amusement.

The hands of the wall clock pointed in the direction of 2:10 a.m.

Tired, I backed up and I noticed the symbol on her uniform; a Caduceus.

She was a Hospital Corpsman.

Just like me.

A single dome light shined from the ceiling just bright enough to illuminate a path to the door. It hummed a faint sound, like a June beetle attracted to a porch light. Distant coughs and the sounds of mattress springs echoed as it was suddenly morning.

"What time is it?" someone asked at a whisper. We didn't hear anything outside, just the heavy snoring of recruits.

I tried to make out the time, but the clock was hidden in the shadows.

"Twenty 'til six," someone said, looking at his watch. He was glaring at the green glow while he laid in the bottom bunk.

Then, the creaking of a door. Footsteps. The jangling of keys.

Just Glow

The door opened and the light switch flicked on. It was Chief.

"Well, good morning!" The door swung open and smacked the adjacent wall with a thud. Startled, we perked up. Some stood at attention, nervous, with eyes half open, trying to adjust to the light.

"We are off to our permanent home! Let's pack up." We all looked at each other, confused.

Is this bootcamp or… I looked around and then at Chief. Khaki uniform, crisp and wrinkle free, it was like she never left the building. Her red hair was tightened in a bun, wearing cherry red lipstick and teeth as white as snow.

In a single formed line, we marched to our permanent squad bay.

Marching was a skill in itself and it was one of those types of things that generally kept us entertained. We used the numbers 1 through 4, odd numbers left foot, even numbers for the right. The cadence caller could get clever and make it into a melodic progression.

"One, two….three, four…forty-one, two…one, two, three, four…threeeee, four," he'd sing out. No matter how many of us, we walked in unison with one sound hitting the ground. And we marched everywhere. To class. To the barracks. To the gym. To the galley. If someone made an error, the RDC would, by the collar, pull them out of the line in such a violent and dramatic fashion and make them exercise in front of us while we all stood there, arms at our sides, facing forward. Rain, snow, or shine.

Augusto C. Cespedes, Jr.

You wouldn't believe it but shining shoes was a form of entertainment because, well, it was a time they weren't yelling at you, and you got to sit on the ground and have a conversation with the others and learn about where they came from. In those first times we shined shoes, I'd found the "clowns" of the Division.

When we got to our home, we all stood at attention in front of our bunks. At least 10 minutes past, and she just walked. She walked along the tiled floor with her arms crossed, and walked like she was trying to skip every other, inspected each row, making sure no one was hiding.

Now, when I said I met the "clowns" of the Division, I meant exactly that.

When she made her way far enough from me and another recruit, he made the loudest popping noise by clicking his tongue to the hard palate of his mouth. It echoed through the restroom into the large community bathroom.

"What in God's. Mighty. Name. WAS THAT?????!!!!" Her head swung around so fast, eyes bulged, and she walked to a random recruit.

I gulped.

"WHO. WAS. THAAAAAAT???!!!" She left his face and quickly went to each recruit's face to see if someone was going to confess, but no one said a word.

Freaking idiot. From my peripheral, I could see the grin from the recruit that made the noise.

Just Glow

"Pray to your God that I do not find whoever did that," she threatened, looking at all of us.

"Line up."

We all ran to the door.

Chapter 5
Ironing in the Dark

The first day was a breeze. It was a full day of classes, learning about the history of the Navy, the ranks and famous heroes throughout the decades.

"Reveille is six a.m., boys. Tomorrow will be a day just like today. We will also be getting our uniforms," Chief said cheerfully. During processing, we only received a cover that had "Recruit" embroidered in gold thread, sweatpants a shirt, shoes, socks, skivvies and a plain t-shirt.

"Goodnight, Chief!" We all yelled in unison. She didn't say it back, just slammed the door. Conversations erupted when her footsteps faded.

"Man, my friends lied to me about bootcamp," one exclaimed.

This ain't nothin'!" said another, laughing as he sat at the top bunk.

It was difficult to get to sleep that night because of the

excitement, but after only three hours of sleep from the previous night, I fell asleep to the midnight chatter.

Dead silence.

You could hear a pin drop.

"REVEILLE, REVEILLE, REVEILLEEEE!!!" The sea of fluorescent lights, like dominoes, lit up from the ceiling as the piercing sounds of wooden sticks to metal cans echoed through the rows of beds.

The last time I looked at the clock, it was 9:03 p.m.

I glanced at it again. 0359 hrs.

"GET UP, WORM GUTS! WHAT ARE YOU WAITING FOR??!!" A deep voice yelled out. It wasn't Chief. Someone was pulling people out of their beds.

Standing at 6'5, he had to be close to 300 pounds. His left chest decorated with five rows of ribbons, the black petty officer walked whilst holding two recruits by their sweatshirt hoods.

With eyes half open, we charged to the middle of the squad bay. Some didn't have socks on, others with just their t-shirts and skivvies on.

"We will learn how to wake up before God," he said. His voice was straight from the diaphragm, deep and bellowing that rattled the cement walls.

"Y'all are a Bag 'O Nasties," he said walking with his hands behind his back, scanning the different varieties of sleep attire we ended up with. Some shook, others were still half asleep but were able to hold their attention. I was always entertained (never showed it) by the choice of names they called us. If I ever smirked, if anyone ever smirked, they'd take an apple to the forehead (literally).

We unintentionally formed two lines facing each other, and he started walking in between us.

Chief came from around the corner, laughing to herself. She knew exactly what she was doing, and she got us good.

"I'm all about the Milton Bradley," he said. "I love games, and we're gonna play lots of them, I promise you that." It took me a few seconds to understand what he was saying, but when I did, I grinned.

At 18 years old, I was considered one of the kids in the division. Division 175 to be exact. There were about fifty to sixty of us, all in one room. All coming from different parts of the world, speaking different languages, of all ages and ethnicity.

Honestly, I was not only missing home, but I was nervous showing it, afraid I would get made fun of. Every day, I tried to see if anyone else appeared homesick, but all I saw were faces of exhaustion; sleep deprived, with darkened bags under their eyes. I missed the Saturday mornings when my mom would cook breakfast, rice and eggs, Filipino style. The rice, lightly sautéed with garlic and the sunny side egg would lie on the bed of rice, the yolk dribbling onto the rice when the fork cut into it. Or when my parents would tend to the lawn in the early hours of the evening, the smell of freshly mown grass. I'd skip behind my dad as he'd make a path, trying to catch the grasshoppers that were hiding in the yard. "Just leave them alone, Jay," my mom would yell out, smiling, overpowered by the sound of the lawnmower.

At the fourth week of no phone calls or television, that all changed when we received our first letters from home.

"Mail's here!" one of the recruits yelled out, raising the cloth bag high up. We all ran to him like it was Christmas morning.

"O'Donnell! Hayward! Perez!" he'd yell out. Their hands would raise in the crowd of recruits, even giving a small shout. The others would smile for them, patting them on their back as they made their way to the front. You'd see the other recruits' eyes dampen as they waited for their name to be called. No one cared. No one made fun of one another. Everyone missed home.

A high ceiling room as big as a basketball court was where we stayed, and in a neat fashion were rows and rows of bunk beds. Uniform and identical, with black backpacks draped over each bedpost. What was special about the beds was the compartment inside. Lifted like a chest were multiple compartments where we placed all of our clothes. In the Navy, there is a unique way of folding every piece of clothing, down to the pair of socks. We learned how to fold and iron and were inspected at any given moment. If Chief or -- let's call him Muscles -- wanted to inspect your things at three a.m., they could.

"My son got his first home run!" someone yelled out, his head poking out into the open. We all cheered for him as the sound of envelopes being opened throughout the room made us forget where we were.

Just Glow

For a second, we were all in our own world. From the time we heard our name called to when we walked back to our bunk, letter in hand. Back to what we left behind. A family. Prison. The streets. Home.

I opened the letter that was addressed from my house and I could feel a lump in my throat start to form. Shaking, I instead used my teeth to open the envelope.

"Hi, JR! We are hoping you're doing well. We are celebrating Dad's…"

I couldn't take another word. I was only gone for 4.5 weeks, but I had never left my family my entire life. I began to bury my head in the compartment of my bunk and didn't have any words to say. I put the letter to my nose and smelled it. It was of my mother's perfume.

"Jay! Your clothes are on the ironing board, ok?" she'd say in the morning as she was getting ready for work. She always had the radio on playing either country or 80s soft rock. I'd sometimes walk into her room and the hard hit of perfume and hairspray would smack me in the face.

"Can you help me with this?" I'd ask, handing her a button-down shirt. I was never good at buttoning the top button.

She'd always tsk at me but smile, helping as she always would.

As I tried to gather my thoughts, I looked to my right and noticed the recruit next to me. His head was buried in his compartment. And the next recruit was the same. And the next. And the next. It was quiet. No one was talking. It was as if our letters broke every masculine wall we built for four weeks, and it all just came tumbling down. I looked at the others as I put my letter on my bed. Some were wiping their tears and looking around, some sharing their letters with others around them. A few laid in their bunk on their back, and stared at their letters, having read it already but reading it again, smiling. Whether I liked it or not, I now had to call this place home.

The building that held the Galley stood tall and adjacent from the gym. A towering red brick building with white stoned pillars decorated the entrance. Flags waved high on metal poles and the sounds of cadence callers sang in the early hours of the morning.

The smell of fried bacon and eggs greeted us at the door as we walked past the giant golden bell with two recruits standing at attention.

When we reached the entrance of the Galley, recruits were silently standing in line. Off to the side were some recruits sweating and exercising, with an RDC towering over them saying in a melodic voice, "Everybody in 'da club doin' 8 counts."

The hall was lined with white tile, with a few recruits wiping each tile carefully with a towel.

"Pop quiz!" Muscles yelled out in his deep voice, startling a few recruits that were not in our division. He jumped at them, laughing. They immediately faced forward and stood at attention.

It was our responsibility to study the material we were taught on our own time. History, ranks, the phonetic alpha-

Just Glow

bet, among other subjects. If we didn't use the time wisely, it affected the amount of time we could eat.

"It would behoooooove you..." Chief would trail off, swirling her index finger in the air as we stood at attention after class, "to learn the ranks inside and out. If you like to eat, you will use your time wisely."

She wasn't kidding. She got Muscles to quiz us in the galley line while waiting to get food, and if we didn't answer correctly, back to the line we went. And time was still ticking.

"Houston! I hope we don't have a problem," he said to me. He either called me Houston or Cesspool, depending on if he was in a good mood or not.

"I want the phonetic alphabet...commence," he announced, as it echoed down the hall.

"Yes, Petty Officer!" that was the only thing I wasn't 100% sure on. After India, I just forgot.

"Alpha, Bravo, Charlie, Delta, Echo, Foxtrot, Golf, Hotel, India, Julia, K..."

"What?"

I stopped.

Some recruits made a noise, while some turned around to see what he'd do to me.

"Juuuuuliet?"

Augusto C. Cespedes, Jr.

"Too late." He sighed, smiled in disgust, looked up and slowly brought it down.

"Houston, we have a problem. Back of the line," he said, as his teeth gave him a subtle lisp.

His hand slowly came up from his side and he pointed the other direction, and like a sad puppy, my eyes followed his finger and my head hung low. For that meal, I was only able to have a few bites of the main entree, meatloaf, a chunk of a dinner roll and I guzzled down the apple juice. That was the last time I screwed up the phonetic alphabet.

Most recruits were consistently able to sound off the right answers, as most would study at night with the help of a red flashlight. Others wouldn't care much about studying and just go to the back of the line, adapting to scarfing their food down. But one day, we finally learned what sneaking around will get you.

Like I said before, Chief or Muscles could inspect your belongings at any given moment. When they walked in every morning, they would walk up and down the rows to make sure there wasn't anything out of order, but they especially inspected the most when it was Field Day because no one was by their bunks.

"Man, I'm beat," a recruit would admit, scrubbing the metal portion of the toilet flush handle. It was the day we had our physical fitness test, swim test and had to March a longer way due to construction. Field Days were usually Thursdays, and it consisted of everyone cleaning, and Chief's boss would come the next day to inspect.

"I can't wait to get some shut eye," another one said,

Just Glow

looking at his watch. It was almost 9:40 p.m. "Twenty more minutes, Fellas," I said, being optimistic. I was scrubbing the same area for at least 15 minutes, daydreaming about my head hitting that hardened pillow on my bed.

"Ohhhhhh shit," Muscles said, grinning. Everyone stopped what they were doing. Scrubbing, wiping, brushing. It all stopped. The noise we were making with the supplies echoed through the tiled walls.

A sinister laugh was heard, and a "Would you look at this, Chief!" was yelled. A loud bang erupted, and Chief came walking out of the office. We all looked at each other and ran to the sound.

Shorter than almost everyone in the division, I tried to look over to see what had happened. Unsuccessful, I forced my way in.

Wrappers of foil scattered the tile floor, and as Muscles started to look under the mattress, pieces of crackers, dinner rolls, and jelly packets flew against the wall. My stomach turned.

"Looks like we have our very first Blue Falcon!" he yelled out, cheerful. Sarcastic. Recruits stared at the trash, others backed up in fear. We were all ready to turn in for the night, and now we were wondering what would happen to all of us.

Muscles, kicking the wrappers, walked out of the room, shaking his head and smiling. We all stared at the recruit who caused it. The lens of his glasses as thick as a magnifying glass, he was roughly 5'6" at 220 lbs. His hairline was receding, with darkened freckles covering his forehead. He stood in between the racks, speechless. Shocked. Mouth half closed; his eyes bulged.

"Welp, there goes our sleep."

"Done. We're done, boys. Thanks, slob." One recruit patted him on the back. Some of the recruits started to stretch their legs and arms, preparing for the worst punishment coming our way. Others walked around and made comments. A few started to pick up the trash because they knew we'd have to do it anyway.

We heard laughter outside, so we stopped talking. Then footsteps.

A recruit bravely asked, "Where'd Chief go?"

"She's gonna go to sleep, unlike you Maggots." He laughed out loud. He walked into his office and walked out with a speaker, and a few bags of chocolate, chips, and a bottle of soda. My instinct was, "Oh, phew, he feels sorry for us. He's bringing us food." That dissipated in a split second.

"Spectacles," Muscles said to the culprit, pointing up, "Get up on your rack."

The recruit, puzzled, looked at him. Then the bunk. Then the trash.

"Petty Officer…?" He began to say.

"I know my own rank, thanks, recruit. Get up there. Sit with your legs crossed. Do it. Now."

Without hesitation, the recruit climbed up, crossed his

Just Glow

legs, and sat facing the middle of the room. From that view, I was guessing he could see the whole room because he started to scan with his eyes.

Muscles turned around and said, "Get in rows, arm's length. Do it. Now."

As we started to assemble into our rows, Muscles climbed up to Spectacle's rack and put his feet on the bottom bunk rails, raised his arms high in the air and yelled, "You can thank Butterball for his actions! While all of you do jumping jacks, he will enjoy all of these delicious snacks, one by one!" He turned to the recruit and said, "if you don't look like you're enjoying it, you will join them. I want you to rub that belly like how you rubbed your belly eating all of those snacks you hid."

He stared at him and then looked at the snacks.

"Go on, recruit. Don't be shy. You know you want it," motioning him to start opening the bag of unknown items.

He turned to the boombox, and…click. The music started. Guitar picking. High hat. Some already knew what it was, yelling out, smiling. Others already looked defeated. It was 11 p.m. It was Metallica's "Enter Sandman."

For the next hour and a half, we exercised.

For those ninety minutes, we only did jumping jacks. The song played on repeat. Non-stop jumping jacks.

And for that hour and a half, he just sat there and slowly ate. Staring at us. He finished off a whole bag of miniature Hershey bars, two small bags of potato chips and a soda. He

Augusto C. Cespedes, Jr.

rubbed his stomach, trying to crack a smile, afraid of what everyone was thinking. Muscles paced back and forth and stood on the bottom rails to stand next to the recruit as he ate. At first, doing a few hundred jumping jacks was okay, everyone's breathing was quiet, calm. At a certain point, exhaustion would set in. The panting became louder, we gradually became out of unison, and the floor… Well, it was covered in sweat. Every jump, every clap, drops of sweat would drip onto the tile floor. Every landing, you'd see a recruit become off balance because of the sweat. The music blared. Repeating. Clap. Jump. Squeak. Panting. No one stopped.

And finally.

"Enough." He pressed stop. "Clean it up." And he left.

From the moment we woke up, to the last light going out, it was always **LOUD**. Yelling. Shouting. But when the lights went out, it was different. Peaceful different. It was your time. You'd only hear the sounds of recruits snoring, the footsteps of the Rover watch going in and out of the rows of racks and the quiet, echoing sounds of irons.

When I was 10, in the middle of fifth grade, I was nervous about going to another school; the middle school. Sixth to eighth grade. I always heard rumors about it. Bigger kids. Fights. Lockers. My mind started to imagine, and I didn't know what to expect. As fifth grade was coming to an end, I started to have nightmares about the fear of the unknown of that next school year. Nightmares that would wake me up in the middle of the night.

Ever since we started school, my mom would iron the night before. Before anyone was awake, she'd go into the

Just Glow

guest room, and iron all our clothes. She would carefully lay each article of clothing on the board with such ease, flattening them out by hand for the iron to make its way across. Most nights, when I'd have another bad dream, I'd make my way to the guest room at the last hours of the night, knowing my mom would be there.

Pretending that I was still asleep, my eyes closed, I'd listen. A familiar tune, she'd hum. The iron against the board, the squeaking of the metal joints. The smell of fresh linen covered the air of the room and in an unexplainable sense, I found comfort knowing that every day, every single morning, she'd be there.

As the ending days of bootcamp neared, the fear of the unknown grew. I didn't know what to expect. A war was erupting.

What was going to happen to me?

With just a red glow from the light, I'd laid my uniform down, straightening the sleeves like my mom would. The steam of the iron hissed as it slid down the board, turning the wrinkles of the shirt to a crisp, neat line. Every night that I was woken up to iron, I felt connected with a memory long ago. As it glided across the board, the metal parts clicking and squeaking, a soft humming of my mom's voice passed gently over me as I kept ironing in the dark.

Chapter 6
808

February 2004

The mirror, partially smeared with evidence of what appeared to look like an attempt to clean it, spanned across the row of porcelain sinks as I approached the last one by the door. Walking up close, I immediately noticed one of the buttons on my striped dress shirt was missing, likely from a consignment shop. I never buttoned the top button anyway. My ears were pierced with 12-gauge plastic horseshoe earrings which my parents hated. And with a partly sideways trucker hat, I stared at myself. Washed my hands quick, flicked them in the air on my Dickies shorts that were down to my knees and walked out. I immediately saw my recruiter standing next to a Liaison Officer.

Augusto C. Cespedes, Jr.

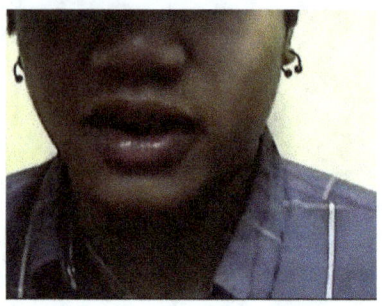

"OK, Cespedes," he clapped his hands together. "According to your test scores, we've got a couple—actually several—opportunities for ya," the Petty Officer said. He was dressed in his utility uniform, sorting out the cards that revealed the occupations and began to place them on the bulletin board.

"Pharmacists Mate, Yeoman, Sonar Technician, Hospital Corpsman, Operations Specialist aaaand Electronics Technician. So…"

To me, that was a lot of information and terms I didn't understand. But I knew the word hospital, so I interrupted.

"What's a Corpse man?" I asked. I knew it didn't sound right the way that I said it, but I attempted.

"It's pronounced Core-muhn, like Fireman. You'll be running with the Marines, Bro," my Recruiter stated, smiling and shaking his head. I've always liked a challenge, I thought.

I immediately imagined myself as a Hospital Corpsman, keeping up with the Marines like I was one of them; strong, confident and ready to take on the unpredictable.

Just Glow

"Alright, well? What're we goin' with?" tapping his pencil, the Petty Officer turned around in the swivel chair.

"I have to call my dad," I blurted out. I didn't know what to do, and I couldn't make a decision on my own. I stepped to the side and flipped open my cellphone, dialing. I stared out the dirty window that viewed the sea of trees that led to the highway.

"Hey Dad, I'm at the Liaison and I have to choose a job…a Navy job," I quickly stated, getting right to the point. I turned around from the window and saw the Petty Officer looking my direction. I looked down at my worn out Converse Chuck Taylors. I'd taken a sharpie to it months ago and drew white and black checkered patterns on the white portion, now faded.

"Ohhh, hmm. Which are they?"

Trying to recall what was told to me, I mumbled, "Pharmacists Mate…Yeoman?…Sonar Tech, Hospital Corpsman, Operations Specialist and something in Electronics."

"Well, with most of those, you'll be on a ship. I don't know much about the Pharmacist's Mate and the Corpsman is good, but I think it's physically demanding. It's medical and they usually call a Corpsman "Doc," he said, with loud bangs on his end. It sounded like he was in the garage, as the sounds were echoing, metal to metal.

Not fully understanding, I thought about what the recruiter had said. "Running with the Marines," and the name "Doc." It was a "Go Big or Go Home" mentality at that moment, wanting to earn that title. Doc. I didn't know what it would take. I didn't know much about it, but I knew I wanted to be something else. Something better.

With a bit of confidence, I pointed to the index card that was pinned on the wall.

"That one," I said.

May 2004

Hospital Corps School, Great Lakes, IL

After a grueling eight weeks of bootcamp, Corps School was a breath of fresh air, but it was still difficult. A different difficult. Monday through Friday, morning until late afternoon, our heads were constantly in books, in classes and running as a class or marching to the galley. Like college, the dorms were Co-Ed, and you spent your free time doing what you wanted. The only difference was you couldn't skip class. You had to be within military regulations. Hair. Uniform. Professional. And at the entrance of every building was a Guard on Duty that we all shared the responsibility of, day or night. Once you were in the vicinity of the entrance, you'd step up on the welcome mat, face forward

Just Glow

and say, "Permission to come aboard" and the Guard would say "Come Aboard."

I'd say the days in Hospital Corps School were generally enjoyable. But the unknown was still there.

Was I going to war? What will my life be like in a year? The Corps school days were fun. But they were numbered.

One afternoon, in between classes, we were, without notice, given pencils and a sheet of paper lined with the numbers "1., 2., and 3.," and said "Wish List" at the top. We were all confused.

"The Navy," our instructor paused, "Or you could call him Santa, wants to know where you want to go after this place; your top three choices," our instructor bellowed from the rear of the classroom, walking slowly after almost every word. He was a hefty black man from the south, with a twang. Gasps and small chatter could be heard with an in between "shh'ing."

"Think hard now and be careful what you wish for," he laughed, almost a belly laugh. For a second I thought, "bad joke," but it was true. I learned that it's not about you, it's about the "Needs of the Navy." "Hurry now, on you write." The banging sounds of elbows and wrists to the desks, you could hear nothing but the scratching of pencils. It was like a race against the clock.

I didn't actually sit and think about it, so I jotted down where I've never been; Italy, Germany, and Hawaii.

Several weeks passed and I knew that our next duty stations were assigned to us because one kid screamed, "I got Italy! I'm going to Italy!" at the top of his lungs, running up and down the barracks hall like the audience members on the Price is Right that got chosen to bid in front of Bob Barker.

I didn't have a computer at the time, so I walked down the stairs, nervously gripping the handrail and saw one computer was unused. I walked across the hall and sat on the chair.

Turned the screen on.

Logged in.

Clicked the bar "Assignments."

It was in bold, blue. "New." My index finger started to perspire on the mouse, missing the click. Eventually, I clicked it.

"3RD MARDIV."

For a few seconds, it didn't hit. But once my mind split up the second word, I sank into the hardened plastic chair. "3rd Marine Division."

The racing of thoughts flipped all the way back to what my recruiter had said to me.

"You'll be running with the Marines, Bro!"

An overwhelming feeling of "I want it, but I don't want it" blanketed me as I slouched in my seat. Something pulled me toward it — being a Corpsman with the Marines — but the sadness pulled me back to my old self. It hurt. I wanted

Just Glow

to continue training and get stronger but a part of me also wanted to go home and go back to what I was doing, grocery stocking and skipping classes. Screw skipping classes, I'd try and go to school again. For real this time. At that moment, I wanted my mom and dad back, wishing I could have done things differently. A part of me wished I never answered the phone. Never spoke to the Recruiter. I should have just walked away because maybe it wouldn't have caused a spark. For a 19-year-old with no military or combat experience, my mind went straight to the negative, thinking the absolute worst. War. Killing. Dying. Never coming home. And I hadn't even graduated Corps school yet.

In 2003, the US declared war against Iraq and Saddam Hussein's regime, and to destroy all WMD (Weapons of Mass Destruction). Summer of 2004 were headlines after headlines of the Presidential Election. Our moment of first-hand war experience was nearing.

One of the benefits of Corps School was once class was dismissed for the day, it was our personal time. To go out on the town. Off to go study. Gym. Dinner. As long as you were back for class in the morning in one piece, you were as good as gold.

Growing up in the suburbs of Texas, we didn't know the way of train transportation. I grew up witnessing the mile-long line of the horses and cattle on the highway making their way to the annual rodeo or waiting, for what felt like forever, at the railroad crossing for the freight train to pass. So, when I heard we could travel by train to different towns, I had to explore.

One day during class PT (physical training), we ran as a

class to the entrance of the Base. It had been several weeks since I'd seen the entrance of the Naval Base, the first time being after Bootcamp. I, along with others, rode a school bus from Bootcamp to Hospital Corps School, which was only a few minutes away. Without a car, you didn't see much of the area unless you were running or taking the bus.

Several days later after class, and days after I'd known I was going to be with the Marine Corps, one of my classmates and I decided to run past the entrance. The sun was still up, and we weren't planning on staying out too late. We took a left at the entrance and headed South.

"Welcome to the Robert McGlory Bike Path," the sign said, distressed and tattered.

"Lake Bluff, 2.4 miles," I said, "not bad." And we started to jog. The trail, a paved path, was surrounded by tall grass and a few trees here and there. The train tracks were to our right but hidden by the brush. "I'd never heard the sound of a fast-moving train," I admitted, thinking out loud. "A train sounds like a fast-moving tornado," my elementary school teacher once told me, as we sat under our tables during a tornado warning. I didn't believe her then, but I'd say she was right. The sound would start at your feet, a rumbling that crept up your body as the roaring crawled into each ear and the next thing we knew, it was passing next to us as we walked down the path. Just right over the grass were the tracks.

"WOAHHH!!" I yelled, but I couldn't even hear myself. The roar engulfed me, the ground shaking from under my feet.

The sun started to hide among the brush, leaving a

Just Glow

bright glow with shadows as sharp as thorns laying across the path. And as we traveled more south, they started to fade, slowly melting into one.

"We're almost there," my friend said.

Only a couple blocks away from the Lake Bluff train station, I looked to the right and noticed the sun had set, and the moon was on the rise. As we started to walk further, the streetlights led to the sign "Welcome to Lake Bluff." Nightfall had set in.

I took several steps past the sign and there it was. Downtown Lake Bluff.

Either it was nostalgia, being homesick or just away from the real world for several months, but Downtown Lake Bluff felt magical. Picture perfect.

I stood in the middle of the street, mesmerized. The shops lined both sides of Center Avenue. At that hour, there was not one car on the road, but the lights of the downtown street brought it to life. Every streetlight served a sheer purpose, illuminating parts of the shops, sidewalks, and trees that almost made it, well, movie-like. There was something special about it. It could have been that I've never seen such a place, or my past self felt…connected.

Nothing was open but I was excited to walk down the streets. As my friend took one side of the street, I stepped onto the sidewalk and started to walk alongside the windows of the shops. An antique store, toy store, a pet store, clothing shop, and coffee shop. Catching myself smiling, I started to imagine it on a busy mid-morning, the opening of the door causing a small bell to "ding," with distant conversations heard. I began to look around and suddenly, I felt a sense of peace. Like I belonged. And at that moment in time, in those few seconds that felt like a lifetime, I felt like I wasn't in the military. I felt like I belonged.

For once in my life, I thought of how I'd like my life to be. I saw myself walking with a beautiful wife on a summer day, enjoying the warmth of the sun and our kids pointing to a shop they saw with toys on display, their smiling faces gleaming on the reflection of a window. And slowly I walked up to the window and began to see my own reflection. And I stared.

A high tapered haircut. There were no earrings. A fitted golden, yellow colored shirt that said "NAVY" in a reflective silver color, and navy-blue shorts.

I began to think about those times waking up at Anthony's.

Miserable. Useless.

I thought about that drive home with the music saying, *"Don't know which way we're goin'. Find a way out, find a way…"*

I then started to think about those moments growing up saying I'd never join the Navy. Always against it. Then, finally, answering the phone call.

Looking at my own reflection, I realized I was doing something bigger than myself. Something I never knew I could be a part of. A part of something bigger, that in time, would bring me to a place like this. A place where I felt at peace. Didn't know how. Didn't know when. Sure, I was excited for the future but honestly…? I was beyond scared of what it would take to get there.

"Ready to go?" My friend said, yelling from across the street.

"Ya…" I yelled, staring but then started to take a step back. "…I'm ready," I trailed off, and finally backed away from the window.

FMSS Graduation, November, 2004

In the Navy, a Hospital Corpsman can be stationed in different types of environments. Because the Marine Corps is a department of the Navy, the Hospital Corpsman provides the medical assistance needed by the unit. Depending on the type of environment, they would need to complete Field Medical Service School, an eight-week program designed to transition the Hospital Corpsman to become "one with the Marines." From learning the parts of an M16 to knowing which Marine to treat in a firefight.

Four rows up, we waited in the bleachers for our names to be called. 7:45 a.m., the latest we had ever been out on formation during FMSS. The California sunrise was already on the horizon, our breaths seen in the air, not of nervousness or fear but excitement. A sigh of relief. Grateful for the grueling eight weeks to be over, some of us leisurely paced the formation grounds for the very first time. It was Graduation Day.

Augusto C. Cespedes, Jr.

We all wore our Woodland Cammies, a uniform commonly worn by Marines and Navy personnel.

"Conte, Kelly, Cespedes, let's go!" Someone shouted. It was the HM1 (Hospital Corpsman, Petty Officer 1st Class) in charge of the formation.

Matt Conte, switching his cover around from it being backwards, yelled sarcastically, "Present!" His smile and sarcasm were contagious, always making me laugh and wondering how he always got away with it.

"Wait, take off your cover, Conte! Let's get one last picture," Ruth said, handing the camera to a classmate.

We huddled together. "Ok, last picture! Ready?!"

It was a question that rang longer than I ever could have imagined.

We all jumped down from the bleachers and got into our last formation. The slab of concrete we used for formation was in front of our barracks, a stone building that was

Just Glow

painted cherry red, with cracks that probably grew over the years, painted over.

"Some of you will be in a clinic, while some of you will be on a ship. A few of you will be in the sand, wondering what you got yourself into. But know this. No matter where you are, know you are all fighting the good fight. Be proud of yourselves. Hoorah?!!!"

And with the deepest yell, straight from our diaphragms, was a "HOORAH." The sky was suddenly filled with our covers, and we all shook hands. And just like that, it was over. We all were to go our separate ways.

"Yup, Hawaii, how about you?" I heard someone say in excitement. I turned around to see who it was, and it was Conte, smiling again, his white teeth shining.

When I met Conte, he reminded me of an actor in those cheesy 90s sitcom shows, like the one who was always smiling, goofy as ever but without a doubt, would give the shirt off their back in a heartbeat. Whenever he spoke about the attractiveness of a girl, he'd always say with a grin, "I wouldn't kick her out of my bed for eating crackers." I'd always laugh and say, "I KNEW you'd say that."

I never saw him sad. And if he was, he always found a way to crack a smile or make a joke. No matter how grueling or exhausting the situation was, he somehow figured out a way to make it fun. And the voice that he'd use was Special Ed from Crank Yankers. We would be humping (another term for walking) as a Battalion on a Friday, up KT Hill, a road that leads to the radio tower on the Kaneohe Bay base, and you'd hear him with his Marines yelling "YEAAAAAAAA." You could see the Marines laughing or smiling, patting him on his back as he'd run ahead. It was almost like him yelling would give him a jolt of energy. The funniest would be that he'd hold the "y" longer with a different pitch, and with that grin of his and his eyes looking left and right, he'd belt out "YEAAAAA." Sounds stupid, sure, but in the midst of going to war, we all needed that. The immature jokes. The laughs. Anything to take our minds off the rough times.

Conte and I didn't become friends until the last days of FMSS. We were in Hospital Corps School at the same time, but in different classes. Once we became friends, we would share stories about Corpsman school, and I told him a time when I got into trouble for reciting the Sailor's Creed over the barracks intercom during my Fire Watch. It was on a Sunday, midday. I had a few hours left, and boredom was setting in. Looking at the intercom, I thought to myself "Noo, I can't..." smiling. I tried to take my mind off it, but I just couldn't. I put my mouth to the microphone and pushed the button. And with my deepest voice, I started to say...

"The Sailor's Creed.
I am a United States Sailor.
I will support and defend the Constitution of the United States of America and I will obey the orders appointed over me..." others started to stop what they were doing and stared, jaw dropped, knowing how much trouble I'd be getting into while others laughed in shock.
I grabbed the microphone and stood up.
"I represent the fighting spirit of the Navy, and those who have gone before me to defend freedom and democracy from around the world. I proudly serve my country's Navy combat team with Honor, Courage and Commitment," I emphasized. "I am committed to excellence and the fair treatment of all."

Just Glow

It fell silent for a moment, but once I put the mic down, everyone came up to me and patted me on the back, applauding.

"Are you kidding me??? That was the best thing this year!" one said, arm already on my shoulder. I couldn't help but smile, thinking it was pretty cool to be "that guy."

"Not such a bad idea," I thought. But my time under the limelight didn't last long.

There was a group of kids that I saw not too far away, huddled and pointing to me. And then I noticed. It was a staff member, the Petty Officer on Duty. I was doomed.

"What do you think you are doing?" he began to say. "You understand you could be kicked out of school for this?" I really didn't.

"No, Petty Officer," I announced, finding myself standing at attention. My proud moments quickly transformed into regrets, and I let out a big sigh.

"What is your name, Student?"

"HN Cespedes..." I shamefully said. My head wanted to hang low, but I stood tall, ready to accept the punishment.

"Your instructors will hear about this come tomorrow morning. Finish the remaining time of your Watch. You should be ashamed of yourself." He turned around and walked through a line of people that were trying to listen in.

"Wait," Conte would say, interrupting me, "that was you??!!!"

"Not my proudest moment," I'd say to him.

"You sounded legit! I remember lying in bed trying to take a nap and I heard The Sailors Creed, so I ran outside and stood at attention!" He was still laughing.

"What's wrong with that?"

"I was in my underwear, man!" he said. We both laughed hard.

Paradise

"Please place all seats back to their upright position and secure all tray tables as we make our final descent into Honolulu," the flight attendant said on the loudspeaker. Everyone started to suddenly move around, mostly anxious to get out of the plane.

The number of things I'd see and do in Hawaii swirled in my head faster than I could probably speak. Of course I was ecstatic for Hawaii to be my duty station, but the inevitable stuck. It sat and permeated. And I, of course, smiled and appeared unaffected.

The Pacific clouds covered our view of the island for several seconds, and then, it appeared.

Just Glow

If I could compare my expression to something to show what it looked like, the most accurate one would have to be like how in the original Jurassic Park movie, Mr. John Hammond first sees the island from the helicopter for the first time. Wide eyed, back suddenly straightens, and says "There it is." Mesmerized.

Ya, kinda like that.

At 10,000 feet, the water surrounding the island was painted in various shades of blue, perfectly misshaped with white specks of what represented waves. The sun beamed down in the lighter blue, almost revealing how shallow it was. I just couldn't stare at only one thing. My eyes wanted to fixate on every detail. The white cotton clouds towered over the terrain, causing some parts darker than others. The famous Diamond Head crater was easily noticed, large enough to swallow the plane. The green turned to white, and as it became clearer, they were clusters of buildings. Honolulu.

Only a few steps into the airport, I'd noticed that even the air was different. A good different. Warm, with a hint of a cool breeze and the smell was pure. Clean.

"Alooooha!" a woman said. She smiled and placed a

Augusto C. Cespedes, Jr.

fresh lei of flowers over my head and around my neck. You couldn't help but feel positive. Relaxed.

It was only Friday morning and our transfer papers stated to report to duty that coming Monday.

We didn't have a car, so we both split the cost of the cab. "Kan-ee-oh…" I attempted to say. "KBay? The Marine base? Sure man, hop in," the driver said.

At first, I was bummed that we didn't get a car for the weekend, but I think Matt and I would have agreed that because it was both our first time in Hawaii, the drive to the base was the most amazing 30 minutes we've ever experienced. Driving down H3 for the first time was a moment I will never forget. Our mouths stayed open as we basically had our heads out of the windows like dogs in complete awe of the wonder. Trees towered over us but in a peaceful, inviting manner. We drove through a valley, the highway surrounded by a rich shade of green, and once in a while, we'd feel a light pattern of rain, and then suddenly it'd stop, the shining of the sun following closely behind.

Once we came close to the entrance, our driver would say, "Hey man, I can't go past the gate. Have to drop you bruddahs off here, ya?" He slowed down, and I started to scrounge around for my ID. Once I had it in my hand, the guard put his hand out.

"Welcome. See some ID?" he'd ask.

Sticking my hand out of the window, I held it with two fingers.

"Can't see your face." I leaned to one side.

Just Glow

"Ok, come aboard. You...ID?" He pointed to Matt. He leaned in and grinned. The guard seemed used to the gestures, slightly grinning back.

"Come aboard," he motioned in. "Know where you're goin?"

"No, actually. We're new Corpsmen for 2/3."

"Ohhh, Roger. Ok. Straight ahead there's a fork, veer towards the right and you'll hit the headquarters. Report there."

Our cab left and we started walking.

It was probably a good half mile to headquarters, but we were in such awe that we didn't feel the exhaustion setting in. Once in a while, we'd turn around and admire the mountains that we had just driven through, now a backdrop for the base.

After about 15 minutes, we stepped onto the sidewalk of the headquarters building. We gathered our bearings, and slowly approached the door, turning the handle.

When we entered, a Marine with a guard belt and a sidearm turned around.

"How can I help you?" he asked.

I was trying to see what rank he was, while trying not to look like I was having problems.

"Reporting for duty, Sir!" Conte raised his voice,

standing up straight. Conte did things that often made me chuckle because it came off as being sarcastic, but I knew that he was being serious.

"At ease, at ease." He smirked, letting out a small laugh. He grabbed his duty belt, straightening it out.

"Who are you and which unit are you assigned to?"

"Matthew G. Conte, 2nd B-" he continued to say in a raised voice.

"Battalion," I interrupted with a calm voice raising my hand towards Matt. "2nd Battalion, Sergeant." Matt smiled at me, still standing up straight. I was nervous and maybe Matt was, too.

"Hmm…Let me make a few calls. Stand by."

"Stand by?" Matt mouthed to me, turning only his head.

"Just wait." He stepped away and walked towards his office, putting a red dial phone receiver to his ear.

After a few minutes, he started walking back towards us.

"Ok, looks like you fellas are the first ones. There are barracks to the right near the small store you just passed on the way here. Report to the guard there."

I guess I had the expression of confusion because he paused and said, "You good?"

As we started walking up to the barracks, I realized it

Just Glow

was the barracks that I thought was a hotel. They looked much nicer than what the others looked like.

"This can't be it," I said, shaking my head.

"I dunno man, this is the only building next to the store." Matt looked around, scanning the area. The mountains in the distance were draped with a shade of white, but you could still see the outline of its vast height. A building painted light gray, the barracks stood out from everything else. The landscape was neatly manicured, accent lights on the lawn highlighting the cleanliness of the walls.

We walked through one of the entry ways, and the common area was clean, bright and lined with a number of doors. In the middle was the guard hut.

"Docs! Welcome!" The guard yelled out from the doorway. It was surreal hearing a Marine say Doc, and especially to us. Conte and I quickly looked at each other then looked at the guard.

"That's us," Conte proudly said.

He fumbled through a pile of papers on the desk and moved his finger up and down on what looked like a list.

"You guys are in room 1106," he said, handing us two keycards. "Just right down the hallway. Let me know if you need anything, ya?"

We exited the hut and started walking. The breeze from the wind made its way through the hallway, and it was refreshing. Gentle yet strong enough to tip over an empty water bottle.

Augusto C. Cespedes, Jr.

The barracks door was heavy. Inserted the card and the metal lock clicked, made a buzzing sound and pushed open the door.

The light from the window came in, shining against the door. It was nothing that I could have ever imagined. Having lived in Corps school and FMSS, this was Heaven.

A microwave on top of an actual refrigerator. Tiled bathroom. Desks were made of worn, aged wood with rickety legs, and all poorly arranged in the room. Carpeted flooring. Being in Hawaii was one thing, but having a pretty decent set up was the icing on the cake.

"Mom! You won't believe this..." his voice trailed off as he went outside, his cellphone to his ear. I could hear the excitement from his voice echoing down the hall.

I plopped myself on my bed, a twin bed by the wall, and placed my hands behind my head as I stared at the ceiling.

"Ok, not too bad. I could get used to this," I said to myself. If it's anything to be satisfied in the military, it's a nice barracks room.

A dresser and desk divided the room, and we spent the afternoon unpacking, telling jokes and sharing memories of Corps school and FMSS. That night, we each just laid in our beds in silence, tired. Content. Still amazed at how we were actually in Hawaii. The exhaustion from traveling kept us quiet but with moments saying, "Dude, remember when..." and another conversation would start. One of us trailed off after a sigh and "ya...," and it was exactly how a Sunday should end.

Just Glow

Welcome

"Buzz, Buzz, Buzzzz!!"

0600 HRS.

"Buzz, Buzz, Buzzzz!!"

A rhythmic hum echoed off the walls and my LG flip phone rattled on my bedside table as I turned over to grab it. Monday morning.

We both had our uniforms laid out with our best attempts of folded sleeves. We were quiet in getting dressed, partly because of the nervousness.

We had gotten word that we were to report to the Battalion Aid Station at 0800 hrs.

With the help of Bootcamp, Corps School and FMSS, it took us merely 10 minutes to get ready.

"If you're on time, you're late," Conte would say in a loud voice, considering that it was only 6am. "Never heard of that?"

Grumbling, I said, "no, what's that…?"

"If you're early, you're on time. If you're on time, you're late," he laughed, restating what he said.

I mean, it made sense. And early we were.

Augusto C. Cespedes, Jr.

The sun was just breaking the surface as we looked at ourselves one last time in the mirror before we left.

"Here goes nothin', right?" he said, confidently. His voice was always so positive. Chipper.

The heaviness of the door caused it to slam with a force, echoing throughout the patio area. We walked past the guard hut and onto the grass, a height at which could have used a good mow. The birds were of a different kind that I've ever seen, noticing that they hop and only fly if they needed to. Common Myna. You could chase after them and they'll hop away.

As I looked up to find the sidewalk, I noticed a figure walking fast towards us. Khakis. No smile. Bow legged. He brought his hand up, finger in the air as he took a few more steps.

"What are your names?" We stopped.

"Cespedes, Sir," I immediately said. As I looked closer, I noticed that he was a Chief.

"Matt Conte, Sir!"

Chief spoke with an authoritative voice. He looked the other way, quickly spun around, looked up and then at us. "Are you freaking kidding me right now? You knuckleheads almost cost me my career!" His hand was shaped like a knife, all fingers were straight and pointing it towards us.

"Chief?" Conte was confused.

Just Glow

"We're moving!" The blades of grass smacked my pant legs as we walked towards the sidewalk.

He started to walk with us but then started to grab our collars. "You knuckleheads were supposed to check in at the BAS! I waited for you all weekend! Didn't know where you were! Thought you left the island!" As we neared the BAS, people were headed our way, so he loosened up his grip and patted us on the backs but still proceeded to raise his voice.

Squinting his eyes, he loudly whispered, "SERIOUSLY. What in God's name were you thinking? And those barracks you're in right now? That was your last night there. You're in different companies, anyways…" His voice trailed off. Groups of Marines could be seen crowding the BAS with a few sounds of chatter, laughter, and cheers.

I stopped walking at everyone's pace, but I knew I had to continue. I swallowed hard. Devastation was an understatement. I was speechless. Thinking that whole time that I'd be with Conte, and now, to be separated. It's one thing to be going to war in the next few months, but to not be with my best friend? It hurt but I had to hold it in.

The sidewalk was lined with thick cement pillars on each side and as we walked towards the BAS, the breeze started to get stronger but still felt comfortable. The dust, dirt, various leaves and a few cigarette butts were scattered along the cement slab path, and as we got closer, the noise got louder.

"So there I was in Waikiki, half naked and waiting for a cab…" one guy was yelling, with his friends laughing.

Augusto C. Cespedes, Jr.

"Man, good 'ol Waikiki… why didn't you call me??!!" They all laughed together.

The Battalion Aid Station, a place where the Marines went for "sick call," was solid concrete. And by its appearance, the building was probably built in the 60s.

The doors were propped open by giant rocks, and the island wind brought in unwanted dirt, making a trail shaped like a triangle.

It was like I'd stepped into a time warp. 30 years back. The desks were of wood, rickety, rusted legs and poorly arranged but could be seen as an attempt to organize the room. Empty, white-washed walls with filing cabinets backed up against them with the color of an off-white fading into a yellow tint. There were probably eight or nine different conversations, along with the row of Marines waiting to be seen by the doctor.

Chief pointed to the right corner of the room and said, "Cespedes. You're there with Golf. Go." He gave me a little shove at the upper back, like I was his kid going into school. Standing at the desk were two people looking at papers.

I had no choice but to walk forward.

Before I got to the desk, I stopped. And then I saw it.

The word "AFGHANISTAN" was written all over the boxes and chests that were lined on the wall.

I continued to just stare and thought about a million different things but couldn't decipher what they were. It was all going at lightning speed. Emotions, feelings. After a few

Just Glow

seconds, I finally gathered it all. I thought about how I left with Conte but ended up getting separated.

What was he thinking? When were we leaving? Would I make it back?

I felt myself still shuffling towards the desk and it was then that a hand landed on my shoulder, heavily weighted, that caused me to break my stare.

"Welcome," he said.

Chapter 7
Dolly

Training for war was often cold. Damp. Dreary. Constant.

In order to get acclimated to Afghanistan's climate and various forms of environment, we first trained on the "Big Island," Pohakuloa Training Center, also known as PTA. Located 6-9k feet above sea level, it sat in miles of faint landscape, rocky terrain.

When we arrived at the island, after what felt like hours of riding in a bus, we gathered as a Company. As the clouds rolled in, the pitter-patter of rain would hit the brims of our covers.

Living in a damp hut shaped like a half cylinder, we called it home for several days.

The Marines coming back from a deployment were considered the "Senior Marines," and the Marines coming from bootcamp were considered "Junior Marines."

Augusto C. Cespedes, Jr.

As the platoon Corpsman, I was considered a Junior Corpsman, but I had a different experience. I witnessed how the Seniors greeted the Juniors, and it wasn't pleasant.

"GO, GO, GO!!! WHY ARE WE NOT RUNNING??!!!" They'd yell, even before the sun rose. As I'd try to organize my medical pack, minding my own business, the Junior Marines would hurriedly run, constantly responding with "Yes, Lance Corporal," or "Yes, Corporal."

Most times, the tension was so dense, you could cut it with a knife.

If a Junior seemed like he had an attitude, the Senior would get into his face, and hope that he would swing at him.

"Go ahead, Private. Give me your best shot. See what happens," he'd say with a calm but threatening voice. Most would not watch, as we were so used to how things were going, and some would just watch for the sick entertainment.

The Junior would just stand there. His lips curled. Nostrils flared. But he did nothing. Huffing and puffing, with clenched fists, he'd stand there at attention.

Just Glow

The other Seniors would look up to make sure nothing was about to happen. They'd have the other Senior's back, ready to defend him at will.

"That's what I thought," he'd say. You could see the Senior stand his ground, hoping the Junior wouldn't attack him. "Sit. Down. Now. Boot."

Junior Marines were labeled as "Boots," and just the sound of it was degrading. The ones to get the dirtiest, the ones to carry the heaviest.

The mentality was simple. Earn your respect.

Being a Corpsman, I did have the luxury of seeing what was going on in the main BAS tent, but I was always told, "Alright, ya gotta go back to your Marines. They're probably wonderin' where you are." The Chief and the other higher ranking Corpsmen would be kicking back and on their laptops while I'd be strolling in from a training exercise, drenched and exhausted. They've earned that, though. They've been on deployments.

Part of the acclimation process was learning how to night patrol. Despite the terrain, patrols were essential to show presence. Didn't matter how rough and rocky it was, we humped it. It's one thing to walk in the dark, but we were told to patrol without a light.

"No lights, Boys. We'll use the moon to guide us. The enemy looks for the red and white lights," Gunny would tell us.

We had set out walking a few miles from camp and the

thought of using no light was ridiculous. The first mile was easy. Flat, dirt roads. The dust from the dirt kicked up with sounds of the rocks hitting together.

"Move right," Sergeant yelled out. I looked to the right and saw that he was directing us off the path. The moon was hidden behind the clouds for a moment, but I could make out the silhouette of boulders. No road. Just a sea of huge boulders.

"But…that's to nowhere," I thought to myself. I hadn't needed to medically tend to any Marines yet, but I was a bit nervous that I was going to have to.

"Sergeant?" A Junior Marine questioned like he had read my mind.

"Did I stutter? I said move right. Let's go." So we did. A few sighs and coughs could be overheard from the shuffling of feet as we stopped walking on the path and started to make our way to the boulders.

A Senior Marine then said, "You heard him! Move right!"

One step into what seemed like the abyss, my foot was already sliding into the crack between two rocks. After that,

Just Glow

all I heard were feet sliding. But no one said anything. We kept moving forward. Pitch black, we continued on.

I pulled my foot out of the crack and was able to gather my bearings.

I stepped onto what seemed like a boulder, but the angle didn't hold. Another crack. I was afraid of completely missing a step and my jaw meeting a rock, splitting open. I started to sweat. My legs started to burn. I wanted to stop, but if I did, it would have been a disaster. I started to wonder how long we were going to be doing this.

Minutes of swearing passed and someone, ironically a Senior Marine, had spoken out for all of us.

"Sergeant....? We are barely-"

"ENOUGH!" He turned around, picking his foot out of what seemed to be a hole.

Everyone stopped.

"Do you think the enemy cares about our struggles? They feed on that shit. Do you want to die because you decided to train easy? What should the CO say to your family when you die an unnecessary death because you decided to train in your comfort zone? Think hard about that and tell it to yourself. You have to approach the enemy when and where they least expect it! Embrace the suck, Boys. Keep moving," he said, grunting. He proceeded to spit on the ground and started to walk.

I started to imagine walking on a dirt road and getting

caught by insurgents because we decided to take the easy route. And something came over me. "Trust the process."

With drops of sweat gathering to the tip of my nose, I started to breathe slower. The burn felt easier to manage.

Just a little longer. Trust the process. No pain, no gain. Don't be a part of the weak. Do it for the Marines.

I looked up and it was then I noticed something.

The moon finally came out of hiding and I stopped.

I didn't smile or say anything. I just stood there. After a few seconds, I sighed heavily and looked forward and my eyes began to focus on it.

The moon had casted its light on the vast landscape, revealing the different shapes and sizes of it all. Relief had come over me, and I swooped my hand over my face to collect the sweat. I looked at my watch. 11:02 p.m. It's been over an hour since we first stepped into the abyss.

With the glow of the moon, it was easier to be out there. My body didn't tense as much as we kept walking, and I noticed I cracked a small smile even as I still slid off the rocks. Onward and upward.

"He's down! Wait, stop!" Someone yelled out. I looked to my left and someone was bent down with their flashlight in between the rocks. It was a Senior that was in trouble.

"He needs help! Doc!" Suddenly, the burning sensation in my legs had dissipated and I started to almost run to where the light was.

Just Glow

Once I got there, his helmet was still on, but the strap was to the side.

Breathing heavily, he said, "I'm fine," spitting out brush and dirt that he had taken down with him. "What... happened?"

My first thought was a concussion. From the looks of it, he fell three to five feet and landed in a pile of brush that broke his fall. But I noticed his Kevlar helmet was scraped. He had hit his head on a branch before the fall.

"You may have bumped your head a little too hard, Bro," I said, checking his pupils. They were dilated, even with the flash of the penlight.

"Any numbness?"

"I'm... ok... just a little woozy..."

"Can you get up?" I asked, placing my hand on his shoulder. "We gotta get you to the BAS."

Slowly, we pulled him up and with the help of several of us, we got him to the nearest road. Luckily, a truck was able to get to us and they picked him up.

Sergeant stepped away from all of us and contacted the camp. It seemed like he was gone for at least 10 minutes.

He raised his hand in the air, pointed to the sky and swirled it around in a circle. "Must be a blessing in disguise because we are going back," sergeant yelled out, and then pointed to the direction of where the truck went.

Augusto C. Cespedes, Jr.

I couldn't believe it. We were going back.

What felt like a few miles, we walked in a relaxed formation, side by side. The burning of my legs had gone away, but the sensation of blisters rubbing on the heels began. Must have been from the constant sliding.

I soon heard familiar sounds. Laughter.

Camp must have been nearby.

A few more minutes and we could take the gear off. My med pack. The best part of it all was the temperature was cool, roughly mid-50s. After sweating for a quarter of the night, the steam was seen coming off our backs as we took off our flak jackets and other gear. The musty, sour smells of our sweat soaked shirts reeked even in the open air, but no one paid much attention to it.

The Marines didn't care much about sleep, so once they took off their gear, they dug into their MREs yelling out what each other had. It was like Christmas.

"Yes! Yes! Jalapeño cheddar!" someone yelled, like it was the Golden Ticket in a Wonka Bar.

"Oh, come on, Cheese Tortellini again??!"

"I'll take it!" And the exchange was quick, throwing each other packets over one another's heads.

Their faces, lit by one single flashlight and caked on with sweat and dirt, all smiled ear to ear over packaged, high calorie meals.

Just Glow

I looked at my watch again. 0202 hrs.

Knowing we only had four hours until sunrise, I rolled out my green mat, laid down and closed my eyes, still chewing on pieces of a muffin that I fumbled blindly for in the cargo pocket of my uniform.

Lucky Enough

I woke up to the clinking of a spoon circling a tin can, and the smell of cigarette smoke. Small chatter was heard in the near distance, with quick sounds of zippers.

It was time to get up.

"Wakey, wakey, eggs and bakey," someone said out loud. The fog of the morning was at its fresh haze and was thick.

"Come get your chow, Juniors! Doc, you're up."

A military truck with a trailer attached was set up for an assembly line of food; school cafeteria style. Huge trays of food were lined up on tables that, well, didn't really look like food. As I stood in line behind the Marines, I leaned to the left and took a peek. The tray of scrambled eggs had a shiny appearance to it like a sheet of ice that glistened in the sun. As the plastic wrap was being taken off, beads of water would drip onto the substance. Then, the metal ladle would bury itself into the thick layer with instant ease, and like a piece of yellow lard, it easily was removed from the tray and plop, onto the cardboard tray.

Augusto C. Cespedes, Jr.

Like children in line for school lunch, we shifted like one moving unit with our trays out, accepting everything that was provided.

Tiny pieces of brown colored sausages shaped like "AA" batteries were in a tray next to the eggs. They rolled around like items in a junk drawer. As it seemed like they've sat out for hours, the lard had turned to white. 50 degrees and slightly windy, it didn't have a chance to stay hot.

"Eat up, Boys! Big training today. We are hiking the mountain."

My head dropped and I started to mentally dig for some motivation. It was deep but I was lucky to gather it. I held out my tray and as it got heavier, I walked to where the rest of the Marines were and sat on my pack. Instead of complaining, the Marines joked about the appearance of the food but surprisingly ate it like it was their Mama's best Sunday cooking.

I took a spoonful of the egg that I carved out and held it up to examine the small craters it had in it.

Yellow tofu that moves like gelatin.

"Wanna know a trick?" A Senior Marine asked.

I looked at him, still holding up the spoon.

"Anything tastes better with hot sauce," he laughed, still chewing on the eggs as he spoke out. He threw me a small plastic bottle of hot sauce from an opened MRE package.

I opened it and shook a few drops on it. Killed the

Just Glow

blandness of the eggs. The taste was a bearable mix of spice and salt. I grinned. He was right.

"Wow," I said, taking another bite. "Pretty good." I let it sit in my mouth to try and enjoy it and it really gave it a better taste. Incredible? No, but it was something I could carry on into deployment.

Training consisted of a six-mile hike, hours at the rifle range and introduction to urban warfare.

The first thing I thought of when the term "urban warfare" was spoken to me, I imagined the movie Black Hawk Down. Buildings upon buildings riddled with bullets, rubble everywhere you stepped and the enemy hiding within.

Luckily, because it was unfortunately the most common warfare we would be fighting in, the military built a mock city the size of a football field, consisting of a mosque, small houses, and a market. All made out of wood. It thrived with actors playing certain roles with most being harmless, normal, everyday civilians. The purpose of this was to understand how the enemy hides within the normalcy; paying attention to how people responded to you if asking about a certain incident or person. Terrorists paid people to do bad things. Whether it was a child on a bike or an elderly man sitting peacefully on a bench, they were able to persuade them to potentially kill us.

In a deep, bellowing voice, the 1st Sergeant said to all of us, "It would be wise…" he paused, spitting chewing tobacco that splattered on the gravel, "to treat this time in training like it's the real thing. If you don't, it'll be your loss."

Augusto C. Cespedes, Jr.

There was fake blood. The actors spoke Arabic. They prayed, showed emotion and never broke character. It was hard at first to take it seriously, but after a few runs of it, it started to become like the real thing.

It was only mid-morning but I wanted to get a head start on things, so I slowly organized my med pack for another night patrol, when someone yelled out.

"Corpsman Up! We need a Doc!" The thought of what happened on the night patrol flashed through my mind, but as I looked up, I saw a Marine being carried by two others, with his right foot exposed. It appeared injured with a closed fracture.

The Marines all yelled out, some with sarcasm and not at the same time.

"Doc!"
"Dooooc!"
"Doc C!"

I stood up, raised my hand and took a deep breath.

"1st Platoon Corpsman, right?"

"That's me, Gunny," I responded with confidence.

"Gonna need you to escort him to the hospital. It's pretty bad. He fell off the ridge, heard a snap. Didn't break skin, though." His words sounded garbled, but I quickly realized he just needed to spit from the chewing tobacco. He shifted his foot to move it out of the way and spit a mixture of saliva and dark colored fluid.

Just Glow

The Junior Marine, writhing in pain, wasn't saying anything intelligible. He had a rolled-up olive drab handkerchief in his mouth, and seemed to be biting hard on it, with threads of saliva on the side of his mouth. He held his knee and just stared at his foot, crooked and deformed. We didn't have to search for a truck, as a medical truck was sitting at the camp site. We loaded up our things with the Marine safely transferring to the back, leg open to the air.

"Off ya go! Hurry back now." Gunny hit the side of the truck like it was some kind of mule and we set off to the island's hospital.

Even though it had only been roughly 10 days, stepping away from the training environment was a relief. The sound of the truck, loud, robust. No radio. No yelling. No gun sounds or explosions. For that split second, I felt like a normal kid again.

We started driving east and the clouds slowly started to disappear. The sun revealed itself and it was beautiful. The temperature increased; the grass was green. As the mountains and landscape moved, it stayed constant, like a suspended article of clothing on a laundry line.

"I think we're here," the driver had said, a Marine who was primarily responsible for the transportation portion of training.

I slammed the door and looked up. The hospital laid beneath the sea of green, a cream-colored building.

Hospital staff started approaching the vehicle.

Augusto C. Cespedes, Jr.

"Hey, we've been expecting you. We can bring him in through the side. Gonna be a few hours ya?" the nurse said.

"We'll be here," the driver said.

"Guess we're gonna have to figure out how to kill time," I said, looking out at the view. I walked across the street and sat at the edge of the bench that was outside of the entrance. Scanning the horizon, I started to think. It was still so surreal to be living in a place like this. It was exciting to think of it, but it felt useless at the same time because I was going to be gone for eight months.

After moments of silence, a few voices were heard from a distance.

It was a family of four leaving the hospital. The boy, probably around the age of five, had a bandage to his lower leg, being carried by his mom. The girl, taller than him and most likely his sister, held the dad's hand while they walked together to their car. I hadn't seen my parents in eight months, so seeing this family stalled me. I froze and focused on them. It suddenly made me think of my childhood. Young. Free. Dependent of my parents. Without a worry in the world because my parents were there for me. I got lost in my thoughts and, in an instant, broke like a hammer to a glass vase.

I blinked hard and realized where I was.

Training for war.

Not sure if I'd ever come home again.

I was a 19-year-old Navy Corpsman assigned to a

Just Glow

platoon of infantry Marines who were willing to die for the person who fought next to them. I wasn't ready, but I had no choice. I already made it this far. A part of me wanted to drop my things, fly back home, and be a kid again. I started to think about being at the liaison, staring at myself in the bathroom mirror. I could've walked away then. I could've walked away when the recruiter at the mall started talking to me. I missed my old life.

My eyes started to water and then I heard whistling. I tried to make out what it was to the tune of, and after several seconds, I knew. I took in a deep breath and smelled cigarette smoke. There was someone next to me.

"Baby don't worry, about a thing, because every little thing…is gonna be alright…"

At the corner of my eye, I saw someone sitting at the other side of the bench. I glanced over to acknowledge her choice of tune, and we both nodded. I wanted to smile but all I could give was a half effort one, like someone put a finger to the side of my mouth and pushed it up.

As she took in a deep breath, I could almost hear the crackling of the cigarette ember, and at the end of exhaling smoke, she said, "You remind me so much of my son." The voice was raspy, deep but had a comforting sound to it.

I cleared my throat, wiped away whatever tears were in my eyes and my half effort smile had turned full.

"Haha, really?" I asked, turning my head to acknowledge her.

She was frail with black hair sitting with her back

slouched and legs crossed. Wearing a distressed pink shirt, shorts and flip flops she appeared like she had been sitting there for hours. Comfortable on a cold, metal bench.

"He always wore his haircut like yours. What do they call it? High and tight?" With her legs crossed, she had her elbow on her knee with the cigarette in between two fingers.

I put my hand to the side of my head to feel the fade. I remember I had gone to the barber right before we left.

"Ya, I think that's the term…," I said, laughing a bit.

"So you're training at Pohakuloa, ya? Where everyone goes. So high up on the mountain. It's so cold there!" She said as she made herself laugh, causing herself to cough. She turned the cigarette away, so she didn't burn herself, and brought it back to her face. And then proceeded to take another drag.

I smiled at the quirkiness and the fact that she kept smoking as if nothing happened, but I think I also smiled because a local was interested in talking to someone like me.

"Ya it's ok." I looked down at my boots and then my eyes looked up to stare at the sky. It was a perfect paint of blue with a few clouds that looked like cotton. The sun was turning a bright orange, slowly making its way towards the top of the mountain.

"Dolly," she then said, turning to me with her hand out. Her shirt said Hilo says Aloha!

I gently shook it and felt the hardness of her bones that were covered over with paper thin skin.

Just Glow

"Augusto," I said in return.

"Augusto…Spanish? Filipino? Sounds Spanish," she said, sounding more interested. She now was facing towards me with her left knee on the bench.

"Filipino. I'm a Junior, they actually call me J.R. back at home."

"Ohhh," she said, as the raspiness of her voice carried. "J.R.….where's home?" she asked.

"Texas…"

"Oh wow! The states….tsk… Ya… I haven't been there in forever," she said, lighting another cigarette. She lit it so quick, it was almost like second nature for her. The quick movements of her hands, one swift flick of the lighter.

"Do you have family there?" I asked.

"Me? Ya…they're all there. Me and my husband are the only ones here." When she said that, I couldn't imagine being an ocean apart from my family. And then I realized that I actually was.

"Oh, sorry to hear… is that tough for you? For you to be so far from them?" I regretted to have asked that at such an early part of the conversation, but I was thinking about my own situation and I felt like I had nothing to lose.

"Sometimes…" she trailed off, taking a longer drag than usual. "My son and I got into an argument a long time ago and he left the island with his family. So, we haven't spoken since then."

It hurt to hear her say that. I could only imagine herself getting older, dying and never speaking to him ever again.

Before I got a chance to say something empathetic, she asked, "How is your family?"

I don't know.

No one has ever asked me that.

And that was when the emotions roared in.

I tried to hold it in as best as I could, but it was the question that drew in the thoughts of home. And it was the smallest, most vivid memories. Mom's cooking. Playing in the backyard while my dad mowed the lawn. Catching dragonflies with my mom. Soccer tournaments. Going to my cousin's house for the summer. My face felt tense, then weak and I looked away from Dolly, afraid I was going to weep.

"I'm sorry," she said. "I didn't mean to upset you." She put out her cigarette and got closer to me.

"No, it's fine," I lied, taking a deep breath. "Don't say sorry. They're fine. I'm sure they're doing well. I just haven't seen them since last year. And I've never left home without them until I joined the Navy," I admitted.

"How old are you?" she asked.

"Nineteen," I said. It was January 2005, and we were

Just Glow

scheduled to leave for Afghanistan in the spring. I would turn twenty years old in June.

"You have so much to look forward to," she said confidently. But I didn't believe her. The idea of war was on my mind and thinking about it put a stop on the thoughts of my future.

I didn't realize I was holding onto my emotions, but I couldn't hold it in any longer. My face let go and I started to cry.

"I hate being away from my family," I began to say, raising my voice, fluctuating in volume and pitch. "I thought it was going to be easier than this. I know I need to be strong for the Marines, but it is so hard," I admitted, letting it all out. It felt good to cry. I didn't care if anyone else was around. I knew I needed to let it go. I had held it in for so long.

When I put the Corpsman caduceus on for the first time, I knew it was going to be a tough responsibility, but the feeling is different when it's actually happening.

With empathetic eyes, Dolly looked at me and said, "Some things in life, you have to take a leap of faith. You're gonna be alright, I know it."

She leaned forward, took another cigarette out and quickly lit it, simultaneously breathing it in and leaned back.

"When I was younger, I was scared just like you. There were things in my life that I didn't know what to do, but I said to myself, 'I need to trust that this is what is right for me,' and I never looked back." She talked as the cigarette dangled between two fingers.

"You won't ever see the other side until you take that step," she said, breathing out.

I thought about Lake Bluff, and how I looked at my own reflection. Someone I didn't know, but someone I became. I thought about the recruiter who stopped me at the mall. I thought about how I walked into that town, imagining myself with a family.

Her eyes started to squint, and she put her other hand up as the setting sun had peaked through the brush, beaming off her face. It was now an orange glow that highlighted the landscape.

The entrance door moved open, making a sliding sound and someone yelled, "We're all set!"

I blinked hard a few times, breathed in deep, and stood up.

"Write to me, okay?" she said.

"I would love that," I replied. She gave me her information and I took a few steps back, smiling at her.

"Thank you, Dolly. I won't forget what you said," I promised. I pursed my lips tight and nodded.

"Good." She smiled, her poor dentition exposing itself to me. "And maybe I'll call my son now," she replied, lifting her cigarette, smiling and showing her teeth. She took one last drag of her cigarette like it was her send off for me and blew out the smoke in a dramatic fashion, staring at the setting sun's last light.

Driving back, I didn't say anything about the encounter to anyone. Never spoke about it for the duration of training. But I felt the change in me. In my perception. I held my head a little higher, and took my steps from then on looking forward but always thinking back of when I first heard Dolly humming, "Gonna be alright…"

April 2005

It was the smallest box I could find at the post office. I just needed something to send my phone home. I locked the bathroom door and sat on the toilet seat with its lid closed. I turned on the faucet just enough to make noise but not fill up the sink. Making sure my roommate was not coming back, I found myself shaking.

I stared at the LG phone, a simple flip phone I had bought in Chicago after bootcamp.

"This is it," I thought. I just shook my head. My body shook like it was 30 degrees outside and I didn't have a jacket. My back started to ache, and I couldn't hold still.

To think, just a little over a year ago, I was driving through Cypress. Skipping classes. And worried about an empty tank of gas. And now, I'm packing up for war.

The phone was like my lifeline to everything back home. My parents. Friends. My sister. I never had a good relationship with my mom, let alone speak more than five minutes with her on the phone, but when I landed in Hawaii, we spoke on the phone at least once a day. Sometimes for an hour or two. Most times to just be in each other's presence.

"Ok so you're five hours behind, right Jay?" My mom asked. I can hear her putting clothes in the washing machine, turning the dial before starting it.

"Yea, Mom. I'll talk to you after work. I'll call when I get back into my room."

"Ok, Jay! Love you!" She'd say in an energetic, excited voice. She loved it. And I loved it, too. I felt like a part of me was home.

"Let's talk this weekend!" My friend would say to me on the phone as she was getting ready for dinner with her family. I could hear them in the background asking who it was, and she'd say it was me and they would greet me. Sometimes, we wouldn't have anything to say, and it'd be me on the phone while she sat and did her homework. I didn't have unlimited minutes, so we either spoke after a certain time of the day or on the weekend. My cellphone would be scorching hot after being on the phone for so long. But it felt like being home. It was as close to being home as I could get.

And now I'm taping it up into a box.

I placed the phone at the bottom. I took a deep breath, but it cut off halfway, halting to a stop. I couldn't hold back the tears anymore.

I thought about what Dolly had said to me, but I felt like

Just Glow

I was packing away a part of myself. The flood of tears came rushing like a pipe had burst in the dead of winter, and there was no way of stopping it.

I tried my best to tape it up, but my hands couldn't hold the tape still, causing them to fold. Eventually, after several minutes, it was presentable, and I stood up. I looked at myself in the mirror. I aggressively wiped my eyes, took another deep breath and said, "Gonna be alright."

I unlocked the bathroom door and when I felt like my face had turned to its original color, I stepped outside. The silence of the room had turned to loud, echoing rock music and shouting. The Marines were packing. And some of their stuff was out in the common area.

I walked down the hallway, staying close to the wall. I wanted to turn the corner to go for a walk, but before I could, the burning of a cigarette made me stop.

"Looks like you need one," a Marine from my platoon had said. He held out the pack like they were a deck of cards and I grabbed one. Cupping my hand over the cigarette, I flicked hard on my matte black Zippo lighter but nothing came out. That never happened. *I swore it could light in the rain.*

I felt the wind form a tunnel in my direction, so it forced me to turn the corner.

On the other side of the wall, I held my hand up to cover the lighter but I didn't need to. I lit the cigarette in a swift motion, and I started to look up. The sun was casting its final rays on my face, and I squinted, holding my hand up to meet my brow.

Augusto C. Cespedes, Jr.

And I thought of Dolly.

The swift motion. The sun in her eyes. I felt like she was there with me. I remembered her dramatic cigarette drag and so… I did the same. Inhaling, I heard the crackling of the ember, revealing a bright, orange glow and felt its warmth on my upper lip.

I felt connected.

Everything will be alright.

Just Glow

My Dear Augusto,
 I am sorry for not writing to you for a long time. Please forgive me. I didn't forget you. I always think of you and how you are doing. The reason for not writing, is that I had to take care of my spouse. And he is gone now and it's very hard after 58 yrs together. Please answer if you get this card. God Blessings be with you.

To Augusto

MAY THE SONG OF
CHRISTMAS BE IN YOUR
HEART YEAR ROUND

"Love"
Always A Good
Friend
Dolly Toutie

Chapter 8
Hotter than Hell

I sat on the edge of my bed and stared at the sole of my left foot. It throbbed in unison with the beat of my heart, and I could barely touch it. The skin that had developed over the plantar wart was thick. I was trying to think of when I noticed it, but the number of miles I'd hiked, I couldn't remember.

I placed my bare foot on the carpeted floor which made my foot tense up. My attempts of trying to peel off the skin were useless and caused even more pain. I'd try and tear away skin, and a flap of it would harden, catching on my sock or a thread on the carpet. I tried to walk, but the sensation sent jolts up my calf, forcing me to put most of my weight onto the inner part of my foot.

"Ain't good at all," I said out loud. It was 0540, and my roommate was still asleep. A large dresser divided our beds, so it was likely he didn't hear me.

I opened the medicine cabinet and popped four Motrin tablets into my mouth, bent my head down and scooped a handful of water into my mouth.

Augusto C. Cespedes, Jr.

It was time to go to work.

Work consisted of taking care of your Marines, whether it was a small scrape, an ankle sprain or an ingrown toenail. As we were preparing for our deployment, medical records needed to be organized with the necessary papers inside each record prior to deployment.

One of the advantages of being a Corpsman was, if you were clever enough, you could escape out of anything.

If the Marines were doing something completely irrelevant to your job, you'd say, "I have a meeting at the BAS I have to attend. It's about Afghanistan, Staff Sergeant."

He couldn't argue with you. The risk, however, was if he tried to confirm it. But you had to risk it and that's where authenticity came into play. You had to make it seem true. Gave a specific time. Elaborated on the details.

"Alright Cespedes," he raised his voice. "Then hurry back, ya hear! We need you for a few things."

I'd walk away, hiding my smile but then doing the famous Kevin McAllister "YES!" motion behind the corner.

Walking across the freshly mowed grass, I hopped onto the sidewalk and turned left. The concrete buildings were perfectly aligned and were in a row which made an outdoor covered walkway. Everything echoed. I made sure I picked my feet up when walking because someone could hear it way down the hall.

Just Glow

After several yards, I saw the BAS and instead of going straight, I had to make a pit stop.

"But first," I pointed up, grinning, "Wiki," and I made a hard right.

A sudden shock of pain ran from the bottom of my foot to my calf.

"Sweet Mother of…" and I took in a deep breath, feeling it pulsate. It felt like a large rock was embedded into my foot, not moving.

I could tell the Motrin was wearing off.

Located close to the BAS, the Wiki was a small convenience store that held the essentials; alcohol, candy and food. But I went there for my all-time favorite, go to meal: Spam Musubi.

I'd say it's a "preferred taste" kind of snack, but to me, it served many purposes: easy to carry, equal parts of carbs, protein and fat, and was easily a "three biter." Ever since boot camp, I learned how (the hard way) to enjoy food… quickly. There was no time to sit down and savor it. That's why I loved the Musubi; you can enjoy it while on the move, fully capable of being eaten in three bites.

Wrapped carefully in plastic wrap, the combination of rice and spam was wrapped together with seaweed paper that created a perfect, subtle taste of salt and the ocean.

Walking in, you could smell the aroma as you made your way towards the small heater they were stored in. And you could tell if they were fresh. The rice would be white, even when it met the spam. If it sat for hours, the rice closest to the spam would turn a hint of light brown. On a rushed day, I'd take anything. But on that day, I was hoping for a fresh one.

I opened the glass door, and low and behold.

Top shelf. Fresh. Spam. Musubi. Just for me.

I felt the heat of the warming lamps as I grabbed the closest one and closed the door.

Once I made my way out the door, I got back onto the sidewalk, and stopped. The fluffiness of the warm rice could be felt through the plastic, and the spam was equally warm.

I unwrapped it and took a bite, first sinking my teeth into the rice. It was one of those small things that you looked forward to.

The hands of the clock moved fast and yet another workday was completed.

Baking in the Hawaiian sun, we all stood around for our last formation before the weekend. "Hurry up and wait," was something we all were used to and because it was engrained into our heads since Day One, boredom was never evident. We always found something to do.

Once you turned the corner, the smell of cigarette smoke hit your face like it was patiently waiting for your arrival. Some guys would be sitting at the wall of the company building or catching a quick nap in the shade with their covers over their face. Others would be standing around, head down, kicking the grass, pacing.

Just Glow

"Saurez versus Jackson, let's go!" You'd hear someone yell out and it was as if it was expected. Whether it was to kill time, settle a dispute or to make a bet, Marines grappled. Once names were called, the cheers bounced off the cement walls that led to the covered walkway. There wasn't any hesitation in it. They gathered in almost like a rock band calling for a circle pit. A few Seniors, with arms crossed, making sure none of the leadership was coming, nodded in acknowledgment at the front of the building. You could see their cracked smiles like the big brother giving the green light to do something mischievous, as if they were the ones who made the rules.

And multiple things would be happening simultaneously. Locker room talk, the smacking of a fresh, newly opened cigarette pack or Seniors having a few Juniors pick up trash or do things that just made you say to yourself, "What in the…"

"Do your best 1st Sergeant impression," one Senior would say to the other, practically laughing at the thought of it.

With specific hand and facial gestures, he'd begin with a deep voice and say, "Corporal! What in God's Heavenly name do you think you're doing? Get in line!" He barely could finish the impersonation as a few Marines would be on the ground laughing.

"Alright that was…" and he was interrupted by a distance shout from the Company office.

"FORMATION!!!!"

Augusto C. Cespedes, Jr.

Sarcastic voices trailed off like dominoes as the scattering of Marines could be seen falling into their squad lines.

"Formation! Get in line!"

"Formation, you nasties!" Collars of the Juniors would be pulled just for the heck of it.

Even with four platoons, not a single sound was heard as the leadership was seen walking down the company stairs. We all stared at their every movement like we were peasants looking at the ruler of our kingdom.

Lines straight, perfectly aligned with the building with a red sign in yellow lettering; "Golf Company."

Like a King speaking to his people, he spoke with a loud, raspy voice.

"Gents..." he started to say. Then a pause. You could hear the silent acknowledgment.

"Monday is our hump. Eight miles. And I don't want to hear the whining from your sucks, or I will make it twelve."

I gulped so hard that I thought the rifleman next to me heard. My saliva slowly veered down my throat avoiding my trachea, with its violent push downward heard in my ears. I thought about my plantar wart.

Humps were organized hikes that tested and trained Marines' strength and endurance. It was done with notice and sometimes as a surprise. There's one thing to walk for miles, but the catch was it was with every single piece of

Just Glow

gear, inspected by your Platoon Sergeant the morning of so no one carried lighter than anyone else.

"It would behoove you to not drink that disgusting, weak fluid you call beer and start hydrating or else your rear will meet that dreaded silver bullet! Right Docs?!!!"

A heavy slap on my shoulder blade shook me out of daydreaming and I smirked.

1st Sergeant continued, "I can't tell you what you knuckleheads can't do but don't make a fool'a yourself this weekend. I'll be with my old lady, and I don't want a phone call at zero dark thirty about you in the tank, ya hear?!!!"

"Yes, 1st Sergeant!" we all yelled together, almost rattling the company building.

"Dismissed! Platoon Sergeants, they're all yours."

From the belly, and sarcastic as ever, it would always be the same person yelling "Libbo!" Shouting, cursing and other sorts of noises were made because, well, it's the weekend.

I walked towards my barracks and tried to hide my limp, counting to 10 to keep pushing through the pain. Every step I could feel a small stab through my boot like a rusted knife digging into flesh.

I closed the door behind me and banged the back of my head to the paint.

I gotta do something about this.

Augusto C. Cespedes, Jr.

My roommate wasn't of age to purchase alcohol but one of the Seniors down the hall was, so I gathered all the courage to ask him. I had to do what I had to do.

"Corporal?" I knocked softly on the heavy metal door, his room blaring Pantera. I knew he didn't hear it, so I used the knuckle of my finger to crack open the door a bit more. He was spitting into an empty Dr. Pepper bottle, the substance appeared coffee- colored. Copenhagen long cut or snuff. The favorite. It was the smell of rubber and licorice sitting in an unventilated garage.

"Doc, what do you want?" Dressed in PT shorts that were way past his knees, shirtless that showed his fading tribal tattoos and wearing black flip flops, he came out of the other side of the dresser. He didn't have a roommate, so he was able to arrange his room the way he wanted.

"So," I started to say, kicking imaginary rocks on the ground trying to find the right words to say so he couldn't say no.

So I said it as fast and clear as I could.

"I need a few beers to cut a wart out of my foot before the hump." Feeling like I had said it quicker than I wanted it to be, I made an expression that looked like "no" was going to be the answer.

In a dramatic fashion, he spit into the bottle, and it seemed like a much larger one because of the wet, splattering sound.

"DOC. Are you serious? You don't need to make crap up for me to buy you beer. We're going to Afghanistan. I

Just Glow

ain't gonna get shot and you let me bleed out because I didn't buy you beer." He laughed. "I'm going there anyways. Need some more Cope." The thought of that widened my eyes so I turned away, letting the morbid scene pass through my head and I quickly turned back.

I sat at the edge of my bed, my left foot exposed to the cold air. Like a surgical procedure, it sat under the light, waiting.

Four empty bottles of Bud Ice sat on my desk across from me next to the empty Ka-Bar sheath.

I turned to see what time it was. 2034 hrs.

I turned my head and felt the slow motion of my body's reaction and made the decision to proceed.

The tip of the blade accidentally pierced the comforter. With hands heavy, I drew it back and held it up, admiring its length and thickness.

I blinked hard and breathed deep through my nose and turned the knife downward.

With as much of a steady hand as I could bear, I held my breath and pressed hard. With its border surrounded by an accumulation of dead skin still attached like a parasite to its host, I winced as I could feel the depth of the blade unexpectedly strike the new tissue, sending neuropathic signals to my head that urged me to stop.

Shaking, I drew it back and quickly grabbed a new bottle of beer off the bed and took a few chugs, slamming it down onto the desk, producing a violent fizz as it tried to settle itself. "Let's try this again," I mumbled.

I placed my hand on the comforter and pulled down, wiping the sweat that was pasted on my palm. I pointed down and dug the tip closer to the middle of the wart, holding my breath.

No feeling.

I let out a sigh and started to breathe, trying to keep the knife still. With careful ease, I brought the blade down and slowly pushed it forward until most of the tip was covered by tough, calloused skin.

Again. No feeling.

And then I noticed it. Blood started to seep from one of the holes.

But I couldn't stop. I had to finish.

So I stabbed it again. And again. Like the numbers on a clock. A perfect circle. Again.

After several minutes, I was at my last few moments of piercing.

My eyes couldn't focus clearly on what I had done to myself, but I knew it was nearing the end. My temples collected sweat and dripped onto my leg as I drew the knife out from my foot and blinked to re-examine the damage.

Can't quit now.

Just Glow

I wiped the blood off the knife with piece of cloth and breathed in slow. I thought about drinking the rest of the beer, but I was already in position. I pointed the knife downwards one last time and dug it in as far as I could. I felt the hardness of metal, so I reached for the cloth and shoved it in my mouth and bit down. Hard. And kept going.

Like a shovel under a rock, I lowered the blade and watched in amazement a massive wart emerge from my foot.

I bit the cloth hard, let out a moan and watched as the blood poured out of what appeared to be a massive crater.

Afghanistan 2005

A cloud of black smoke rose from the roaring seven-ton, a military transport truck that took us to our base. Armored to the teeth, we piled into the back and sat on metal benches bolted to the ground, feeling every bump of the terrain.

"Guns out, eyes peeled, Boys! Don't be complacent!" Staff Sergeant yelled out from the passenger seat. The smell of diesel overpowered the ripened stench of the city's sewage as we parted from the base.

Out of nervousness and excitement, the sounds of metal and steel banged against the armored plates of the truck as the Marines held out their M16s and M249s. I looked down and was reminded that I only had a sidearm, the M9 service pistol. I looked up and began to crouch down.

A Senior Lance Corporal looked at me and said, "Doc,

pull out the pistol." I looked at him and smiled, waiting for the joke that followed.

"It's a weapon, ain't it?" he said, repositioning himself and continued to look forward. He was a fireteam leader, equipped with his M16 and an attached M203, a grenade launcher. Fumbling for it, I unholstered the pistol and drew back the upper receiver, hearing it load a round into the chamber. I held it out like the rest of the Marines, finger straight and off the trigger.

As we drove into the heart of the city, the sounds uninvitedly engulfed us and I felt a tighter grip on the pistol.

In what appeared to be in a median stood a sign, tattered with bullet holes, that wrote in Arabic, "Jalalabad Welcomes You." My eyes followed the words as the truck passed it by, paying more attention to the riddled sign.

The streets were flooded with people. Merchants, children being pulled by their parents, shops with various provisions that dangled in the sun, motorized scooters and cars. It was as if there were no road signs, but everyone seemed to understand where to drive. Distant and nearby sounds of motorists zoomed past us in different pitches and decibels, filling the stagnant air with fumes that collided with the pungent smell of meat, fecal matter and poor hygiene.

It seemed that some citizens weren't paying attention to what was going on as they crossed the street, almost being hit by our truck.

"Back! Back!" The turret gunner yelled, motioning with his hands. He had two hands up in a pushing motion. It was

Just Glow

then that our Interpreter, George, stood up from the back and yelled in Arabic.

إقف!
إقف!

or "qif!" he yelled, saliva seen sticking to the side of his mouth. He repeated it in such a manner that his voice started to crack. I learned a little later that it was an Arabic command for "halt," or "stop." His Kevlar helmet loosely fitted, his hand motioned in and out.

With swiveled heads, each Marine turned to see what was going on. Some had stood up, eager for an early fight.

A four-member family looked up as they rushed across the street, the parents dragging the children to the side cursing and yelling at our truck.

Once we passed a certain point, it was as if we only heard the thunderous sound of our truck hitting several potholes causing us to all shift on the bench. We had left the city.

The crowds started to slowly minimize once we passed a few yards of concertina wire, which led to a makeshift "checkpoint," a gate made up of a large PVC pipe and a man dressed in a camouflage uniform holding an AK-47. He nodded as our truck approached, lifted the gate by cranking the wheel and we passed through.

It seemed like we were in more of a "neighborhood" type setting, with houses ranging from small shacks made of tin roofs, painted wood and cement walls to actual small houses of brick. People stood outside their doors and raised their hands up to their eyes as to block the dust and light from their face as our truck picked up the dirt.

The next checkpoint was built in a fashion where the truck had to zig-zag to the gate, with barriers made of giant cement blocks and concertina wire. Once you reached the gate, it was heavily guarded by camouflaged men with AK-47s and a few Marines carrying M4s, a smaller version of the M16. The gate itself, made of thick steel, was operated by the guard at the post, which was 20 to 30 feet high, manning an M2, a .50 caliber machine gun.

One man with red hair, dressed in camouflage, forcibly held up his hand in the direction of the truck with his other hand on the butt of the rifle, causing the truck to stop several yards away from the gate. Four Afghan soldiers walked to the truck with black sticks with mirrors attached to ends and started to inspect the underside of the truck, walking around it with serious expressions. The sweat on their heads could easily be observed from the inside of the truck. Once the inspection was complete, they made a motion of "All Clear," and the truck proceeded into the FOB (Forward Operating Base).

Even though the sounds of the engine grew, the tires crunching over loose gravel could still be heard as we entered the base.

I couldn't see much of what was going on outside, so I grabbed the thick side of armored plating to lever myself up.

"AHH!" I hissed at myself, waving my hand in the air, "that's hot as a mug, Bro!" I yelled.

The Marine next to me just chuckled, and said, "Well

Just Glow

whadyuh expect? It's almost 115 degrees out here. That's some dry heat." Like a leaky faucet, his sweat dripped from his chin onto the dusty truck bed, making a small pool of mud.

He pulled me up from the shoulder of my flak jacket and we all peered over the side. We stared down at the rows of wooden shacks that stood below the raised path.

"Welp, at least we made it in," Staff Sergeant said, wiping his brow. He jumped off the passenger stair step and made a crunching sound as he landed onto the ground.

"Well? You just gonna sit there? Let's go. The faster we move, the faster y'all can rest."

We all moved at once, shuffling to the back of the truck and each jumping off.

Once we got our assigned hootch, we grabbed our gear and made our way to the door. A makeshift rectangular handle made of wood; a Marine opened it. Like a group of kids discovering a hidden room in a 200-year-old house, we all piled at the doorframe to see what it looked like inside.

Augusto C. Cespedes, Jr.

The air in the hootch was a thick, stagnant wall of heat. Once I took a step in, the air wrapped itself around my head with my ears smothered in the intensity of its hot breath. Inside was floor to wall to ceiling plywood with the exposed beams revealing where the nails have been hammered through. I slowly took a few steps forward and I could feel the bending of the wood, giving off a cracking sound.

I walked across to the other door, and with it being empty, it echoed. As I opened the door, three Marines were right outside about to enter.

"It's a tad bit warm in there," I jokingly said, holding up two fingers like I was measuring a millimeter. But honestly, it was nothing to joke about.

I had never experienced a type of heat like Afghanistan's heat. It's dry, unforgiving and utterly brutal. Most of the time, you don't even realize you're sweating that much. The first thing you'd notice is that you don't have the urge to urinate, no matter how many bottles of water you drank.

"Fifteen water bottles, Gents. That's how much we are packing. We're told we will get a supply drop when we've reached the mountain," Staff Sergeant bellowed out. He was wearing a desert boonie, and Oakley sunglasses that were tied to his neck. The sides of his face were glistening with sweat, and making its way down, formed a horse collar made of sweat that darkened his shirt.

As we tried to pack our things under a shaded tree, I looked to the North towards the mountains we had planned to scale in the coming days, repeatedly blinking from the sweat that caused my eyes to blur.

Operation Red Wings

We were given word that a Chinook helicopter carrying a dozen or so special operators trying to save Navy SEALs who were pinned down by multiple insurgents was shot down. No one survived the crash. One SEAL who was left alive in the firefight, ran to a nearby village. Our mission was to set up a blocking position on the valley to close the gap.

"Gather 'round, Gents," Lieutenant said, motioning us all to the middle of our hootch. He then pulled out a DVD player.

"What I'm about to show you is some really gruesome stuff, but I want you to watch it and get angry. I want it to motivate you," he said, looking at us. I kneeled down onto the olive drab cot and watched him insert the DVD into the player. He pressed the silver triangle, and we all heard it spin with a deep wheeze.

First, it was horizontal lines running down the screen

like raindrops and you chased it down with your eyes but focused on the next ones at the top. Then it gradually turned clear.

It was a muffled voice of a man through a megaphone, most likely Arabic, speaking in an aggressive manner. Next, a grainy video of men in black clothing running an obstacle course, and as I put two and two together, it all made sense; a propaganda video for recruiting terrorists. Initially, it looked sped up, but it wasn't. They were fit, lean and couldn't see their faces. Crawling under barbed wire, effortlessly climbing onto eight to ten foot walls and careening through a set of horizontal bars. I gulped hard and imagined myself being captured by them, on my knees with a hood over my head, thinking about my life. The video didn't make me angry but rather worried about the Marines. *Were we ready to face them?* The question didn't matter. We were leaving the next day for the mountains.

The video went black for a few seconds, and everyone started to get up, stretch and make juvenile comments like facing an opposing team.

"We've got this! Let's go!" one Marine said, high-fiving another as they walked to the side.

"They're that ashamed to be hiding their faces?! I'm ready for 'em," another said, pounding his fists together.

As most of us started to get up, the screen came back on, and we paused our movements. It looked like a home video. A time and date was stamped at the bottom, and it was of this year. This month. Actually, just a few days ago.

At first, the camera was pointing at a blue sky, filming a

Just Glow

helicopter that was seen through the trees. A few series of noises and rustling were heard, even though the quality of the video but it was the noticeable sound that was heard at the end. A boom so loud that we all focused on the small DVD player.

With the cameraman shaky, he was panting and running down a hill in a wooded forest, trying to speak in an apparent exhaustion. He was seen following a few men that were also doing the same and, in a few seconds, we noticed what the camera was attempting to focus on. And it finally did.

It was a fiery crash of a helicopter. Its remains were engulfed in flames with black smoke rising into the tree-line.

"Gents, I want everyone to understand what is happening in this video," Lieutenant started to say. There were whispers of curse words and some can be heard yelling out.

"This helicopter was sent in an attempt to rescue the Navy SEALs from enemy fire and unfortunately was shot down by an RPG." We didn't look at him while he spoke as we were fixated on the screen.

We all watched it in horror.

The cameraman, panting and speaking in Arabic, repeated the same phrase over and over. Trying to keep still, he focused on a few bodies on the forest floor, tattered and covered in blood and dirt. Their faces stared at the sky, lifeless. Fixed. It was then we knew who they were. They held up the military IDs close to the camera, and it was the same card that we all had. The ones issued to every military serviceman. As the terrorists rummaged through the men, you could hear the astonishment in their voices, as if they had found gold. They started to pull off their dog tags and dangle them in the camera screen, smiling, the cameraman acknowledging their actions.

A few Marines got up and walked away. I, on the other hand, just stared blankly at the screen. I was thinking of a million different things but all of it aligned with how I might die. I held onto my holstered M9 like it was something that would actually protect me. My stomach turned as my naive imagination completely took over, exploding into the "what ifs" like a disorganized array of combustible particles piercing the air. I started to imagine myself being dragged out of a wrecked helicopter, another language being yelled in pure frantic and my fingers digging through the dirt as my childhood would repeatedly rewind and fast forward in my head, wondering exactly how they would kill me.

A sudden slap on the shoulder and an arm wrapped around my neck.

"Don't worry, Doc. We won't let anyone hurt ya. We've got your back!" a Senior Marine said to me, smiling.

I had no choice but to believe him.

Day One, The Climb

Our truck stopped at the base of the mountain. It stood tall, intimidating, endless. Like its surrounded counterparts,

Just Glow

it was a vast ocean of greens, browns and tans of infinite valleys.

"This is as far as we're goin'," the driver said.

When we climbed off of the seven-ton, I heard the noise of a peculiar sound. An animal.

I looked on the other side of the truck and donkeys were with a few Afghanistan soldiers who were tending to them. I couldn't help but laugh.

"What's, uhh, going on here?" I asked, pointing at the animals. For a split second, I had forgotten about the mission and focused my attention on the purpose of the donkeys.

"They're goin' with us, Doc. Duh. They're apparently good at hiking up mountains," a Marine stated as he exhaled a cloud of smoke from a newly lit Lucky Strike.

He was right. Donkeys were incredible hikers and could endure extreme temperatures and terrain while carrying a lot of weight on their backs. The sounds of donkeys were something new to me, though. It was a loud screech in one breath and then a mixture of hyperventilation and wheezing that lasted about 10 more seconds. Over. And over. Times that by eight donkeys. From the looks and sounds of our furry travelers, we wanted the enemy to notice us. Flush them out.

Once all was unloaded from the truck, we took our first steps to scale the mountain. With about 5-10 feet apart, we walked. And walked for hours. Sometimes it was silent, sometimes not. Sometimes you'd hear the occasional start of a cadence call but would then die out. Other moments would be someone reminiscing about their past, or a few would sing their favorite tunes.

"Out of all the songs, you choose that?!" a Sergeant would yell out to another Senior Marine. With a dangling cigarette stuck to his lip, his question was a loud mumble. We'd all laugh but not miss a step, and it'd go silent again, waiting for the next thought or sarcastic comment.

The terrain was of various forms of rock, soft sinking sand and heat. Couldn't forget about that heat. I felt myself already trying to catch my breath as the nervousness tightened my accessory muscles. But I knew to keep silent, dig deep and find strength. For myself. For my Marines. To get home.

Just Glow

I tried to remember to take sips of water every few minutes but the more I drank, the more my head uncontrollably dripped. Drip by salty drip, my nose like an annoying leaky faucet, intermittently released a drop of sweat onto my boot or flak jacket. And the water was warm, almost hot. I drank it, as it mixed well with my sweat.

"Save. Your. Water!" Staff Sergeant yelled to us, temporarily walking backwards to announce his order. His head was covered by his boonie, but could see the line of sweat that had already been established on his neck armor.

And the walking went on like a sick, monotonous cycle. Left then right, a continuous lifting of the foot and heel trying not to drag your feet. It was like as if your next step onto the ground would follow with powerful waves of enemy rounds zipping past your head that sent you to the ground. It was a mind game. And not a question if it was going to happen. It was a matter of when.

Augusto C. Cespedes, Jr.

Blurry waves of static were heard from our translator's radio and after minutes of choosing a channel that had anything sounding like the enemy, he'd put it up to his ear and yell back in Arabic, almost fighting with the person on the other side. We'd look at him in curiosity of what was said, while the Afghan soldiers would respond, yelling back in Arabic, laughing and gripping their AK-47s holding them up and chanting. In a sick sense of humor, it helped the grueling process of walking and the continuous sweating, knowing we had more firepower than anyone in the area.

During the familiar sounds of repositioned gear and weapons and boots hitting the gravel, a Marine yelled out, "What are they saying??"

"They're saying they can see us and they will not let us out of the valley alive," he said, with a thick accent, holding the receiver up to his ear as if he was confirming the threat. I couldn't see it, but I felt the Marines' strength as they gripped their rifles tighter, despite the temperature and conditions. It was like hearing our Translator arguing with the enemy created an immediate anger in the platoon, stronger than anything around them.

Despite the constant threats, we still scaled, constantly exposing ourselves to our full potential. The hellish warmth

Just Glow

of the sun beat down constantly like an unforgiving ball of fire. And in each exhalation of my breath, I knew it wouldn't end anytime soon.

However, in such conditions, it was easy to search for any form of entertainment. Humming, smoking a cigarette and counting steps. And having the Afghanistan soldiers with us was one thing I found to be smiling at. From their mannerisms to their motivation to keep up with us was something that kept me going.

"Woah there, Comrade!" a Marine sarcastically yelled, ducking from the swaying gun muzzle, "muzzle check!" The Afghan soldiers would immediately point their rifles up, motion with their left hand with palm out and then touch their chest, smiling, revealing their poor dentition.

They had a bit of quirkiness to them but with the strong hospitality of a fellow serviceman. They didn't follow any military regulations that we were used to, but you could easily see the passion about their religion and country, knowing exactly where the sun would set and laying out their individual prayer rugs. Wearing a camouflage uniform paired with leather sandals, they would carefully remove their footwear and place them neatly next to them. The translator and soldiers would group together, say a few words and all do the same exact thing. Kneeling east towards Mecca, they'd intermittently bow and this went on for several minutes. With our cigarettes burning and the smell of smoke carrying through the sparse breeze, we carefully watched them while the bizarre sound of donkeys didn't even seem to bother them.

The language barrier was evident, but we enjoyed trying to understand each other through body language, like a weird game of Charades. It was the jerk like movements that connected us in that moment, and we'd all laugh, knowing it was all fun and games. It made time pass quicker, and for some weird, sad reason, it boosted our motivation that seemed to burn helplessly in the heat.

"Staff Sergeant, we're runnin' low on water," the Squad Leader would say, shaking the warm bottle of water and dangling it in the sun, disturbing the already established small bubbles in the container.

"Supply drop sometime tonight. Try and hold on a little longer. Once the sun goes down, it'll be cooler. For now, stop bein' such a weak body, Corporal," he said, smiling. You could see the sweat fly off his head as he moved in a fast motion.

What made it even worse was we ironically came up to a stream, and the sight of it was beautiful. It was a relief to see some form of cooler water than the ones that have turned hot in our packs. The form of it twisted and turned in the valley as the misshaped rocks and boulders appeared to have been thrown in. Looking at the flow of water made our desire of thirst worse, almost teasing us.

The Afghan soldiers slowly started to drop their

weapons and began squatting on the rocks. They cupped their hands and hurriedly drank the water, bringing it to their faces.

"We probably shouldn't do that," someone said, with his hands in the upper part of his flak. He bent down to relieve the pressure from his shoulders and back, as the flak jacket weighed roughly 20-30 pounds. As he bent down, you could see the sweat create a darker shade of the uniform at his lower back.

"I'm on my last bottle," one of the Riflemen said, taking a small swig.

Please God. I was trying to back track on how many bottles of water I had consumed over the past eight hours. My pack was feeling light, so it was then the feeling of worry engulfed my desire to drink.

I took off my pack and opened it. None. My stomach started to hurt, and I started to lick my chapped lips. "I am screwed," I quietly mumbled. I dug with my hand aimlessly like some miracle would happen and a bottle of water would show up but no, it was immediately destroyed.

Augusto C. Cespedes, Jr.

One of the Marines saw my expression, and threw a rock at me, hitting me in the boot.

"What's wrong, Doc?"

"I...uh...have no more water," I said, looking down in shame. I felt defeated, like it all just snuck up on me and I'm the one left to suffer. No time stamp on the supply drop.

"Let's keep moving. We'll set up camp when we get to the top," Staff Sergeant yelled out. Our Lieutenant was standing with one leg on a large rock, the map laid out like a blanket and slightly bending forward, motioned the compass protractor in different positions. He then yelled out, "Only one kilometer to where we need to be!"

I looked at my watch. 1503 hrs. The hottest part of the day. It was when the sun had already been repeatedly beating on the earth, and with no mercy or regard to its victims, it still continued to scorch.

And up the ridge we went, and it was in that moment we dug deep. The change in elevation caused our breathing to change. Our muscles tightened. Quivered. Anxious to get to the top. Some guys threw out their cigarette as it may have distracted them from focusing. I turned around to check on everyone else and saw one of the machine gunners and the expression on his face. His eyes fixed, an intermittent squinting from exhaustion, then, instantly bulge out to keep up with the ground. Relentless. The hardened, unforgiving steel of the M240 laid across his shoulder blades and I could see the pain in his every step. His head was at an angle and unintentionally lowered because of the weight of the weapon.

Just Glow

"Doc, don't you have IV bags in your med pack?" someone asked, still panting. He was pale, as the flushed appearance of his fair, Irish skin had diminished. He was right.

Out of desperation and a grain of excitement, I whipped around my med pack and unzipped it. Its plastic, Vietnam era zipper disconnecting. And there they were. Four, one-liter bags of Ringer's Lactate. An isotonic fluid solution used for fluid resuscitation in critical cases and, surprisingly, weren't hot. Whether it was the protective plastic covering or buried in between the dressings, Quikclot and tourniquets, its temperature seemed cooler.

I gripped one side of the covering and ripped it off with my teeth. Then, I removed my Ka-Bar from its sheath. Using the blade's tip, I turned the blade sideways and made a careful slit at the top. Initially I was willing to be adventurous and drink the fluid, but once I took a small taste of its salty concentration, I rethought the desire. But my parched mouth needed something other than dust and a constant grittiness of sand. I didn't remember the last time I had urinated.

The Marine next to me noticed my hesitation and him being just as thirsty, said "I get some after you, Doc."

Augusto C. Cespedes, Jr.

We glanced at each other, hesitated, but the thirst quickly overcame and we devoured it. It was refreshing and punishing. I held my nose to hide its strong, briny flavor. The intense, warm taste made me gag but I needed to keep going. I swallowed the fluid in huge gulps, in an attempt to distract myself. I didn't want to drink it. I needed to drink.

After what seemed to be an hour of climbing, we had reached where we needed to be. Our mission was to provide a blocking position at one part of the valley that keeps the enemy in control, and if they decided to leave the mountains, they'd have to go through us.

I looked at the other side of the ridge and saw a small unit of Army Rangers. Some were sitting, others looking beyond at us, hand at the brow, shading their eyes. It was a small relief to see it. One gave a friendly wave. There were only about six to eight of them and it appeared that their mission was the same; to provide a blocking position. When I thought about it, firepower wasn't an issue. We had a whole platoon of Marines, thirty-five to forty men with a few fireteams consisting of heavy machine guns and a mortar team.

After setting up camp, we arranged the fire watch schedule and once we all were able to sit down, it was a sheer game of "sit and wait." The sharing of MREs, stories being told, the burning of cigarettes and the natural thumping of smokeless tobacco cans.

Because of the lack of lighting and industrial gases, the Afghanistan sky was nothing I had ever seen before. It was like having your own planetarium. Over the past few days, I'd attempt to admire one section of the sky and then start to notice another section, more luminous than the others. Then the next. And the next. After several moments, I paused and took a deep breath and realized, it all deserved to be looked at as a whole. Every star seemed to have been visible, beaming at their brightest. Like it was free. Absolutely nothing was able to harm it. And for a split second, you'd actually forget where you were; one of the most hostile environments in the world and a starry night could take you away. My back on the uneven, rocky surface with unclean hands behind my head, I stared at the blanket of stars and finally, for once, felt a cool breeze brush across my face. My mouth, cracked, reddened and tender, slowly twitched that may have resembled a smile.

July 4th, 2005

"BRRRRRRRT!" Like a mysterious beast in the distance, the instant roar woke us up in the dead of night. The sounds of weapons moving, the metals clanking together in a scurry.

"Geezus, what was that??!" I asked, rustling around and grabbing my Kevlar helmet. The echoing of a deep, thunderous crackling sound made me jump. The sound of it was like a monster in the forest, something we've never heard before.

"Those are A-10s," Staff Sergeant calmly said, looking at the ridge.

Moments later, the monstrous sound was even louder and suddenly a ball of fire appeared on the other side of the valley, scorching the land like gas-soaked tinder to a flame.

The sight of it was distressing, watching huge forests being scorched by a plane's weaponry, but comforting to know we weren't exactly alone in the mountains.

Hollering of excitement erupted as we all got out of our sleeping bags to watch the action.

"Woaaaah," a Junior said, mesmerized.

"Ya! Get some!" a Senior bellowed, putting out his cigarette.

As two hands connected for a high five, a spark in the distance lit up the sky like a firework.

"Get ready for the next one!" My Dad would yell out.

We excitedly positioned our lawn chairs in a semi-circle around our dads as they took the lead on lighting the fireworks. After all, we were all under the age of 10. One dad, my uncle, would sort out which firework to light, my other Uncle would hand it to my dad and he would carefully sit it down, try to make us laugh in the process and then light it. Our cheers rang down our street as the colorful sparks flew in the air.

And the chanting began.

"Bottle Rockets! Bottle Rockets!" We'd all chant, scream and laugh, feeling nothing but pure joy and comfort knowing our dads handled the work of it all.

As time passed, the sounds of the A-10s became more distant and the smell of smoke began to dissipate. One by one, we all went back to our sleeping bags. A few of the Marines would light a cigarette before hitting the rack, still watching for any remnants of a light show.

"That's a Fourth of July we'll never forget," someone yelled out, as the sounds of rustling continued. And it was not more than several moments later, only the sounds of the occasional call of a donkey would be heard in the dead of night.

Day Two

Day after day, we sat and waited. In the blistering sun, we waited. In the dead of night, we waited. And it became repetitious. Wake up. Eat. Smoke. Shoot the shit. Eat. Sleep. The boredom had set in and made its way deep inside that forest and we had another dreadful week to go.

With the sun at its highest point, I sat on what seemed like the last bit of shade for the next few hours. Everywhere else was hot to the touch. I didn't remember when I last urinated, as I was trying to save my water in case we had to patrol or we got into a firefight. I looked around and found no one was moving much. Like several crocodiles basking in the sun, they lied around. Or paced. Or did what I did, tried to find any bit of shade to not overheat. They cleaned their weapons, strengthened their crude humor by making fun of each other or slowly ate their MREs. Not because they were hungry or unkind to one another but because boredom was as powerful as the heat that scorched the Earth.

I heard footsteps getting louder towards me and

Augusto C. Cespedes, Jr.

suddenly, out of nowhere breathing heavily, a Marine rushed over to me panting.

"Doc," he gasped, "We need you! Grady…he's literally crapping his brains out." I made a "Why me?" face but also thought, "Well damn, at least there's something to do." I quickly got up, brushed off and walked fast to where the others were.

"He doesn't look too good, Doc," one of the Seniors said after taking a long hit from his cigarette. He exhaled out his response with a small shake of his head.

Grady, a Junior PFC and a rifleman for 3rd squad, laid motionless on his left side, his face smothered in an old MRE warming bag. The stench of fresh vomit was sour and basted the air like a thick lather of beef fat. I slightly turned my head and opened my mouth to gag, dry heaving in the direction of the ground.

"Can't handle that, Doc?! Come on, Squid!" Staff Sergeant teased, hitting me across the back. It almost knocked me to the side, but I felt like my body had prepared for it. I stood my ground, wiped my eyes, grinned, and began to focus on Grady.

I squatted next to him and started to breathe from my mouth. He was pale and covered in sweat with chunks of undigested food on his shirt and neck.

"Hey…." I started to slowly say, clearing my throat. "What's up, Grady…?"

Before I knelt down next to him, I looked to make sure my right knee wasn't going to land in vomit. As I lowered

Just Glow

my head, the warm drips of sweat ran down my nose almost tickling it before it dripped into the sand.

"Arrrrgghhh…" Grady moaned, rolling over, unaware of the vomit he was starting to lie on.

I subconsciously started to breathe from my nose and smelled a strong scent of feces.

"Grady," I said, sniffing carefully in small spurts, "Did you shit yourself?" I asked, bluntly. I looked around and heard another Marine moaning in agony with the sounds of wet flatulence sounding off in the near distance. McMahon was a Senior fire team leader for 2nd squad. He was bent over, unable to stand up straight.

"What's going on with us?" he said, panicking with a cracked voice. His eyes grew big, and it was as if he could feel something happening inside his body. Growing silent, he looked down and the bubbling sound of bowels curdling in his stomach began. Groaning in pain, the Marine slightly squatted down as if he couldn't help it. Like a busted faucet it started to run out of him.

Feeling overwhelmed, I took both of my hands and swiped my head of the sweat and walked over to the other group of Marines. In the middle was their Corpsman, Doc Nieto. Only the Marines called us Doc. For me, as respect, I called him by his rank.

"HM3, hey…" I'd started out saying. "Small," I paused, clearing my throat, "ok…er- maybe bigger than small-problem on the other side," I said.

"What's up?" He was just starting to eat his lunch, an

MRE that he had made into a sandwich. The glorious beef patty. While I stood there, he continued on, revealing the dark brown patty that laid on top of a dusty, hardened fortified biscuit. Holding it in the palm of his hand like a silver platter, he carefully began to squirt the jalapeño cheddar packet onto it. Contents of oil squirted from the packet then bits of the "cheese."

"Dang it," he said in disgust, "did it again." The oil ran down the tiny crevices of the block of cold beef, and he stuck his tongue out to catch the first drippings.

"Boot move," he said to himself, slightly embarrassed, "Go on..." He started to chuckle, but no one was paying attention.

"Few of the Marines on the other side are coming down with a bug. Might need your help with puttin' in some IVs," I continued to say. I wasn't the best at inserting an IV catheter, and I definitely wasn't going to start learning how to be better then.

"That bad, huh?" he asked, his mouth partially full. This was Doc Nieto's second deployment and, compared to me, he was more calm and less anxious. He held his right index finger in the air and took a few more bites of the sandwich, chewing vigorously as the biscuit was most likely dry and tough. Once satisfied, he brushed his hands and got up.

"Alright, let's see what's goin' on over in Crap Town," he dramatically sighed and chuckled again.

As we walked over, we both immediately noticed the ripened stench and caught ourselves watching each other cover our noses.

Just Glow

Not only were Grady and McMahon down, but two others had fallen from the thick smell of bodily fluids. Hart, a Junior Lance Corporal, with hands at his knees, was bent over, spitting on the ground. The saliva appeared stringy and viscous, not actually leaving his mouth as he tried forcing it out.

"Dude, this is horrible," he admitted, belching.

Only a few feet from him was Michaels, another Junior Lance Corporal who had his body draped over a boulder, seeming embarrassed.

"It's been 10 minutes," I said, "what happened?"

"Hahaha," a Senior started to laugh, "Hart and Michaels were making fun of them and ended up getting sick from the stench." His speech sounded slightly altered and I assumed it was because of the smokeless tobacco he had in his lip. In his left hand he held a worn-out water bottle with thick, dark, tar colored fluid inside. He was spitting in it.

"Doc, help, please! I feel like absolute garbage," Grady yelled as he rolled over. I saw his behind marked with a large, darkened area. My immediate thought? Definitely poop.

"Grady," I started to say, "you need an IV…" I breathed in deep, stood up and walked over to my med pack. I took out an LR bag and some supplies and walked back over to him. I looked up and pulled a tree branch, testing its strength to hang the liter of fluid.

Augusto C. Cespedes, Jr.

"Gonna hold still, right?" I asked him, realizing he really had no other choice.

"Doc, I can barely hold my shit in," he said, half effortlessly chuckling and hearing his exhaustion.

Using a drape from my med pack, I laid it down, spread out all of my supplies and took one of Grady's arms. It was clammy, fair and weak. I wrapped a tourniquet around it trying not to be distracted by the cold sweat. With vigorous force, I wiped the inner aspect of his forearm with an alcohol pad and stopped. I took it off and looked at it. The pad had turned a dark brown and his arm with circular swirls. I took a piece of gauze and in forceful motion, wiped away the excess.

"Use the smallest needle, Doc…please," Grady moaned, his voice slightly muffled in the bag. His hair, dirty blonde in color, was damp and caked with sand and bits of rock.

I looked at the size of the catheter, "18g," it said.

"Smallest I have, Devil," I replied, showing him the wrapper.

He slowly took his mouth out of the bag and his eyes met the wrapper. "Ooo," he said, his eyes in a fixed haze and trying to grin, "I love green."

I felt like I was shaking but maybe that was just in my head. My vision started to close in, transforming itself to tunnel vision as I directed my eyes to his arm.

Please don't screw up. It would've been such an embarrass-

Just Glow

ment if I had. All of the Marines watching and I missed? They wouldn't respect me.

"Alright Doc, better not screw this up," Staff Sergeant yelled out. I swore he heard what I said to myself.

I grinned, took a deep breath and held the catheter with the most confidence I could get. The sweat from the sides of my head and the tip of my nose started to distract me but I shook it off and kept my focus.

Just commit, dude... Bevel up. Right angle. Taut the skin. I focused on the bevel as it connected with the first fibers of the epidermis, like a nervous worm into the soil.

"Damnit, Doc..." Grady grimaced. His eyes, glazed over, still seemed to respond to the insertion. His expression exposed his teeth, filled with plaque and remnants of an MRE biscuit that had stuck to his yellow tinted dentition.

"I'm in, Grady. Hold still. Don't move," I ordered. I felt confident. I was in.

I just need to lower it down, advance it a little more and slide the catheter in. Of course it sounded simple in my head.

Sweating, my eyes turned heavy, but I lowered, saw flash and pushed it in a little further. In seconds, I advanced the catheter and with no resistance, it was over.

"Done," I said. I breathed in and didn't let it go until someone said something.

"Nice, Doc," one of the Riflemen said. I didn't smile, forcing myself to look serious. Wasn't over yet.

Augusto C. Cespedes, Jr.

I looked around and Doc Nieto was already inserting an IV into Michaels, with McMahon and Hart waiting for their turn. Both were lying on a flat rock against a tree, sprawled out and exhausted.

With sure confidence, I unwrapped another IV supply kit and studied McMahon's arms. I could hear the curdling of his bowels and the discomfort on his face. He had already emptied himself behind a huge boulder roughly 20 yards downwind. Pale, in a cold sweat and dazed, he silently moaned. He smelled of a sour, musty sweat and fresh fecal matter.

"Ready?" I asked. He didn't answer.

I took his arm, clammy, almost lifeless, and wrapped the tourniquet above his elbow.

Wiping it with now two alcohol swabs, I noticed a single vein and pressed it. Plump, soft and exposed at the surface.

I thought of how Grady's IV insertion and acted quicker this time.

Bevel up, angle it, in. Flash, lower down, advance further, done.

"Well look at that! Atta boy, Doc," Staff Sergeant said with a voice of confidence. It felt good to hear him say that. I finally was able to wipe my head of the sweat that had been sitting, getting heavier but not enough to drip onto the ground.

After securing it with tape and hanging the bag on a tree branch, a bulky MRE was flying towards me. With the last bit of alertness I had, I put my hands up and caught it.

"Enjoy Doc, you earned it," a Senior Corporal said, and then proceeded to thump a new can of smokeless tobacco.

Chili Mac. I smiled. One of the best MREs. It was a favorite amongst everyone and a Senior gave it to me.

Walking slowly, I made my way to one of the last trees that gave shade and plopped down, facing the Marines.

I did, didn't I.

I grinned, wiping my face. I couldn't remember when I last urinated, so I chugged a warm water bottle before indulging myself into the MRE.

The Drop

I blocked the sun's blare with my last water bottle, tilting it completely upside down to enjoy the last bit of water I had. Squinting not because of the light but my sweat had crept to the corners of my eyes, giving it a slow burn.

"Staff Sergeant, we're runnin' low," one of the Squad leaders had yelled out. He was pacing along his row of Marines who were seated on a small incline of terrain. Their heads were down, and each uniform had a darkened shade of sweat below their neck extending to their chest.

"Patience, Marine, Lieutenant is sending in our coordinates. Start drinkin' your spit," he said, laughing to himself. He took off his boonie, revealing his reddened shaved head, dripping.

I turned to look at where Lieutenant was. His face was directed downward with the handset to his ear and his right hand covering his right ear. I moved slightly to glance at what he was doing, and he was reading a map. He must have been calling in the drop. He then looked up and started scanning the sky. I thought I almost caught what he had said, as it looked like he said, "thank you." He turned around and I immediately looked the other way.

"Alright, Gents, listen for the bird. They're on their way," Lieutenant yelled out, his left hand next to his mouth like a megaphone. Everyone gave a half effort cheer.

Because of the risk of losing the supply drop, a team was organized to set out to locate the drop. Considering I was the Junior Corpsman, I was chosen as part of the team. We started to put on our gear, which had been sitting in the sun for hours, now cracked, hot and smelled of ripe sweat.

Several moments later, a Junior yelled out and pointing to the sky, "I see 'chutes! Incoming!" And there they were, olive-colored parachutes floating in the sky carrying small, dark colored objects. At first they were close together, but as they approached the ground, they appeared to be separating.

Just Glow

"Oscar Mike, Gents. Don't let the villagers get to them first," Staff Sergeant yelled out as the Marines started to load their rifles. I repositioned my med pack and looked at the sky. We started to quickly move.

The terrain was far from easy to maneuver around. Trees with giant, uprooted limbs, various sized rocks scattered the ground, and every step was unpredictable. Our flak jackets, bulky, thick and heavily weighted, kept us closer to the ground placing most of the weight into our backs and knees. We felt every foot placement on uneven ground. But it was our thirst that drove us to find the drop.

Running to follow the parachutes, the open sky slowly transformed to a heavy canopy of trees, and it became more difficult to see where they'd landed.

"Keep your ears open, Gents! Most likely the trees will break their fall," one of the squad leaders had announced. We slowed down our pace and breathed slower, giving our ears control to take over our other senses. My eyes bulged in desperation for just one sip of water, and I listened.

A single, high-pitched snap echoed in the distance, and I ducked nervously. I barely caught my fall, feeling the unpleasant outward roll of my right ankle. Initially thinking it was a "pop shot," I covered my head and felt my eyes scanning the area. I almost felt embarrassed for my reaction, but I saw a few of the others made the same reaction. When we all realized what it was, we slowly raised as a unit and looked at each other.

"I heard it! East! Three 'o clock! Let's go!" Corporal said. Violently slinging his rifle to his back, he started to run, pumping his arms to gain momentum up the incline of terrain. Tired, thirsty but desperate, we followed.

Weaving through the thick brush for nearly 10 minutes, we finally approached the parachute. Abnormally out of place, it was an enormous piece of cloth that draped over the trees with and on the ground was a pallet of what appeared to be cases of MREs and water. It was absolutely beautiful. The cases of water appeared fresh. Like it was wrapped just for us. Not a speck of dust on them. The boxes of MREs were of cold and hot rations.

"Cold weather MREs!!" a Senior said, practically gasping. "These are on another level, Doc!" He began to hold it up like it was Christmas morning, smiling from ear to ear. Seeing him smile in that way only made me smile back.

"We gon' eat good tonight!" Corporal said in his sarcastic, "horribly made up" Southern accent.

The happiness eventually tired out and the only sounds were of the rearranging of gear.

"Uh…" someone slowly started to say.

"Wasn't there more than one?" someone asked, panting. It was one of the Juniors. He was leaning forward with his

Just Glow

head down, his hands under the shoulder areas of his flak jacket. I could see that it had put pressure on his back.

"Damnit," Corporal said, quickly forgetting, "we gotta find the rest of them." He was shaming himself, banging his head down while making a face. I felt the same way. I couldn't believe we had to find the rest of them.

Exhausted and obviously upset, no one said a word. But after what seemed like an hour trek, we located all of the pallets.

A static of what seemed like English was heard from the radio a Junior was carrying, followed by a series of high-pitched frequencies.

"Mobile 1, this is Base. Radio check, over," the radio blared.

"Roger, Lima Charlie, Over," Corporal Harris said, a red haired 24-year-old and native of West Virginia. He stood next to the Junior and mouthed the handset, sweat dripping on the backpack and over the mangled plastic.

Continued, monotonous static traveled through the waves of heat as we stopped to listen to their response.

"Roger," it said with a following click. "Requesting SITREP," the voice said in a clearer transmission. It seemed like it was held longer to speak, so we all heard it.

"Roger, break,"

I could hear the exhaustion in his voice as he said, "we have the goods."

Augusto C. Cespedes, Jr.

The Descent

I rolled over to the sounds of my "Battle Buddy" snoring next to me and the small, familiar whispers in the background. Listening carefully, it was gear being assembled. After two grueling weeks, it was the day we were finally leaving the mountain.

Keeping my eyes closed, I listened to the distant sounds of miscellaneous things being secured and the distinctive, familiar rattling of rifles moving from the ground to propped up against a rock or slung over a shoulder. Instinctively, I looked at my watch. The screen, scuffed with small bits of sand, stuck at the edges.

0330.

It was the time that the temperature would fall ten to fifteen degrees. When the sun is finally at its lowest point, before sunrise, this side of the earth would finally be able to cool off. I stuck my head outside of my sleeping bag like an animal out of hibernation and slowly breathed in. A noticeable, cold sensation stunned my nares as I inhaled through my nose. I didn't want to let it go but knew it was time.

"Wake up, Dude, we're leaving," I said, nudging the Junior next to me. For two weeks, we each had a "Battle Buddy," and he was mine.

LCPL Rawlings, a 21-year-old from Texas, was a Junior Marine attached to the Machine Gun team. He was fully responsible for the care and well-being of the M240G, a

Just Glow

bulky strapless machine gun weighing a little over 25 pounds. It took him several seconds to come out of sleep, but he snorted once and his eyes quickly opened, and for a split second, forgot where he was. In one fluid motion, he looked around and then at me, and dropped his head back down to the ground. Next to him was the M240, perfectly placed and immaculate, like the baby you were responsible for in Home Economics class. With closed eyes, he reached for it and the hand to metal connection made a deep clicking sound that instantly eased him. He slowly breathed in and out, pushed over his sleeping bag and stood up but bent over, touching his neck.

"Man, this gun is killin' my shoulders, Doc," he blurted out. "But whatever," he sighed, "as long as we're getting off this mountain. Been here too long," he said.

"Let's huddle up, Gents," Staff Sergeant said. In the pitch black, his voice seemed much louder and traveled.

He brought his hands together and started to say, "Fourteen days, Gents. I know you feel it. 'Cause I see it. We did what we needed to do, and with our combined efforts, they've recovered the SEAL," he said, but there was not a response. A low "Rah" could be heard in the group. "He was hiding in a village for days and a Spec Ops team rescued him."

Silence, yet again, and only more jostling of gear as no one couldn't stand in one spot.

"You're probably wonderin' why we're up before God," he continued to say. There were a few small laughs but died in an instant.

Augusto C. Cespedes, Jr.

He dramatically breathed in and slowly raised his hands. "You noticin' it's cold right now?"

A heavy pause filled the air.

"The hump down is gonna be long, but we ain't stoppin'. Gotta move fast…" he looked at each one of us almost as if he wanted to see our reactions.

"Figured we start now while it's cool because when the sun is out, we're gonna slow down. It's gonna be hot….but quicker we get off this mountain, the quicker you'll be at the bazaar buyin' your dirty bootlegged DVDs, Rah?" he smiled, looking like he wanted to laugh at his own joke.

A few low laughs and "Rahs" rang in unison.

In a straggled, modified line, I stood directly behind one of the Junior riflemen and couldn't see past his pack. His desert backpack was of a different, lighter shade from his uniform. Once he started to walk, I gagged, as my sense of smell caught the horrible stench of what his body had endured. The smell from his uniform was of fresh and days old sweat that had dried over and over again, layering on itself.

"0400," my watch said. And we stepped off.

I walked in the middle of the platoon in between two riflemen, while Doc Nieto hung in the back to make sure no one needed medical attention.

"Boot-legged DVDs," I laughed to myself, exhaustedly placing one foot in front of the other.

Just Glow

The DVD

Going to the bazaar was one of, if not, the only things to do during downtime. Not only did you get to go outside, but you didn't have to wear any heavy gear; just your uniform, a cover and a loaded weapon was all that was needed, slung over your shoulder or holstered. Once a week, merchants from town lined the gravel path that was outside of the base, laying out their various items to sell. From ceramics to leather goods to weapons, things were there for us to buy. But it was the bootlegged DVDs that caught most of everyone's attention. If I could describe the DVD section of the bazaar, think of a Blockbuster Video's "Clearance" section but on the ground. In an attempt to organize their merchandise, the plastic cases of DVDs were arranged in a way that you were careful not to touch it, as the merchant would basically stand over you, arms crossed. So we'd just look, slowly moving our legs as we looked at the covers of them all. And the covers were not the ones you would typically find; great quality photo with a gloss finish. No, it was the complete opposite. They appeared to have been printed from a low-quality printer on economy paper. The colors were faded in a lighter shade with water spots and stains that seemed to have dried in the process. After scanning through all of them, the merchant would feel a sense of dissatisfaction and speak.

"You want good DVD?" the merchant asked, as he bent down next to a darkened sash. It was laid out next to the poor quality DVDs, and I could see there was something under the sash, slightly raised and with straight edges.

I looked at the Junior who went with me, who was also looking at me, and we both smiled, knowing what each of us was thinking.

Augusto C. Cespedes, Jr.

"Yes," we both said together, anxiously waiting to see what was under the piece of cloth.

He stood up from squatting and pulled the sash.

"Wooooahhh..." we both said, eyed widened in childish amazement. They were so different than the uncovered displays. Even the casings were different; untouched, dust-free, picturesque. The DVD cases were solid black, and not like the ones that sat in the sun that created a grayish tint to it. The most obvious difference was the decorative cover that was on the front. Vivid, radiant colors on a shiny gloss paper. It looked real. The Junior and I couldn't take our eyes off it.

"So...what you like?" the merchant said, interrupting our daydream. To the corner of the organized pile, I chose a few comedies and an action movie. The Junior, on the other hand, was interested in the other section.

"How much for these?" He was pointing to a few others, with women dressed in lingerie.

"For you? Special price.... $15," he said,

I gasped. I didn't know whether to pat my friend on the shoulder or walk away.

"Wow, better be a good one," I mumbled, hoping the Junior heard me.

"I'll take it," he said, not thinking too long on it.

We gave him our cash and not paying attention to where we were walking, we kept our eyes on what we had purchased.

The Junior and I went our separate ways, and I noticed him

Just Glow

smiling before he opened the door to his hooch. *"I'll let you know how it is, Doc,"* he said, laughing. *"It better be worth $15 or I'm returning it!"* He laughed, opening the wooden doorknob and it slowly closed with a water bottle attached to paracord, preventing it from slamming shut.

The next day, I caught him at the smoke deck, and I yelled out to him, *"Well?! How was it??"* Catching him mid smoke, he took the cigarette out of his mouth and said, *"Worth every penny, Doc,"* and hysterically laughed, coughing out bits of smoke. So I decided to buy one.

"Good DVD, Sir," I said, showing him my money. He smiled at me, bent down and removed the sash. And it was all there. Like nothing was touched. I scanned them all at once but then feasted my eyes on the corner section. I pointed to the one that had a cover with a woman in lingerie. He grabbed it and took my money and like a kid with a new toy, I held onto it with both hands. I wanted what the Junior had experienced, who was smiling at the smoke deck, but I knew I had to wait until it was nightfall.

The childish anticipation lingered on for hours. Like a worn-out valve that slowly seeped, the continuous, expected drip of thought made it difficult to relax. Every now and then I would move the DVD out of my backpack just to see the cover then pushing it back into my backpack.

I laid in bed, uncovered, with my eyes wide open and stared blankly at the bare boards of wood that hung at ceiling of the hooch. Like sheep, I started to count the amount of nails that had pierced through the boards, exposing sharp bits of wood, like a bullet that had been shot through. I lied there and waited for everyone to fall asleep.

A slow, grumbling snore casually floated through the air and into my ears, so I gave it a little time. Once I heard no one speaking I reached down, grabbed the DVD and turned on the DVD player that was sent to me. A silver, bulky electronic device. I pressed it open and inserted the disc.

It hummed as it spun at a high rate of speed, the light of the monitor glowed against my face as my heart palpated, feeling like it was skipping beats.

A fuzzy, white and gray series of lines showed up on the screen fell like rain as the sound of a woman was heard in a foreign language.

"Fifteen dollars…good DVD, let's see." My eyes wider now with pupils dilated to capture it.

As the blurred lines had cleared, my eyes focused on what was happening.

A home video of low, poor quality showed a single woman, with her shirt on in a birthing position, breathing heavily as a few people had surrounded her. I felt my face change positions, my eyebrows now crooked. I couldn't make out exactly what was going on, but I knew it was not something that I, at all, anticipated.

The woman was giving birth.

My eyes widened even more, and my mouth dropped. Beyond embarrassed and with a heavy feeling of disgust, I moved the earbuds out of my ears and put my palm to the monitor, causing it to slam.

I laid in silence and from that day on, I never asked to remove the sash ever again.

"How was it, Doc?" the Junior asked. He was sitting at the smoke deck as I passed him before heading to breakfast.

Just Glow

"It was good man! Worth every cent," I said, smiling, lying through my teeth.

I shook my head out of my memory and caught myself laughing. Giving myself a few yards back behind him, I let the Junior walk ahead of me to not catch the odor again.

"Heeeeeere we go again," a Senior Marine said in a loud, sarcastic and melodic tone. His smile, present but fading just as quick as his step onto the terrain, was a brief reminder that there was an unending battle between humor and pain. The pitch and volume of his voice were like tiny fragments of pain fleeing from the deep fibers of his body. The more we sang, laughed, or joked, the more we felt as if the pain was departing.

I could tell he was waiting for someone to repeat him, but the jostling of gear was overpowering his voice.

"Same 'ol shit again," I scoffed, saying to myself, mimicking the same sarcastic melody. And with a deep breath, I took my first few steps onto the descent.

We didn't speak, especially at that hour, but we didn't have to. We all knew what each of us was feeling. Exhausted. Sleep deprived. Homesick. The desire for real, hot food.

Before we left the area, I slowly blew out a breath into the early morning air and a brief mist appeared. Impulsively, I put on my fleece, an olive colored sweater and then my flak jacket over it. The smell of the flak, musty sweat mixed with dirt, slowly raised to my nares. The total weight was burly, heavy and tighter than usual but it stopped the morning shiver.

Augusto C. Cespedes, Jr.

"You'll be sorry, Doc," a Senior said to me. He clicked his tongue and shook his head, almost laughing. "I'll give it five minutes before you rip all of that crap off," he continued to say.

I didn't believe him, but it did feel different. The flak usually had room in between it and my uniform. But this time, the extra layer caused it to stick and within seconds, felt a tingling sensation that ran up my chest and into my neck.

"Well, I'll take my chances," I said to him, my pack and its contents bouncing around as I made my way down the path. Within several seconds, it was already harder to breathe.

And the more I moved, the more heat generated inside the fleece. The gradual build-up of a warm feeling made me itch and I had to admit it.

"Okay, you win. You're right. I'm sweatin' bullets already," I said, pulling to the side and ripping my flak jacket off and removing the fleece. The crackling of the Velcro made a few Marines turn around.

"Told ya," he said laughing, causing a mist to pulsate from his mouth into the air.

I smiled, embarrassed but quickly did what I had to do and got back in line.

The descent felt like hours. The weary twists, turns and the left then right repetitious movement of our feet created

Just Glow

this bizarre desire to look at my watch again, a Casio watch with its Velcro strap barely catching anymore.

0610.

The neon green glow of it had statically blurred in my eyes as I tried to adjust to the darkness of the descent. Almost tripping on a few jagged rocks, I was able to position myself and keep my balance, causing tension in the muscles of my abdomen.

"I cannot get injured," I mumbled to myself, "One last leg until we're home."

There were several moments walking down the mountain that made me recall the climb. A specific divot in the ground I remembered, placing my foot on it, even in the dark I was able to see it. I was not as tired now as I was several days ago. But then I remembered that we were just a couple of hours into the descent.

We had reached a part of the descent that had forgivingly plateaued, giving us a small break on our bodies. The blistering sun, now awakened, had made itself comfortable on the surface of rock and our skin.

The familiar ache from the climb started to uproot itself.

"0938," my watch showed, and I silently cursed to myself.

"Corporal," a Junior had spoken out slightly out of breath, "if you could eat or drink anything right now, what would it be?" I could hear the nervousness along with excitement in his voice, possibly trying to keep his mind off the painful reality of the long journey down.

"Ha," the jingling of his gear intertwined with his laugh as the terrain caused him to make a few, small jumps.

"This might sound strange, but I want some good 'ole fashioned biscuits and gravy, Brother," he said, licking his upper lip that was dry and crusted. Corporal Harris' accent was more pronounced, maybe out of sarcasm or the thought gave him a burst of energy.

"Gonna be honest, Corporal," he said, "I've never had it," he admitted.

"WHAT??" he attempted to slow down but his gear kept his momentum.

"I'm from New York," he laughed, "we don't eat stuff like that." He paused and then asked, "What is it exactly?"

Like a speaker on a podium, it was like he had prepared a speech about the dish. He positioned himself and directed his face towards the Junior, wiping the lingering sweat from his face.

"The biscuit and gravy are a staple of the south," he said with confidence, "the contrast is undeniably one of, if not the best symphonies of culinary creations." His voice had caused a few others to look at him, entertained by his impromptu-esque monologue.

"I mean, it's good but not tha…" someone started to say.

Just Glow

"Captivating the palate," he continued on, raising his finger as a signal to everyone that he was still talking, "the elegance of warm, freshly baked biscuits, tender and flaky, united with the velvety caress of savory gravy. A symphony of flavors unfolds as the gravy, rich and aromatic, blankets the biscuits, infusing each bite with savory perfection," he said. His eyes appeared glazed over, and cracked a smile like it was right in front of him.

"Harris, you're an idiot," a Senior laughed, shoving his shoulder to snap him out of his daydream.

"Man, to me, it's that good. I'll never forget the first days off from school for the holidays, I'd only need to open my door to be hit with the aroma of those biscuits baking. And I was an early riser growing up. And knowing my mom was up that early, measuring, mixing, already having that sweet smell for me to wake up to was comforting to me." He started to have that glazed-over look again but blinked several times and looked away to wipe his face.

It grew silent and somewhat awkward, leaving the jostling of gear to take over. It took several seconds for Corporal to say something.

"What about you, Bergman? What's so good at the Big Apple?" he asked, clearing his throat.

"Good ole' New York Pi-..." he excitedly began to say but was interrupted by yelling in the front.

"He's down! Doc is down," Sergeant yelled out.

"Doc, I think you're needed up there," Corporal said,

giving me a push on my upper back as I started to walk faster up the line.

It was Doc Murray, a Corpsman from Michigan who was in his late 30s, who had collapsed.

"Your buddy is down, 'Speedus,'" Staff Sergeant said to me. I could hear the disappointment in his voice as he stood over him. I acknowledged him and thinking he never could say my last name right.

"Murray," I said, kneeling down. "What's going on?"

I placed my hand on the shoulder of his desert uniform. It was crusted and faded. Dusty and noticeably white, salty lines of old sweat that had dried and wet again. The smell his body gave off was like sour, curdled milk that had sat outside for days. He had turned over on his own and I saw that he had vomited on himself.

"I can't go anymore," he admitted to me, whispering it, "I really did it this time, Bro," he then said. His breaths were shallow and reeked.

"Listen man, we gotta try and get up," I pulled on his arm and lifted it. It was flaccid, and his sleeve was hardened with sweat. An arm suddenly came into view and grabbed him by the collar.

"Let's go, Doc! I ain't dyin' out here for some weak ass Corpsman," a Senior had yelled out. The sweat dripped from his face and onto Doc Murray's uniform, creating small little drops on his chest.

Grabbing him by his collar, the Senior tried lifting him

Just Glow

up, and Doc Murray's eyes widened in disbelief and as did mine.

"Stop! STOP! We are not doing that," I demanded but he continued.

"Got any other ideas, Doc?!! I ain't carryin' him, that's for damn sure," he said confidently. He let go of his collar, took off his own backpack and started to rummage through it, taking out a few yards of paracord. Unsheathing his KBAR, he cut it in one swift move and made a loop. He put it around Doc's neck.

"If you're not gonna walk, I'll make you," he ordered. His voice, now deeper, had flown viscous pieces of saliva at him. My mouth made a smile but in complete shock and disgust, and I shook my head.

"You're crazy!" I yelled, putting fingers around the cord, "You're gonna kill him, Man!"

The paracord, a thin, black nylon rope, was centimeters away from tightening, but I ripped it off before it dug into Murray's neck.

"Enough! Murray, man, come on, you GOTTA walk!" I yelled at him, my eyes focusing on his. They were sunken in, glazed over and barely open. I had to keep my hand on his shoulder as he swayed, unable to keep his balance.

"Move," said another Senior, a Sergeant, shoving me aside. Dawkins, a quiet, soft spoken guy from Chicago, was the squad leader for 2nd squad. Roughly 6 foot 4 inches, he bent down and pulled Murray's arm and put it over his back. One swift movement and Murray was on his back. A fireman's carry. In deep relief, I sighed and watched him carry him like a heavily weight rag doll.

Distracted by the yelling, my mind turned itself back onto the descent.

Dawkins started to walk ahead of me, and my eyes looked up at what surrounded us. Overpowered by enormous cliffs, I kept my eyes towards the sky. I took a step off the rocks and my foot sank deep into the ground. My muscle tightened, feeling the tension that sent messages to my brain to look at what I had stepped on. Soft, dry, and scorched sand. Miles of it. We were in a dried out ravine and didn't see the end of it.

My arms swung in a slow motion, and before I could read the time on my watch, I noticed the sleeve of my right arm. A thickened, dark shade of brown matted on the digital pattern. I stared at it and wiped my face on it, adding more to its accumulation.

1158 HRS.

With the sun reaching its highest point, we moved slower and every forward step took an extra effort. As our boots sunk deep into the sand, we had hoped for some sort of relief. Rain was way out of the question but even if it was just a gust of wind, it would've been absolute Heaven. The air was thick, a complete standstill and with the heat radiating off the sand, I could feel the skin on the bottom of my feet start to slide.

"Almost there, Gents!" Staff Sergeant yelled out. No one was talking much at this time. We knew that opening our

Just Glow

mouths would make them even more dry, causing a desire to drink.

Over seven hours of humping. And by this time, we were down to only six donkeys, as most of them had fallen out from exhaustion. Luckily, the Afghanistan soldiers, carrying only their rifles, a metal canteen and a sack for food, still straggled behind us.

There were several things I had thought of since stepping off at 0400 HRS; home, food, my future and my past regrets. But urinating wasn't one of them.

Over those 14 days, we barely did any of it; once a day, if that. We did not leisurely drink water; it was only the desperate desire of thirst that demanded it. We drank warm to hot bottled water and what we ingested just came right out of our pores. Surprisingly, at that very moment during the descent, I had the urge to urinate.

My uniform pants, heavily weighted from the days of sweat and dirt, were difficult to unbutton but I felt a lower abdominal pressure and knew I needed to do this.

With dirty hands, I unbuttoned. The waist area of it was pasted with mud like dirt that caked itself on.

I pulled to the side and instinctively felt a slow-moving rush.

"Doc! What are you doin'?" A Junior yelled out.

"I think I gotta piss, Man…" feeling it at the end, I tried to relax and what came out made my eyes bulge.

Thick, amber colored urine slowly dripped out and it was more of a shock to me rather than a relief. Its viscosity was like of a heavy malt beer.

"Anyone have another water bottle?" I frantically asked. I felt my voice crack, but no one cared at this point.

"Almost there, Doc…" a Marine said, passing me as I hurriedly buttoned my pants. He handed me a warm water bottle, half drunken. The outside of it was dusty, and the plastic gave off fine crackles from its overuse and days of handling.

I forced myself to drink the warm water, hoping my urine would clear up.

I looked ahead and the ravine seemed to almost disappear. Sergeant Dawkins was still walking with Murray on his back, and that made me feel relieved.

A little more than several moments later, we hit a down slope and suddenly, out of nowhere, heard others. Marines. And a roaring sound. *Could it be a seven-ton?* Already fatigued, I felt a small jolt of reserved energy and started to walk past Dawkins. Just up ahead, down a dirt path, was a tree line providing an immense amount of shade with Marines under it. Seeing them there made me anxious to sit down.

I waited for the others to come down the slope. With my hands on my knees and panting, I wanted to make sure Murray made it down safely. As I looked up, I'd noticed Dawkins started to walk faster towards me and I stood still. Once he got close to me, he paused, lifted Murray over his shoulders and he was on the ground, the dust kicking up into the air.

Just Glow

"Shit, I'm tired," Dawkins said in one breath, walking towards the tree line. I watched him take his final steps towards the shade as Murray just laid there baking in the sun. My eyes, now focused on Murray, noticed he needed water. Extremely parched, barely awake. I couldn't just leave him, so I opened up my med bag and took out the thermometer. An oral temperature wouldn't be sufficient, so a core temperature had to be taken.

Nervously, I unbuttoned his sweat-soaked pants. Fumbling with the buttons, they were matted with dirt and mud. He smelled of intense body odor and old vomit.

"Murray, I need to get a core temp," I said, raising my voice. "Can you move to where I can see where I'm going?" I asked nasally, trying to close off my sense of smell. He only mumbled, his speech in a drunken stupor.

I pushed his leg over as he lied on his side, and I held the thermometer. I guessed where to place it, inserted and held it there.

Trembling in my attempt to stay still, I waited for what seemed like forever, my sweat dripping from my chin and nose.

107.2 degrees Fahrenheit.

I scrambled through the pack for something, but searching was muscle memory. I stared at it blankly. Something. Anything. I fumbled through rolled and packaged bandages, tourniquets, shears. My mind seemed like it was on overdrive. Not only physically exhausted but mentally checked out. And seeing everyone already taking their gear off, it screwed with my head. But I looked down at Murray. Then my med pack. Tylenol suppository. I took it out of its compartment.

"Dude, I'm sorry," I apologized and with my bare hand, inserted it into his anus.

He moaned louder, wincing.

Light footsteps that slightly dragged were heard and it was a villager. He bent down and he appeared to look sorry for us. Everyone was in the shade and 40 yards away were Murray and I in the blistering sun.

"I, er, get…?" he started to say, and motioned to his mouth like he was drinking something. After a few seconds of Charades, he saw we weren't understanding him, so he got up and scurried away. I instinctively put my hand on the M9 thinking he was a threat and kept my eyes on Murray.

As I turned to Murray, at the corner of my eye, the villager was in focus, hobbling to us hauling over a huge container. The sloshing sounds of water and drops of it came out over the sides as he was struggling to make it back to us. And it was then my guard was immediately brought down. Relaxed. Relieved.

With sweat steadily dripping down his face, the villager picked it up one last time and the familiar, forgiving rush of cool, clean water splashed on Murray's torso, causing him to open his eyes, take a big gasp, and find himself sitting up.

It only took a few small splashes of village water to cause me to take in a deep breath.

Just Glow

Holy shit. I actually made it down.

Operation فيل (Pil)

After Operation Red Wings, I felt pretty confident that nothing that exhausting would ever happen again. Okay, not exactly, but I felt I would be prepared for anything to come my way.

Operation Pil was a bit different.

Gathered in an overcrowded hooch with the stench of wet socks and a rancid, sour smell that soaked the air, we all had our eyes forward as we listened.

"Listen Gents," our platoon commander spoke out.

"I hope you utilized your time wisely during these days of rest." I could see the beads of sweat started to accumulate on his forehead.

"Alright so, everyone get all your crap at the bazaar??" He laughed and some did follow suit, but he could tell we were only anxious to hear about the next assignment.

"As you all may be aware, our efforts in Red Wings made a significant impact." An uproar of applause and a few grunts followed with what he said, "A Navy SEAL was recovered and we've woken up this terrorist group."

"So here's the thing, Gents…"

Augusto C. Cespedes, Jr.

It was way too early in the deployment to rest. It was only the end of July. And the statement he said next just put a sick feeling in my stomach.

"We're attacking again."

The thought of driving up to the base of the mountain and walking up several feet every few hours was something I wasn't looking forward to.

"Starting from the top of the mountain."

I was confused. I felt my eyes start to wander around, involuntarily drifting off in a clockwise manner. My eyebrows felt like they forming into a puzzled look.

A Marine that seemed to observe me asked, "Doc, ya good?"

"Yea…yea, I'm just trying…to…"

He sort of knew what I was thinking and immediately said, "Rappelling down, Doc,"

"From what…?" I asked.

"A…helicopter?" Some Marines laughed at me.

My mind instantly ran itself back to the day our platoon commander made us watch the DVD. The terrorist propaganda video. The shaky, grainy footage of the helicopter in the air and the next thing we saw was it in flames in the forest.

That'll be us, I know it. I tried to not show my face of fear.

Just Glow

"Eh, it'll be fine, Doc! We got you!" one said, followed with a hard slap on my back.

"Let's get a few more days of rest and then we're packing up for another operation, Rah?!" And with barely a pause in between, everyone would "Rah" back.

Rah.

'Rah' or 'Hoorah' was a special word that, depending on when or how it was used, only a Marine or a Devil Doc truly understood its meaning.

During painful, enduring moments, 'Rah' was yelled out and exaggeratedly drawn out to create this surge of motivation when you're at your last bit of energy.

"RAAHHH!" Like "Hell ya! Let's go!!!!"

"Gents, listen up…" someone would say, "we're low on water but the supply drop is about two clicks (kilometers) away…give or take…"

Drenched in sweat, lips parched and chapped, a Marine would inhale hard and just say, 'Rah…"

Or it was used in a sarcastic meaning, the louder and quicker it was said.

"I need every swingin' dick to fill five sandbags after post," Sergeant would say, voice deepened and bellowed.

"Rah, Sarnt!"

Augusto C. Cespedes, Jr.

With an exhaled, exhaustive breath.

"Rah!"

"Rah, rah, Sarnt…"

But no matter how shitty things were or how shitty they were going to get, 'Rah' brought a spark to things.

'Rah' made you want to overcome it.

Go head-to-head with it.

It was back to packing for the day's long operation and word on the street was the LZ, or landing zone, was "hot."

"Gonna light 'em up!" Someone yelled out. The sound of fuzz from a worn-out speaker connected to a CD player played rock music.

"I don't wanna hear one weapon that misfires, Roger that?"

"Yes, Staff Sergeant!!!"

The statements from everyone created these juvenile thoughts that ran through my mind like a runaway freight train.

Roaring. Frightening. Completely over the top.

I've never rappelled in my damn life.

What if I…I fall halfway through and break my back, end up getting shot? I'd be the reason my unit would all die.

Just Glow

Thankfully, we took a full day's class on rappelling before the operation.

"Gents, we're going to another base for someone to teach you numbskulls how to rappel so you don't screw up," Staff Sergeant yelled out, grinning as he walked out of the hooch.

Once he left, someone blurted out, "I just hope they have good food. You think it'll have a Burger King or somethin'?"

We all laughed, salivating just thinking about it.

But the joke was on us.

Yes, there was Burger King.

And Pizza Hut.

But it was on the opposite side of the base, nowhere near the airfield where we were to spend the day.

So, sadly, it was just MREs that day.

Augusto C. Cespedes, Jr.

If you didn't let a huge part of yourself detach from your family before deployment, it was likely you'd have a harder time adjusting to your new life.

A life of daily patrols.

Of abruptly awakening to the sounds of mortars making impact right where you slept.

Operations that lasted for several weeks.

The fear of dying alone.

Some guys accepted it. Some guys didn't have the support like others did so it was easier for them. And you could see it in their behavior.

For me, at 19 years old, I felt like I was doing well.

Sure, I had picked up the poor habit of smoking Lucky Strikes with my very attractive, matte black Zippo lighter I had bought at the Wiki Wiki store, but I didn't feel the heavy sadness I'd thought I would feel once we had hit country.

Until we were introduced to the room with the telephones.

"No…nope…not doing it," I'd say to myself. For weeks. I had already gone so long without talking to my family and I wasn't going to give it all up now.

No one could really avoid the small stone building as it stood in between our hooch and the chow hall which, in

Just Glow

actuality, wasn't anything to write home about, but it had hot food, and it wasn't MREs.

So every time we passed it, I'd look the other direction. Every single time.

And the days turned into weeks and passed as quickly as it came.

"Ya ready, Doc?"

"Let's go," I'd say. And it was off to the chow hall once again.

But one day, I didn't turn away.

I was curious.

How was the telephone room doing?

I walked up the hill and as ground leveled out, I looked to my left.

And there it was. A dark blue, plastic chair tucked under the plywood table.

I squinted and noticed the usual dusty, black, wired telephone that sat there. Alone. And for once it remained unused.

"I see you eyein' the phone, Doc," he said, interrupting my daydream, "ye'gon use it? I mean, I'm good, so…"

I stood there like an innocent fool and only could think

of the lyrics from Jude Cole when he sang, "Time for Letting Go."

"You should get a job before you ship off, don't ya think?" My dad had his head buried under the sink, fixing a leak. It was Saturday morning, mid-August of 2003. At that time, I had already signed the papers to leave in March. All of my friends that I had graduated with had already left for college.

"Probably..." I mumbled.

"What was that? You can't just sit around and not do anything for the next eight months." He continued to make noises that went 'tink, tink' under the sink, like a wrench to a metal pipe.

I raised my voice a bit louder and said, "I'm gonna think of where to apply."

But it didn't take long for me to find myself at the local grocery store. I walked in on that Monday morning, asked for an application to complete and I was called to come in for an interview that Wednesday.

"You're hired," the inventory manager of Kroger had said, "but there's a catch." Jim, a small but burly man, crossed his arms and leaned back that caused a creaking sound in the worn-down swivel office chair.

"Oh?" I asked.

I tried to think of what kind of catch there was in getting hired as a stock boy.

"It's a ten p.m. to six a.m. shift."

Just Glow

"Oh," I said.

"Ah, shit," was my actual thought.

As an 18-year-old, I didn't know how a night shift would even pan out.

Is it like an all-nighter while getting paid?

Can I eat snacks and stock shelves?

"I'd try and get a few hours of sleep before your shift," my Dad suggested.

"Psh," I thought, "ya, if I was a wimp…"

I thought I'd be okay not doing that. Dead wrong.

On my first day, I went in with the biggest smile. New black Dickies pants, my lucky black Velcro shoes I had bought from Walmart that I loved so much and a plain black polo shirt.

I was ready to eat snacks and stock.

"Ok," Jim said, clasping his hands together, "you're going to start in the canned goods aisle. Ya know, vegetables, tuna, marinara sauce… that aisle." I looked up and the number "9" was displayed on the overhead sign.

"Hey, Jim, you got it," I replied, my hand motioned like a gun.

I looked at my watch, 10:29 PM, and turned to the aisle.

But when I stared face to face with it, I felt myself turn a different shade. Uneasy. Intimidated. The aisle was COVERED in boxes. Littered with pallets stacked high of boxes. Thickened, plastic wrapped, canned goods that needed to be on the shelves.

Wide eyed and feeling this funny smirk on my face, I whispered to myself, "Ok…easy enough…"

So, I started from the top.

Ripping open box after box with my bare hands, it slowly became repetitive.

"Rip the box open, take out the cans and place it neatly on the shelf. Label out and flushed. Walk over and do it again. Over and over.

My statement to myself of "psh, ya, if I was a wimp," I had started to regret. I was tired, sleepy and started to feel nauseous.

After what seemed like more than an hour, I looked at the gigantic pile again, and to my surprise, had barely made a dent.

"You've gotta be kidding me with this sh-…"

"Well, how's it goin' over here? Y'gettin' the hang'uh things?" Jim came from around the corner of aisle 8 and stood there, examining my aisle. He then grabbed the waistband of his pants and bent over to pick up a piece of plastic wrap that was left on the floor.

I looked at him and said, "All good, Jim!" I was hoping my face didn't have an expression of exhaustion.

"Great," he said. "Try and get this done before six a.m. You can go for your lunch around two." He scanned once more over and left.

Just Glow

I exhaled like I was holding all of it in — the exhaustion, frustration — and then let it out when he left.

So I went back to work. And the same motions. Rip, take, bend down, can with label out and neatly flushed.

As I bent down for what felt like the millionth time, I'd noticed the soft music coming through the speakers. Echoing down the hall, its faint sounds of drums and singing made my arm stop midair with a can of green beans in my hand.

"How'd I not notice this?"

"Ohhh, I like this..."

It sounded familiar. Like I'd heard it once before at a party or in the mall as I waited for my mom to come out of the fitting room. I couldn't whip out my phone and search it like the present times, but it was catchy enough for my head to bob and instantly stock the shelves with a pep in my step.

It was a quick few minutes of feeling a burst of energy and it was gone. Just like that.

But all of it still rang in my head.

I didn't think anything of it other than, "okay, that was cool. Super catchy." I had heard that song five times in the shift that I had worked, assuming it was part of a rotation of songs that were picked for that time. And I did most of that aisle by myself, walking out of there with a tired but surprising smile.

And I went to work. Again, and again.

I had this routine. The sliding entrance doors made this jiggling noise when it opened. And its beep sounded weak, like it was tired of doing it.

"Y'all gotta fix that," I thought.

I always tripped over the black, rubber carpet that was riddled with dirt and what appeared to be paper receipts.

Walk down the cereal aisle, #4, and pass by the man with the mop. I didn't know his name, but I saw him the exact same time before my shift. 9:50 p.m.

"Qué paso, Bro?" he'd said, sliding the mop around on the tile floor, making streaks of brownish water that glistened muddy waves. He tried wiping it away but just kept making it worse.

"What up, Amigo?!!" I'd say back. Every time. Expected. Mundane. Every exhale I had given with every other step felt like an expression against it all.

"Yer back in thuh canned goods aisle, Mah Man," Jim yelled out from the entrance of the receiving doors. I could see the top of his head, nestled with strands of reddish-brown hair, that barely overlooked the stacks of food on the pallet.

A part of me loved the canned goods aisle. There was an unexplainable satisfaction when turning all of the labels, making all of the cans flushed with the edges of the shelves. But also, it had its own speaker right above the aisle. And when I started that same routine of "rip, take out, walk over and cans flushed," my mind was actually waiting for the music rotation to start.

70s disco.

Elevator music.

Just Glow

90s soft rock.

Then it came on again. It was the echoing of the drums. The raspy voice of Jude Cole.

I felt a sense of relief when hearing the lyrics. The words "time for letting go" hit unexplainably like it was made for me.

And I realize now that, at that time, I didn't feel pain. Or loneliness. Or a fight to battle homesickness. Just a catchy melody. One that helped me get through a shift of stocking shelves.

"I'm okay for now, Brother," I said to the marine and we both walked to the chow hall. I hummed the melody over and over in my head until the thought of calling my mom had dissolved.

Flying in the Dark

We stood outside the hooch and waited for the day to turn to night. And the more we waited the more anxious I became. I kept hitting my cargo pockets, ensuring I had all of my medical supplies in the right spots; tourniquets, abdominal pads, Quikclot packets in my left cargo pocket.

Augusto C. Cespedes, Jr.

I could feel everyone's uncertainty linger as we just stood there, the small jagged rocks colliding against one another under our boots.

The smell of cheap cigarette smoke started to permeate itself in and around us as we waited for our orders.

"What's that sound…?" someone asked.

It was growing. The sound started off like when you put a playing card in the spoke of your bike to make a small motor sound but only going about three miles an hour.

"Blip blip blip blip blip…" and it grew louder.

"Helo?" I asked.

It couldn't be for us. Not just yet. I felt like having a cigarette.

"Apache, right?" someone asked.

The marine next to me slightly raised his head like he was smelling something in the air.

"Chinook."

"Damnit," I looked down and took a step to my right, almost hitting the hooch next to us and said in a crippled weak tone, "I need a cigarette."

Calmly, a pack of Marlboro Reds was put in front of my face, and I felt my hand shaking as I pulled one out. A pink colored lighter sparked in front of me and when the ember burned, I felt its warmth in between my eyes. I gave it a few

Just Glow

puffs out of nervousness, instantly giving me the biggest, nauseating buzz.

"Uhhhh…"

"Doc, you good?" A Senior had asked, placing his gloved hand on my shoulder, "What's wrong, scared of heights?!" and he belly laughed like a mall Santa Claus.

"DUDE. Do you NOT remember what happened to the team that was shot down in Red Wings?"

He was in the middle of inhaling a cigarette and like a calm French man he said, "I do, but," and exhaled, "we're here now and there's nothing we can do about it but just smile."

"Shit, you can say that again," another Senior said, readjusting himself as his gear appeared heavier than the others. A coyote drab flak jacket that looked bulky, neatly organized but stacked with small pouches that contained 30mm rounds, a few grenades and rifle magazines. It looked like there wasn't any way he could move silently so when he bent down or twisted, the pouches that contained double magazines clanked together like he was Bert in the Mary Poppins movie.

I needed something to keep my mind from wandering into a haunt of assumptions. It was getting bad. The cigarette didn't help. It only made me numb and nauseous for a few minutes. I was stuck in a world of negative thoughts and the thought of the burning blaze that engulfed the wrecked Chinook consumed my mind.

"Guys, listen," I'd started to say. The familiar stench of

body odor and the intermittent rotation of dried sweat and soaked gear filled the air. Everyone seemed to be in their own world.

No one heard me.

"Guys! Listen," I'd said a little louder. I was afraid of being made fun of and ending up earning an embarrassing nickname for myself especially by the Seniors, but I didn't care at that point. I needed to verbalize it. It felt right.

"Guys…I'm not okay. I don't know how to say this, but I need to say it. Something," I then said.

"Well damn, Doc," a Senior turned around to say, "go on then, say it." He wore an olive drab bandana that wrapped around his head, his bottom lip stuffed with chewing tobacco. Its stench was strong enough for me to get a secondhand whiff.

"If I live through this, ahem, I will lick someone's armpits…" and I grabbed the closest Marine, a Senior from the West Coast.

It went quiet for a second, but it brought the biggest laughter in the huddle.

"HA! What?!!"

"You Navy boys are some'n else…" one said.

"That is some sick shit, Doc," a Senior said, almost emphasizing every word. His cigarette was almost done, and he let it hang at his lips.

Just Glow

"But," the one who I grabbed started to say, "I'm probably just as sick as you! It's a damn deal, Doc." He placed his heavily weighted hand on my chest. It was in a black glove with the top of it inked with white skeleton bones.

Easy enough. Either I die and didn't have to do a disgusting promise, or I live and lick the armpits of a sweaty marine with gratitude. I'll take the latter.

"Where're yer friggin' war faces??!!" Staff Sergeant yelled out, turning the corner of the hooch as he began to face us, "listen up, Gents!"

"Ah shit," whispered someone loudly, "…SHIT…" A cigarette fell onto the rocks as his voice roared over us, stunning some of the Juniors.

His head swiftly looked down at the ground and saw the glowing ember but brushed it off as if he'd let it slide.

"ETA is 10 minutes," he began to say, his two thumbs inside the chest portion of his flak jacket. "The LZ is hot. I repeat the LZ is hot. No more games. It's show time."

"Let's go," he said, and calmly turned towards the path that led us to the field.

And for the next few minutes, it was nothing but the sounds of weapons, their metal parts bouncing off the equipment that were attached to flak jackets. Our boots made crackling noises as we trampled over the rocks towards the Chinook.

It was roughly 60 yards away and when we crossed the field of the burnt summer grass, the "blip blip blip" was now a loud, heavy and pulsating sound accompanied by a whistling, whooshing noise.

"Keep yer head down 'less you want your buddy't pick it up for ya!!!"

I was a few feet behind Staff Sergeant and all I could hear was the sound of him yelling and when he turned around, his mouth violently moved up and down like a deranged puppet. The grass, now moving in unison with the movement of the helicopter's double blades, flickered and waved left to right like ocean waves.

The ramp was slightly elevated; a thick, metal, draw like platform that led us into a space full of dim lights, hanging ropes and plastic seats that were off to the side. I kept thinking, "I've wanted to ride in a helicopter, but not like this. Not in the middle of the night in a fucking war zone."

It only took a few minutes and the platform folded towards us and we were up in the air. Quick. My throat and gut felt the hard push into the sky, and I held my breath trying to think of every reason not to show I was scared.

But it was too dark to even see me anyway.

Everyone probably felt the same way.

The first thought.

This is it. This is how I'm going down.

Damn, that didn't feel good. Second thought.

I wonder if it hurts…dying…Hopefully it's quick.

Just Glow

Goddamnit.

I slowed my breathing down.

I'm surrounded by everyone who would fight to the death for me. If I die, I die with them.

That thought seemed to give me relief and forget that we were flying through the valley towards the landing zone.

A bit of positive energy.

I had to let it go.

He wore cut-off, frayed jean shorts that were way above his knees but that's how they did it in the 90s. And he made a plain white t-shirt look good. No wrinkles because he ironed all of them. Yes, he had more than a handful. And no matter if he was sweating from working in the yard or after working the second shift at the local supermarket, he always smelled like aftershave or Drakkar Noir.

Grandpa, my mom's father, was named Antonio. But like any other grandparent, we just called him Grandpa.

Grandpa stayed in the front room of our house in Cypress, Texas and raised us for roughly a year. My parents went to work and before I entered Pre-Kindergarten, Grandpa basically took care of us. He cooked our meals, cleaned the house, washed our laundry, and of course made sure we didn't "horseplay" too much.

The man had impeccable aim. Of COURSE he had impeccable aim. Every Filipino parent had impeccable aim. And it was with whatever was accessible at the time of you running away from them.

Augusto C. Cespedes, Jr.

"Woah!" I'd dart towards the door to the hallway before a house slipper smacked me in the leg. My mom had the common pathways in the house covered with plastic carpet runners and if I'd knocked it on its underside, I'd feel the small little spikes on the bottom of my feet. Ow!

"Stop. Stop it! Stop now!" My grandpa would yell out, his accent was more noticeable when he raised his voice in anger.

But we were kids.

We didn't know any better.

At times, when a shoe was thrown at us, I'd look back and he'd have this grin on his wrinkled face, almost like he was enjoying it. So of course, it made us smile but also afraid because that shit was gonna hurt.

But it was the days when he went to work, and everyone was asleep that I'd never forget. I'd crack my door open so the headlights of his car would pierce through into my room, hitting the opposite wall.

In the dark, my eyes would open to the slamming of a car door. The front door opening, creaking.

"Jay...?" Grandpa asked, his shadow outstretching itself onto the floor.

"Hmm?" I'd whisper out.

"Got your favorite..." he would say, and so I climbed out of bed.

Wrapped in his work apron was what I had stayed up for. Sure, it was wrong. And we both knew it.

The gold wrapper caught my eye as I unfolded the apron.

Just Glow

A *Twix* candy bar.

"Thank you…." I felt myself drawing out the words in a whispered manner, eager to open it in the dark.

My two front teeth sunk into the caramel, and I always anticipated hitting the cookie at the end.

"You're the best, Grandpa."

He stuck his head out of the closet and said in a low whisper, "your mommy would kill me if she knew this…" and we would just both laugh, and I ate both chocolate covered cookies in his room inhaling the room's scent of his aftershave.

My leg started to shake. My ankle, never touching the ground, vibrated. It was just the left one and only up and down — somewhat controlled. And it took some time to get the rhythm, but once I had it down, I couldn't stop, and I'd play this game with myself to see if I could stop it. But it didn't come from just anywhere.

My mind raced. I tried to think of who I got it from.

My grandfather used to do it.

It was a night we had chosen to watch a scary movie. We felt bold and picked out *The People Under the Stairs*.

We rarely stayed up to watch movies, but it was the weekend and my parents had thought we would like it.

"One mike!" a voice yelled out. Even over the sounds of the propellers I could hear it.

Augusto C. Cespedes, Jr.

I must have gotten so spooked by a movie scene that I curled up right next to my grandpa. He wore his usual cut off jean shorts that had the loose threads and I immediately noticed his leg was vibrating.

He leaned towards me, and said, "it's okay. I'm scared, too."

I focused so heavily on the rhythmic movement of his leg and how violent it shook but it was the one and only thing that distracted me from the scene. I held onto it like a tired swimmer would hold onto a piece of wreckage in the middle of the ocean. I felt like it was all I had.

The high-pitched sound of the helicopter seemed to slow down, and I felt the motion of the aircraft decrease its speed.

Although with only the glow of a small amber of light, I looked down and felt my right leg shaking. Vibrating. I couldn't make it stop, and I didn't want to make it stop. I focused so hard on it, the only thing I had to hold onto.

"Thirty seconds, Gents!" Lieutenant yelled out, now standing up with his hand on the rope that hung from the ceiling.

I thought of everything. My life back home. The moment I left my house one last time. It felt so sped up in my head, fast forwarding itself to that very moment.

It's ok, I'm scared, too. It was my grandpa's voice.

But it was the drawbridge that met the ground and someone nudging me forward that broke the trance.

I was waiting for the horrible sounds of being shot at.

Just Glow

The popping noise. But all I could hear was the pulsating noise of the propellers.

I found myself running.

For a moment, the powerful gusts of wind took my mind off the talks about the "Hot LZ." And honestly, I just wanted to find cover. And quick. But I didn't know where to run. There was a bush here, a dirt pile there. I didn't want to be off on my own, so I followed the group of Marines that seemed like they knew where to go.

And before I could even find cover, the Chinook had left. The powerful sounds of its blades had dissipated into the blackened sky, and we were at the top.

Out of instinct, I tried to ignore the adrenaline rush and try and feel if I was shot or I'd sprained an ankle.

And I immediately remembered the talks.

"Gents, it's a hot LZ!"

"Prepare for the goddamn worst."

"Oh, the LZ is hot! HOT!"

Still nothing.

But the echoing sounds of the Chinook's blades kept my thoughts so vivid and violent that that was all I'd thought.

Why am I not hearing anyone yelling?

Or shooting?

Augusto C. Cespedes, Jr.

I feveverishly patted my cargo pocket to make sure I was prepared for the worst, but still, nothing.

Miraculously I found the closest heavy dense of brush and I could feel the sweat dripping off my face. But still, no pop. No yelling.

Once I realized we were in the clear, I could feel my breath start to slow. Deeper. Calmer. That crisp, stinging feeling of the air to my nares was more recognizable now.

"Spread out, spread out. Open your eyes, boys. We only have the moonlight now," Lieutenant said.

I initially didn't understand what he was saying, but I took a good look at the area. The moon, a shiny white object that hung high in the sky, made it glow a sheer, ghostly white.

I glanced at my watch like it even mattered and saw that it was only 0130. I knew it was going to be a long night.

We walked what felt like for several hours, but it was barely an hour and became a total mind fuck.

Walking with a sixty-pound ruck on your back in absolute darkness was one thing. But doing it on uneven terrain put a different wear on your body.

Not only was your body trying its best to feel and absorb every bump and rock on the ground with every step, but you could feel the frustration of your accessory muscles working harder.

Just Glow

And they only worked harder so you didn't eat absolute shit.

I was pretty certain no one wanted to fly off of the cliff and crack their skull wide open.

"Here we go again…" someone started to sing the melody we were all familiar with.

"Dude, shhh…"

Rustling. An occasional sniffle. Cough.

"Man, where the hell are we going?"

My eyes started to feel heavy. Double vision, 'eyes bout to roll to the back of my head' heavy. Heavier than usual but I knew I couldn't lose focus. But it was the waves of stress that kept me in and out. Fear of the unknown. Who knew what would happen to us on the mountain.

Like cattle following one another, I carelessly bumped into the Marine in front of me. With the heaviness of the pack, I couldn't stop on a dime. But it appeared everyone bumped into everyone as well.

"We're stopping…"

"What…?"

"Why…?"

"Anyone know what's going on??"

Augusto C. Cespedes, Jr.

But with everyone's ruck being taller than their own heads, it was hard to see what was going on.

But once I had stopped, the bulkiness of the ruck swayed like a giant pendulum. As if I was bowing to an opponent, I bent down and felt a stretch in my lower back.

"Screw this, I'm poppin' a squat right here," someone yelled out. He was slow to get in position, but he started to bend down with the giant ruck towering over him.

"Nope," Corporal said, and he put his hand under the ruck. "Get up, Private,"

"We've been stopped for like five minutes…"

"It'll be harder for you to get up once you're down. Stay standing," Corporal had said, his voice a little louder than the last.

So we all did.

And we stood around for another five minutes, and another five.

I'd felt the gurgling of my stomach.

Someone coughed. A sarcastic, drawn out clearing of one's throat.

Finally, out of impatience, Corporal began to walk to the front of the line and suddenly disappeared in the line of rucksacks.

Just Glow

"Took him long enough," someone said. The statement made us laugh.

It was unpredictable. Out of the blue.

Just that small bit of humor, after what felt like hours of silence, was what we all needed. Like I had forgotten the rucksack was on my back. A moment of energy.

Corporal's silhouette emerged from the dark like a lone straggler, and he spoke out, "We're stopping here for a bit. Do whatever you gotta do, just don't use your light."

I needed to hear those words. It was our green light to ease off the tension.

I took full advantage of it and immediately plopped down.

I didn't care where I was, but when I started to realize it, the dirt mounds were in an equal formation, much like a garden. I looked around, squinted, and waved my hand to my right feeling the hardened, crisp leaves brush against my fingers.

Farmland.

We were in someone's farmland and with the packs on our backs, stood within the tall stalks of vegetables.

When I sat down, the heaviness of my sweat beaded off and slid off my eyebrow.

Without hesitation, I dug my dirt ridden nails into the MRE I had been waiting for.

Substance. Something other than the salty viscous fluid that entered my mouth.

I ripped open the pink colored foil wrapper and shoved the biscuit in my mouth like it was escaping from me.

"Geezus, Doc," a Senior marine spoke out next to me. He took a drag from his cigarette like it was his entertainment. "You're a straight savage."

I really didn't think anything of it. I was hungry.

"We're hot rackin' tonight," one of the marines said. It was in a tone of delighted sarcasm.

Damnit, what is that again?

"Doc, y'know what that is?!"

I guess I didn't respond in time, so he responded back, "You's 'bout to find out, Squid. Bring out those green mats, Gents." He slung off the rucksack onto the ground and reached for the rolled-up mat that was buckled at the front.

He started to unroll the green mat.

Ahh, the reliable green rubber mat.

It was thin, roughly 3/8th of an inch thick, and barely provided cushion. But when you're tired, that mat was pretty damn comfortable.

We split up into fours but only three mats were taken out.

"Private, you're up first," Corporal had blurted out, "then wake Doc up in two hours."

Two hours. PLENTY of time to sleep.

I placed my hand on the mat to lay myself down, feeling the hardness of the ground through its rubbery film.

"Two hours," I mumbled.

I laid on my back and shut my eyes.

"Doc…"

"Doc…"

I felt my body shaking me.

"Doc…"

"What…."

"Doc Cespedes, you're up."

"I just shut my eyes."

"It's been two hours."

No goddamn way. My mind, now awake from astonishment, started to work now. I was more curious as to how that even happened.

I dug my elbow into the mat, propping myself up and asked, "Are you sure?"

Augusto C. Cespedes, Jr.

"I'm pretty sure," he said. "I smoked a handful of cigarettes and sang to myself every song I knew, so I'm almost positive." He reeked of freshly burned tobacco, the cheap stuff we'd bought before we'd left for the mission.

I made a grumbling noise that stirred one of the ones next to us.

"No Mama, I'm good…I had enough…" one of the guys said, slurring his speech as he trailed off. Once he started to smack his lips, I knew he was still asleep.

We both stared at him. Not out of shock or what was happening but more out of jealousy that he was asleep.

"Alright," I said annoyed, "I'm up." I quickly sprung to my feet and breathed in the air that was now cold.

Damp. At least ten degrees colder than what it was hours before.

Morning dew. 0415.

"Can I bum a few cigarettes from you?" I asked, trying to be quiet. Private, now on the mat that I was just laying on, handed me a small white box. I flipped it open to see four white sticks of cigarettes that were covered with bits of free-floating grains of tobacco.

"Night, Doc," he began to say. He smiled, closed his eyes and kept smiling like he was smelling something sweet.

"Shut up," I whispered.

Just Glow

For the next few days, we were on a steady descent, patrolling through each village that we had encountered.

Each village seemed to be somewhat connected to one another, whether it was a small trail or a dirt path.

At such high altitudes, the mode of transportation was very different from Jalalabad. We only saw people walking with poorly fitted shoes or loafers that you'd find in a consignment shop. Or a donkey or even a bike.

When entering a village, "A salaam alaykum" was what we would usually say with a right hand to the chest. As a sign of respect.

"Mistuh, Mistuh, it's nice… time? Time?" They'd say, pointing to their wrist and then yours. They'd inspect you from head to toe, admiring the gadgets you had on your body. A watch or even a radio.

The rural way of life we had encountered during our descent was eye opening, to say the least.

It was different from the hustle and bustle of the city life.

The statement that always ran through my head was, "I feel like I'm in the Bible." Like we were in another world. Wooden, rickety watermills, mud houses and straw beds.

Everything seemed simple.

Quiet.

Plain.

Dirty.

Several scattered, bent plastic and metal buckets of various sizes were stacked beside water pumps or on the side of houses.

Villages were not all created equal. Some seemed more advanced than others, especially if it was closer to sea level. The higher the elevation, the more the villages seemed to have used materials from the environment. Straw, sticks, and mud.

But it wasn't the appearance that threw us off. It was the various odors that made us always ask, "What is that smell?"

They had housed their livestock in the same area they had slept in, especially in extreme temperatures.

Just Glow

"Doc," Lieutenant had said, "there's a boy in that house that is sick. Can you see him?"

The house was made of hardened red colored mud with pieces of straw piercing through and dried.

"Okay," I replied, wiping the sweat off of my head.

I pulled it open and silently gagged. The smell of spoiled food, animal dung, and unwashed clothing was overpowering.

"Salam Alaikum."

Houses, or shacks, were made from scraps of discolored metal that looked like it had been destroyed in a rainstorm and reused again and again.

Clotheslines that hung different styles of clothing.

Kids with no shoes. Or kids with "barely even considered" shoes. Their clothes, which appeared to have once been seen in bright colors, now dirty and darkened from the dust and sand.

Whenever we patrolled into a village, our constant awareness always, no matter what, noticed the eyes. People stared. Hard. Like a doll's eyes. The heads didn't move, just the eyes.

It was the end of a patrol and we had gotten intel from our Translator that a small terrorist cell knew we were present. So, we stopped in between two villages. The sun had gone down at this point.

"Find a spot, divide into fours and don't get killed. They know we're here."

Two squads in the middle of a road. Out of all places, middle of the road.

I started to look around the area and found myself a crevice that was made from a few big boulders. In it laid a bed of damp, multicolored leaves.

"Out of harm's way, and I could crawl up in a ball," I thought. I felt childish but it was better than being exposed.

"No WAY you're sleeping in that, Doc. You think you're a baby deer or somethin'?" he blurted out, almost trying to get someone else's attention.

And he did.

"Gonna nestle with your buh-wankie, too?"

Just Glow

I understood we were all delirious and needing any joke to keep our sanity alive so I just said, "Ya, give me yours."

There was a time when my parents bought a new appliance that came in a box in the shape of a rectangular prism.

"Can I have it??!" I asked, inspecting it, completely admiring its size.

"I don't need it," my dad replied, "sure, go 'head. What're you even gonna use it for anyway?"

I wanted to use it to sleep in — aaaaand imagine myself as an animal.

But, of course, I didn't tell him that.

"I was going to make a fort," I lied.

"Oh…" he paused. "….sure, okay."

So, I took it to my room and placed it against the wall.

It was huge. It was at least 8-10 feet long and two feet high. And at seven years old, that was more than plenty.

I took one of my school scissors and cut a door into it and crawled in. "A bit hot," I thought. So, I cut a small roof.

During dinner, my sister asked, "what are you doing with that big box?"

Augusto C. Cespedes, Jr.

"I made a fort."

She choked on her food. "Really? Looks like a doghouse to me."

"Don't say that. That's not nice," my mom said.

"It's true. Have you seen it?"

I ignored her and hurried to eat my dinner to get back to the box.

I finished my last bite, put my fork down, went to my room and closed the door.

I started to take the pillow and blankets off my bed and put them into the box.

When I opened the door to go brush my teeth, my sister peered in and said out loud, "You're SLEEPING in there? No way." She paused, then burst out laughing. Like the hyenas from The Lion King when little Simba growled at them, and they all thought it was hilarious.

I just brushed my teeth, held my tongue and when I was done, I didn't say a word. Just crawled into the cardboard box and I felt happy to be in it.

I felt myself tossing and turning, the hollow sounds of the box close to my face.

"JR…"

"JR…"

A creak of a door pierced through the cardboard sound.

Just Glow

It was my door that creaked.

"JR..."

I wiggled myself towards the door of the box and peeked my head out.

"What is it..."

My sister started to whimper.

I thought it was a joke, like it was her last "you look dumb, I get the last laugh" way to say goodnight.

So, I asked, "What else do you have to say about the box?"

There was a long pause and she only started to sniff.

"Can I sleep in your bed?"

I was stunned. Only the pathetic rustling of the cardboard box as I inched my head out of the box a little more.

"What happened?"

She started to whimper, "I was lying in bed, and it was the weirdest thing..."

She paused again, but still sniffling.

"What...?"

"They were everywhere. Spiders. I could see their little legs. Crawling all over the walls and the ceiling. I wanted to run out of my

room, but I couldn't move." She stared past me like I wasn't there, like she was reliving it all over again.

She paused again. It was silent for a few seconds and then she spoke.

"Can I sleep on your bed?" Her voice sounded weak, vulnerable, like she knew what she did was wrong and was hoping I would say yes.

I replayed it all in my head and I just took a deep breath and said, "Okay."

We never spoke about our conversation again. Or her bad dream. Or even the box.

But the next day, we ended up playing a game that involved her Barbies, my action figures and the big cardboard box.

First

Stepping on bubble wrap. Crushing each of the plastic pockets of air under your feet as the soles of your shoes meet the ground. High pitched sounds of popping.

That's what it sounds like. If anyone asked me what being shot at sounded like, that's what my answer would be.

And there was something phenomenal about your first firefight. Maybe one of life's greatest initiations. It was a part of life that no one ever expects to be in but damn, if it came around, it did something to you.

Just Glow

Fear was an emotion that was never spoken about. It was never formulated into words so the guy next to you could hear it. It was an emotion that just quietly seeped through the cracks of everything else.

It was in between your teeth next to the remnants of the MRE you had just eaten.

Fear was that annoying bead of sweat that lingered what seemed like forever that never dripped off your nose.

Every single word of the sentence that made someone hysterically laugh.

Fear were those seconds of dreaded silence that someone would desperately break through and say, "anyone got an extra smoke?"

We found ourselves walking through the dried-out irrigation fields of a farm outside of a village.

"Heeeeere we go again…." someone said, in the tune of a cadence we had heard a million times. In my head I ended up saying the rest of it.

"Smells like shit out here," one said.

"What's new…" a Junior chuckled.

"I'm actually getting used to it," someone admitted.

I wondered if he was being serious.

When we entered the village, I stared at the thick, gray

water that sat in huge puddles next to pieces of trash that were scattered everywhere.

"In and out guys," Staff Sergeant said out loud.

"Ya, can't wait to— ..."

Now, I am not sure if you've ever shot a weapon, whether it'd be a rifle or a handgun. What's funny about that is... It actually doesn't matter.

Being shot at is a Completely. Different. Experience.

It's an indescribable, powerful gust of wind that, God willing, doesn't melt your flesh.

"Contact front! Contact front!"

The violent, whizzing sounds shot past me like some sort of fictitious alien invasion, and I could do nothing but pin my chin to the ground, violently inhaling the dust and sand, feeling every force of each round as it passed by over my head.

The sharp popping sounds followed with the firing off of the Marines' rifles gave me relief. A relief that I didn't

Just Glow

hear "Corpsman Up!"

It instantly let me know we were on the offensive.

"Doc, we're moving! Come on!" In the midst of smoke yelled someone pulling the arm hole of my flak jacket.

If it wasn't for him, my face still would've been buried in the dirt.

"Get behind me," he said, stepping in front of me with his fanned hand out.

He walked swiftly but kept his rifle's muzzle in a "ready up" and I held onto his shoulder like I was blinded.

"Dare f'that sunnavabitch to come out," he said, loud enough for me to hear it. A rancid, sour smell reeked from his clothing, like wet clothes that sat out for days. Musty. Foul. My only way of protection. But at this point, I felt like Juba in the movie 'Gladiator' when he held onto Maximus as they were down to the last opponent in the arena.

We both leaned hard against the mud wall and I, only equipped with a 9mm handgun, kept looking back to make sure no one was behind us.

"We good?! We good?!" he kept saying to me. I could feel his hot, moist breath shouting the words.

"Good," I said, feeling my head twisting and turning, "Keep moving…"

Moving in unison, I forced myself to remind myself why I was there. What I was trained to do. I shoved the thoughts of my childhood into my pocket and clenched my teeth feeling the tense pressure in my jaw.

Then a shout from a distance, like if you were in the attic of your house and someone from the inside of the house had called out.

"Y'guys good?!!"

After all of the cracking and popping, it suddenly fell silent.

"That our guys?!" I thought.

It sounded like an American. He didn't have an accent.

Then that voice was heard again. "We're clear, all clear!"

It was as if a heavy weight had been lifted from my chest. That I could finally take a full breath.

When we got back to base, it was like those wholesome sports movies where the team wins the game and all of the players walk back to the locker room, smiling from ear to ear.

"Man that was insane!"

"You should've seen your face, Bro!"

"Man you were the one who didn't move!" A roar of laughter erupted the room.

Soon after, Staff Sergeant walked in.

Just Glow

"Shut up," he said putting his hands out, "all of you." And we all did. No one made a sound, not even the scuffing of boots on the concrete slab.

His face showed no smile and his head like a rusty oscillating fan, scanned the room so we all could see his eyes.

Then out of nowhere, his lips curled a smile.

"Now that's what you call a fuckin' bedtime story, am I right?" He yelled out. Laughter erupted again, but I couldn't help but let out a single breath.

That night, I laid on my side and tried closing my eyes but I couldn't get it out of my head.

Get down, contact front!

My face to the dirt.

Zipping sounds flying over my head.

I tried to regulate my breathing. Tried to calm myself down.

But even despite the growling, overpowering snores of the Marines, my eyes forced themselves to close, anticipating the abrupt, popping sounds of bubble wrap.

Augusto C. Cespedes, Jr.

The Last Days

I felt an aggressive tap at my left shoulder. It was a violent nudge that moved me off the plywood that laid on the cement slab.

Reality sunk in.

0245. My watch glowed a green light that made me squint in the dark.

1/1/2006.

I rolled over the thin, rubbery mat and a silent celebration of "Happy New Year" came and went through my mind.

"You're up," someone said. It wasn't a pleasant way to wake someone up, but it was the end of his watch, and it was my turn for fire watch.

Over the last few months of the deployment, we gained a place to stay — a forward operating base, or FOB. It was in a town just north of Jalalabad.

"Few more days, Doc," he said, a Senior Marine who was to walk fire watch with me.

The opening of the room gave a clear view of the castle-like doors of the FOB. Gigantic, towering French-like doors that seemed a few feet thick that were partially open.

I started to walk out to get some fresh air and then realized the horrid stench that came from the room. It was of

Just Glow

smelly feet and a sour, odorous body odor that made me silently gag.

"Take my rifle, Doc," someone said, pointing to the wall.

Alone by itself in the corner, an M16 with an attached ACOG laid against the wall. Throughout the whole deployment, I only admired them, never held one during a patrol or a mission.

"You sure?" I said, nervous. I felt stupid to go on a perimeter patrol with my 9mm, but I felt like I had no choice.

"If you guys get contact, at least both of yas will have guns down range. Take it," he insisted, leaning over to grab it. He outstretched himself but I started to move.

"I got it, Corporal," I said, and moved quicker so he wouldn't grab it before me.

I grabbed it by the rails, the cold metal sending a jolt of energy through my body. Nervous. Excited. I felt bigger.

"Gotta show 'em I know basic weapon safety," I thought.

Finger straight and off the trigger.

Muzzle awareness.

I kept it pointed towards the ground, carefully slinging it over my shoulder.

Augusto C. Cespedes, Jr.

"You got it, Doc! You only learned from the best, right?" he joked, trying to keep his voice quiet.

And out we went. The sky was clear and the moon was so bright, it cast its light on the sand, causing it to illuminate in such a way that the sand appeared white.

"No need for light. That's good," the Marine said.

As we made our way back, someone yelled to me, "Doc! Wanna use the SAT (satellite) phone?? Call your family?"

Throughout the deployment, I tried so hard to avoid it. I felt like hearing my family's voice would bring me back to "square one" of learning how to cope, so any chance I got, I turned it away.

But this time, it was New Years. It felt different.

It was a bulky, heavy phone with a worn-out plastic casing on it that felt greasy from everyone who had used it. The antenna was as thick as a wooden drumstick.

Shaking, I dialed the number I knew. My home number. A few numbers before it and then the seven numbers.

The one I grew up with.

373-0420.

The line was full of static but as it continued to ring it was able to clear out. The speaker of the phone melted to my ear as I waited patiently for somebody. Anything.

And then a voice.

Just Glow

"Hello?" I could hear others in the background. "…is someone there? Who's this??"

It was my mom. The emotion that I had held back for all those months toppled over me like a powerful, rogue wave.

"Mom," I started to mumble, finally being able to say the words.

"I'm coming home."

Chapter 9
The Presence of God

Surrounded by small pastures, farms and a few restaurants stood a church on a road called Huffmeister.

Christ The Redeemer was the church that we went to growing up. The one my sister and I were baptized at as babies and where we went to church every Sunday. Now, I am not known to remember people's names, but I do remember Father Dominic's; he reminded me of an Abraham Lincoln without the top hat. If you're not much of a churchgoer, Catholic services are traditional. You could literally recite every word they say during the service.

"Through Him, With Him, In Him, in the Unity of the Holy Spirit," my sister and I mocked. The more you closed your throat and tucked in your chin, the more the voice made us laugh. You just knew it all. It was muscle memory at that point.

As I grew older, our parents slowly stopped taking us, most likely due to our extracurricular activities and lack of interest. When I started fourth grade, things started changing; I stopped sitting in the back with all of the babies and wondered why everyone came to church every Sunday.

"What's a sermon?" I asked my Dad.

At nine years old, I thought a sermon was a part of the Communion.

My parents did not tell me certain things and I ended up finding it out for myself.

Like in the sixth grade, a girl once told our class her mom was pregnant.

"Wow, that must've hurt coming out of her behind," I'd said confidently. Everyone laughed at me, but I thought it was because of me saying "behind."

"JR, do you even know where babies come from??" Two girls turned around and asked, giggling. I stared blankly at the chalkboard and imagined babies being covered in poop and knew that wasn't the case.

"A sermon is a part of the service where the Pastor chooses a section of the Bible and relates it to our lives," my dad said.

What I noticed about the Pastor during sermons was how his voice changed; it didn't have the distinct robot sounding pitch or monotoned. It was real. There were pauses. He'd look at the crowd when speaking and there were genuine smiles in between.

After each service, Pastor Dominic would greet everyone with a genuine smile, laugh, have conversations, and ask

Just Glow

what they were up to those days. I never saw him that way, or just never noticed because I always mocked him. But seeing him differently during those times made me really wonder.

And the only thing that was anything church related outside of church was my Lola.

Lola was my Dad's mom, a woman of few words. Well, at least to us kids. She primarily spoke Tagalog (one of the main languages in the Philippines), but could speak English and have a small conversation. She moved slowly but with purpose. She smiled, but also had a stone wall face as she walked from room to room.

"Make sure you bless Lola," my mom would say, every time we would walk to up to my cousin's house. I didn't understand why we had to do it, but I knew she was old and that it was a sign of respect. I did what I was told.

Whenever I was by myself with Lola, which was very rare, only a few words were exchanged. A pleasant smile, but not much was said.

Lola lived with my aunt and took care of my cousins ever since they were babies. And ever since we were kids, we went there as a family. For dinners, various celebrations, like a birthday or Christmas Eve.

My parents and I stopped by one day. No celebration, just a random day to pick something up. My cousin usually would greet us at the door. But that day he didn't.

"Probably hiding so you can find him," my mom would say, pushing me to go play.

So I went to look for him. I went up the stairs, and at the top, was a small hallway of rooms.

I decided to walk slower and hide behind the corners and jump out.

Careful to make sure he couldn't hear me, I hid behind the wall outside of his room, counted to three and turned around, quickly showing my face.

"Gotcha!" I said. His room was empty. A bed, nicely made, seated high on wooden drawers.

"Definitely over there," I said to myself, grinning. I looked at the two rooms across from his.

I crept up to the wall and with my back against it, I heard something. I was ready to make a big scare, but something made me hold my breath. I heard someone mumbling. I peered around the counter and saw her.

It was Lola. Her back was turned towards me, and she was kneeling at an array of candles.

Several of them. Big, small and in different types of

holders. But it lit the room in a way that casted small shadows, with the flickering of lights that danced on the walls. And in the center appeared to be a small statue of a woman that looked familiar. I tried to think of who it was, and it turned on like a light switch. Church.

I stopped and watched her. My heart stopped racing and I felt myself breathing slower.

I had never seen her like this. When us kids were over at the house, she'd always be cleaning or helping my aunt with things. But to see her praying, I thought of how she was. Quiet. Kneeling in the dark with only the glowing of candlelight.

What was it about this statue that was so special?

I backed up from the doorway, went downstairs and didn't tell anyone.

"Find him?" my mom asked, sitting on the couch.

"Nah, but it's okay."

NYE, 1994

"Put your shoes on, JR! We're leaving!" My mom would yell from the front door.

"Jaaaayyy!" Her voice would linger on until I responded. Knowing we were going to my cousin's house, I had to pack up a few NES games.

Augusto C. Cespedes, Jr.

She'd click her tongue and say, "Hurry! Dad's waiting…"

And we drove off.

"Oh cool, you brought Bubble Bobble??!" My cousin would smile, greeting me at the door.

"Ya! They finally had it!"

We'd play for hours, legs crossed, sitting on the floor with our other cousins. The TV would be blaring with our parents trying to talk louder.

My Uncle would come into the room and say, "Hey kids, it's almost night out so you know what that means?"

"Starlight Moonlight!" My cousin and his sister would both yell out. I was confused. I tapped my cousin on the shoulder and asked at a whisper, "What is that?"

"It's like Hide and Seek with the game of Tag. I'll show you when we get outside."

My cousin's backyard was gigantic. And it wasn't just gigantic. It had a garden with pieces of rail wood that shaped each section, giving a lane to walk in (for us kids to run through), a greenhouse that was sort of run down, various potted plants, tall trees and outdoor furniture that lined the back. And at night, it seemed like the perfect place for hiding spots.

My cousin grabbed a flashlight and there was probably eight of us.

Just Glow

"So here are the rules. One person has the flashlight. We all start from home base. Everyone has one minute to find a hiding spot, and once the minute is over, the goal is to get back to home base without getting caught. You can only get caught by getting the light to shine on you."

We were all giggling and getting excited, some rubbing their hands.

"Okay! Are we ready? I'll find you guys," my cousin said, volunteering to be first. He hit the flashlight against the palm of his hand.

"One minute, counting...now." We scattered like field mice.

Already breathing fast, I ran towards the back. I didn't want to waste any time. I put my hands out to make sure I wasn't going to collide with anyone or anything and I made a left. The greenhouse. The door was already open, stuck on a bed of pebbles.

The crunching of small rocks echoed as my foot turned and I scanned the room of what I could see. Complete darkness. I took a few steps and hit a broken plastic pail as it bounced off my foot.

"Oh come on," I said to myself. I put my hand out again and felt glass. Doorknob. Another door. Opening it, I found myself in the back part of the yard.

"Fourteen more seconds!" Someone whispered loudly as they sprinted past me. Startling me but I didn't stop, I couldn't waste time. I randomly picked a spot that appeared to be the corner and I hurriedly walked to it.

I quickly crouched into the brush, making sure I could also get out of it and my knee had hit something hard. Something that didn't seem to belong in a yard.

I put my hand out and it felt like the paint was chipped, making a scaly like sensation on my hand when I touched it.

I started to get up to see what it was, and I saw two white dots about one to two inches apart. I backed up a few inches and focused on it. *Eyes. It was a woman.* Her eyes sent goosebumps traveling down my arms, and the hair on my neck stood up. I was frozen. The eyes seemed like they would follow me even if I moved a few inches to the side. She looked sad. I couldn't stop staring at her, but I also couldn't move.

I remembered seeing the same woman somewhere. *Lola's room. Praying. Church.*

I quickly shook off my trance once I heard a rustling and saw the flashlight's beam towards me, so I hid behind her. I put my hand out again to feel the chipped paint and put my head down. I felt the flashlight pass me and sounds of twigs breaking as my cousin walked past me.

Once I felt like I was in the clear, I made a run for it. I darted back into the greenhouse and jumped over the plastic pail, subconsciously remembering where it was before and scurried through the other door, jumping over the pile of pebbles that laid at the door frame.

Looking like the area was clear, my eyes were set on

home base. With high knees, my legs moved in a forward motion and dug my feet into the grass as I ran as fast as I could.

"Made it!" I said as my fingertips touched the wood of the deck. I looked back and I was the only one there. A few of my cousins were sitting on the couches of the deck, in awe.

"You're the only one who didn't get caught!"

I looked around and my cousin with the flashlight pointed the light at me, causing me to put my hand over my face.

"Where were you hiding?!! I looked everywhere!" he said, smiling but you could see the shocked expression in his face.

"Not telling," I said and thought about the eyes in the dark and how they made me feel. The brightness of the painted sclera were seen in such darkness. I was in fear at first, but still. Curious. I never went back to that spot, but I always wondered. I never mocked the Pastor again.

2001

One of the most difficult things to find in high school was a circle of friends. Whether it's the three of you or twenty, a circle of friends was essential and when you were able to obtain it, you were as good as gold.

Augusto C. Cespedes, Jr.

"That shirt is awesome," I'd said to him. It was sophomore year of high school. Health class. One of those classes you just had to take to graduate. There were a mixture of grades in our class, from freshman to Junior.

The shirt was of The Get Up Kids, an emo band that rose in popularity in the mid to late 90s. A navy blue shirt, with two identical flying robots on each side of the band name.

He looked down at it, smiled and said, "Thanks, Guy!"

After several weeks in Health class and finding out we both liked the same things, David introduced me to his friends.

"We play tons of Ping-Pong," he'd say, scarfing down the last remnants of a Frito pie he had bought at lunch.

I didn't know what to make of it all, but I knew, in my heart, it was good.

I gathered up the courage and decided to drive my '91 GMC Sierra to a different part of town, northeast of where I lived.

I had just bought an anti-shock, sports edition CD Walkman from Sam Goody and inserted the tape deck into the cassette player with its cord connected to the player, and pressed play, the silver triangle on the front. Of course the cd was of The Get Up Kids.

"Something to Write Home About," by The Get Up Kids. Track 1, "Holiday," was the best opener for, really, anything you're preparing for. A full sounding pick slide with

Just Glow

the bass drum preparing a full band intro. Once it was a full band sound, the drums went all out with the guitar, and you noticed it fill with a few half time beats and it was just, most creative. Positive. It always put a genuine smile on my face, even at seven in the morning. I always tried to enter the school doors with it playing, imagining myself as the main character in a movie or book, ready to take on the world. Or just first period.

Passing a few stop lights and turns, I'd noticed something. I'd never been to this side of town. Pastures with rickety fences turned into manicured lawns and every car was parked in the driveway. Even the cement was a different color. Brighter. Cleaner. New.

Taped to my speedometer was the printout of MapQuest directions I had cut smaller to fit onto the plastic covering. After several minutes of multiple up and down glances, I eventually found myself parked at a two-story house. Towering high stood a house made of light stone with four cars parked in the driveway and two cars in front of the house.

Intimidated but excited, I knocked nervously on the heavy wooden door. I felt like I didn't knock hard enough, so I attempted to knock again, but the door opened mid-air.

"Hi! JR???! How are you? David said you'd be coming! We're all upstairs," she said. Her smile was radiant, contagious, as if I felt like I was smiling back. It was hard not to. She was talking to me like she had known me for years. 'Soccer is Life, The Rest is Just Details' is what her shirt said, slightly tattered.

I walked in and the smell of the house was fresh. Like

new. A crisp, clean breeze of finished oak that had just been cut.

One step after another up the stairs, I followed David's friend to the top and heard the sound of a rhythmic tapping and a few cheers. A ping pong ball. I smiled at how it seemed like everyone knew each other. The high fives, the inside jokes. It was wholesome. And everyone seemed to have their own spot. A few sat on barstools, two were sitting comfortably on bean bags and one sat by the stereo, seeming like he was controlling the music.

"What do y'all want to listen to next?" someone asked. He looked over to the stereo.

"Play that cd you just burned!" Someone else said. He suddenly looked up to the air and motioned like he finally thought of what she had said. He started to look through the booklet of CDs, sleeves that were filled four to a side.

"Summer....of...2000. Got it!" He pulled it out of the sleeve and popped it in. Just the sound of the guitar made everyone cheer. All at once.

And we played for several minutes. Rotating players, the random circle of high fives after each point or extended rally. And when I didn't hear the music anymore, it was actually a pause in between tracks, as a catchy yet sappy piano intro started with a guy suddenly singing,

"I can only imagine what it would be like…"

Everyone laughed.

"What is this???!!" someone asked, looking around the

Just Glow

room for acknowledgment. Other comments could be heard as he laughed.

"Next!" one would say.

"Oh, come on! Haha!" another laughed.

Of course, as the new guy, I laughed too. But it didn't last long because deep down, I actually liked it. His voice was something I'd never heard of. A soft yet deep tone that continued to linger on.

The closest to it was probably something my mom would play, like Phil Collins or Garth Brooks.

Someone ran over to the stereo and skipped to a more upbeat song and, just like that, the moment was over. But after everyone was starting to go home, I went over to one of the girls to save myself from embarrassment, and asked at a loud whisper, "So who was that earlier on the music player? When everyone was laughing?" I smiled and looked around, trying to make sure no one heard me.

"Oh, before? When we were playing ping pong? That's Mercy Me! Never heard of 'em?"

"No," I thought. I just shook my head.

"We sometimes go to Bible study at a friend's house every Wednesday, if you'd like to go," she'd say.

The next week in class, I went up to David, and said to him, "Hey, one of your friends was telling me that y'all go to Bible study during the week."

Augusto C. Cespedes, Jr.

"Yea! What's up?"

I looked down and thought about the guy who said, "What is this???!" and I was embarrassed to ask, but I just risked it and asked.

"Can I tag along?" I was hoping for a yes.

His mouth, going from relaxed to the biggest smile, said, "Of course."

The house wasn't too far from where we all lived. It was a nice neighborhood with humongous trees in everyone's yard.

There were about seven or eight of us. A quaint living room, with dim lighting. I didn't know anyone except David and his friend, but everyone introduced themselves to me with a smile and a sturdy handshake.

I had never been to a Bible study. I didn't bring a Bible, nor did I understand the things he was talking about in the Bible. Then the host of the house grabbed the guitar from behind him and started to sing and everyone started to sing like it was planned. I felt completely out of place.

Everyone's eyes were closed. Mine remained open, trying to stare at something else except their faces. I tried staring at the guitar. It was a beautiful Martin acoustic. But I couldn't hold my stare any longer. And as if I didn't feel comfortable at that moment, I felt even more uncomfortable when some of them raised their hands and sang.

I immediately looked down with wide eyes. I pretended to pray. I didn't even know the words, and I honestly just

Just Glow

wanted to leave. "Why are they raising their arms?" I was asking myself. It felt so awkward. I swallowed hard and waited patiently for the song to end.

We left, and I didn't go to another Bible study. Like a coward, I made up excuses if I was asked.

"Oh! My sister has a soccer game I have to go to," I lied. She didn't play soccer that day, nor was I ever forced to go. I felt horrible for lying but I couldn't bear the thought of being uncomfortable again.

February 2006, Six months before Iraq

As every week went by, we'd get word on the happenings in Iraq. Either from the chatter in the BAS or in formation. Another IED, another ambush, more dead. With Saddam in trial, there was more eruption and anger throughout the cities. Of course the rumors would go around as someone would say, "I heard our base is going to be the worst."

Oh. Great.

Every weekend, I'd see more parties, more loud music being played and more guys stumbling around after a night on the town. Everybody had a different way of coping, of preparing for that dreadful day we were to land on the sand.

"Can't wait to fire some rounds down range, Sarn't," one would say in the middle of formation. And the comments would trickle down the squad line like gasoline to a flame.

"You'll get your shot, Private," he'd say, "don't you worry. You've got eight months of it. Heard it's a hell of a fight out there. I'm buddies with a guy from 3/3. They're getting their asses kicked. Low supplies, hot as all hell and they're ready to go home." He spat out dark colored spit onto the grass and looked around to see if anyone else saw him.

"Well I didn't join the Corps to sit around and fumble my thumbs, so I hope it hits the fan on us."

As a Corpsman, you never wish anything bad on a Marine. "More guns down range," is what was taught to us during FMSS's Mass Casualty training. Bandage up the less wounded first to win the firefight. Worry about the less fortunate ones until the last round falls.

Hearing the comments, and what was happening in Iraq made the preparation unpleasant. Was I ready to face this type of warfare? It didn't matter. Less than a hundred days left whether I was ready or not.

"Yo, Doc, we're all going into town tonight. You should come along." My roommate was always inviting me out, but most of the time I made something up.

"Man, I wish I could. Me and some other Corpsmen are doing a seven-mile run in the morning. Been planned for days now. Next time, okay?"

I'd venture off on my own to the PX, the chow hall or walk the grounds of the Wiki Wiki to the BAS. And just walk. Or try and chase the "hop only" birds without anyone thinking I was going crazy.

Just Glow

I would try and call my family, but the times were so off. Either it was their bedtime or mine, and the best time to talk was early to mid-afternoon.

"Doc Cespedes!" Someone yelled from down the hall. It was a Marine who once shared music with me in Afghanistan.

"This Sunday, me and a couple of other guys are going to church. Wanna tag along? It's called Hope Chapel."

Hope Chapel sat on a hilltop of Kaneohe Bay, overlooking the bay. In 90 days, I'd be in one of the most stressful situations, fighting for my life to come home and I finally found a place like this. Peaceful. Friendly. Refreshing.

I'd go to Hope Chapel a few times here and there and every time, the Pastor would say, "if you feel it in your heart to invite God into your life, come forward." But I never did. I was either nervous, too good to go up there, or I didn't think I needed Him. Or I was too frightened to say I did. I kept my head down and pretended to pray.

Baptized

Before I was even two years old, my parents had me baptized at Christ the Redeemer. In southern Catholic Churches, being baptized at a very young age was standard.

And go figure, they dressed me in a sailor outfit. When I felt the cold water on my head, I feel like I remember it so vividly, thinking my parents and my Godfather were letting some strange guy try to drown me. Tears ran down my face, but the water barely touched my forehead.

"Let Augusto Junior be baptized in the name of the Father, The Son and the Holy Spirit."

And that was it. After that, I went to church every Sunday with my family. It became a routine.

Deciding to be baptized was different. And it happened at Hope Chapel, months before I had left for Iraq.

"Today we have a very special Baptism. Recently returning from Afghanistan and in only a few weeks he will be off to Iraq. May we all pray for him, and may God give him strength and courage as he protects the Marines that are with him," the pastor stated to the audience. There was a silence, and honestly, I didn't blame them. It was a situation that no one wanted to imagine themselves in.

I stuck my feet into the water and didn't expect it to be lukewarm. With no time to hesitate, I placed my whole body in, holding onto the cool metal railing that angled itself into the pool.

I could feel pressure placed onto my upper arms and it was both the Pastor and Brandon who were directing me to the front of the pool.

The heat from the stage lights radiated onto my face like the afternoon sun, and I watched the floating particles of dust dance in the rays. I stared away from it and onto the crowd. Suddenly, they all became blurry. I started to feel myself tear, and a slight pressure was felt onto my forehead, and I went back and under.

A muffling sound. Cheering. Applause.

What felt like several seconds I was under, I was lifted back up and a loud applause was heard through water clogged ears.

The sound came full force, and I wiped my face, felt myself smile and…that was it.

I wasn't sure why I was going to cry. I guess because I was sad I was leaving, yet again. Maybe I was going to cry because I thought something magical was going to happen? That it would make me feel better? But it didn't. Through weeks of preparation, nervousness, and excitement, I felt deceived. It didn't do anything except make me cold, sad, and wet.

Augusto C. Cespedes, Jr.

August 2006, Thirty days before Iraq

I stared at the ticket stub as we walked into the auditorium. Careful not to crinkle it, I held it delicately with two fingers.

"Chris Tomlin, Sold Out" it said as we entered.

We got to stand in the front during the concert and it was an unbelievable feeling. Like no other.

A familiar set of notes rang out, and loud screaming was heard because it was a known song.

"Great song," my friend would yell, in an attempt to overpower the sound. I smiled to acknowledge him and mouthed, "yea."

I then started to look around and noticed people with their hands raised. Many people with their hands raised high and their eyes closed. Immediately, I thought about those moments during Bible study. The uncomfortable feeling of being the only one without raised hands. How I kept my eyes open and stared at everything in the room except the people, the guitar playing softly as I waited anxiously for the song to be over.

I shook it off and began to look forward. I started to think of how I was so upset after getting baptized, not feeling anything different. And how I was going to miss home. And if I was ever going to come back.

Like the flick of a switch, I began to miss my family. My parents. My sister. My friends. I wouldn't potentially see

Just Glow

them until after the deployment, April of 2007. I thought a second deployment would be easier, but it wasn't. Iraq was and felt like a different beast.

Phone calls home didn't help. Hours on the phone with a friend couldn't take away the unwanted feeling of possibly dying.

"I'm really sorry," they'd say, with few words as other people could be heard on the other line. I understood how they felt but also needed them to understand me. But how could they?

Partying or the excess drinking didn't help either. Nothing in the world could help and I felt…helpless.

I need You. I suddenly felt myself with heavy eyes. I couldn't think of anything else.

As the shopping cart zoomed past the aisle of candy, my six-year-old self hung onto the side and ended up jumping off at the sight of it. I ran a few feet towards the aisle and picked it up. Cookies 'n Cream Hershey bar. My favorite. I held it with both hands, a white wrapper that showed black and white cookies being dunked into milk.
  I turned around and ran back to where I thought my mom was, but it was just a massive crowd going in different directions.

"Mom…where are you…?" I thought to myself. I saw something in the candy aisle I hadn't seen before so I decided to part from the shopping cart. After feeling like several minutes, I had lost how to get back to where my mom was, and started going in circles.

"Have you seen my Mom?" I asked a stranger, as if I found hope in asking someone walking by. At only 3.5 feet tall, I was lost.

Augusto C. Cespedes, Jr.

"Hun, I don't know where your mom is, sorry," they'd say.

I felt myself starting to sweat. Like heavy beads, they uprooted from the pores of my temple. I began to panic. I regretted everything I did in order to see that chocolate bar, and I just wanted to be back at the shopping cart. I tried to clench my fists but felt weak. I opened my mouth in an attempt to ask someone, but they would turn away. It was like a bad dream and all I wanted to do was wake up.

My lip curled and I bit it. I felt completely helpless. My mom was going to leave me. The store was going to close, and I was going to have to sleep in the bread aisle or something.

I started to feel my face scrunch, my eyes water and feeling like I had no other choice, I cried out.

Something pulled at me, and I felt an ache in my heart, and as the melodic sounds of that familiar song echoed, I slowly unhinged my hands from my side, raised them and began to close my eyes.

"If your name is JR, please come to the front of the store. Your mom is waiting for you," the announcer calmly said over the intercom. It was as if my mom was standing next to her, smiling.

"Aww, that must be you," a woman would say, looking down at me. She grabbed my hand and we walked towards the front of the store.

Almost synchronized with the music, I lifted my hands and felt ….alive. It was a feeling that I'd never understood. The hairs on my neck stood straight up.

And it was in that moment, a warm, gentle weight was felt on my left shoulder. Not abrupt. It was as if the palm

Just Glow

was initially placed and fingers had followed through, almost in an attempt of grabbing my shoulder.

A low, deep voice was felt from my bones.

I'm here. It's okay.

It sunk far into my blood and honestly, it scared me.

I didn't let it linger any longer, and I opened my eyes, dropped my hands, and looked around. No one was around me. The music blared and the singer sang out.

What exactly was that feeling?

I looked over to my left shoulder and wondered how I could've felt that.

I thought about how I stared at the pair of eyes in the dark. How much fear I was in at first, but after taking a step back, it had disappeared.

"What an amazing concert," my friend yelled as we all exited into the escalator. Our ears were still buzzing from the sound.

I was speechless. I didn't know what to stare at. I didn't know what to say or think.

My eyes chased passing cars on the way home as I sat in the backseat of a beat-up Honda Civic. The smell of the interior was of days old French fries with a hint of cigarette smoke. As the streetlights danced in a horizontal beam, I felt myself squinting, staring in wonder. What truly happened in that concert? Was someone playing a trick on me? I had so many questions, but I knew no one would understand.

No one was even around. I kept running those moments through my head over and over, trying to make sense of it all, but I just couldn't figure it out.

I laid in my bed that night listening to my roommate snore, hoping to feel that mysterious weight on my shoulder again. I wanted to give it another chance. After a few moments of feeling nothing, I just let out a sigh. The buzzing of the fan grew louder as it oscillated in the room, the breeze gliding across my face as it passed over me. Papers on the desk flickered like a gentle flame under their paperweights of cigarette packets and rifle magazines and the half empty beer bottles sat at the sill.

But I knew, in that moment, it was going to be okay.

I was going to be okay.

Chapter 10
Just Kids

March 2006

With black framed glasses and squinting towards the Hawaiian mountainside, he stood at attention. His neck at an angle that appeared slightly bent, sizzled its sweat in the sun as we waited for the last call for the weekend.

It was 1600, the moment the sun was at its hottest.

"What's with the face, Warner?" Sergeant asked him as we all stood in formation.

"Beg y'pardon, Sarn't?" Warner, confused. It was as if the same muscles involved in squinting caused him to involuntarily grin.

He laughed. "Wipe that smirk off your face, Private. You'll get yourself in trouble."

"Roger, Sarn't," Warner replied as his grin slowly faded away. With his head still bent, a Senior Marine chimed in.

Augusto C. Cespedes, Jr.

"Are you deaf, Boot?! Wipe that stupid smirk!" With both hands, he grabbed Warner's face and proceeded to almost treat it like molding a pot. His actions made his neck straight, which caused him to change his position, now with shoulders back and awkwardly leaning forward. His glasses now crooked, he ironically stood at attention. Most of us didn't have to look at him as we could feel the waves of tension beam off the squad line.

Once I came back from Afghanistan, I didn't get a chance to meet all the new Marines as most of them were being "tended" to by the Marines, now Seniors. I guess I was considered a Senior Corpsman, coming back from an eight-month combat deployment, but I already had Iraq on my mind.

Before formations, I'd watch the initiations at the barracks, and it dawned on me. The new Marines had arrived.

And I didn't laugh. Because no one did. Every time I left my room, there was always a commotion. Something down the hall or in the yard, and all you could do was stare. A Junior Marine doing push-ups in the hallway at eleven at night, another Marine cleaning his room because he didn't do it properly during Field Day. There was always… something.

With sweat glistening off his face and neck, the Junior Marine would be swinging an imaginary golf club, looking at the ground and then staring off into the distance at what he had "hit."

Just Glow

"How far do you think that went, Boot?!" A Senior Marine would calmly ask him.

"Two hundred and fifty yards?" He replied nervously.

"Doubt it! Not with that form. Try again!" And this would go on for another ten minutes. And no one would laugh. It was part of the initiation.

"I know you're moving faster than that!" Another Marine would belt out, causing a new Marine to scramble aimlessly in and out of his room while the Senior would stand outside, arms crossed. Every now and then I'd exchange glances with the Senior as they did these things and we'd both crack a smile, knowing that they once were in that same exact position and now they had their turn. So I'd just shake my head and keep walking.

And this went on for weeks.

Weekdays.

Weekends.

Didn't matter what time of day it was, you'd see or hear the hazing of the next batch of Junior Marines.

"Libbo!!!" The sarcastic yelling of Marines would end the formation. And just like that, it was another Friday. Scrambling towards cars or barracks, it was one more weekend away from Iraq. Before turning towards my room, I looked back at the now dispersed platoon and saw Warner fixing his glasses as he began to walk towards his room.

"Hey Warner, wait up!" I yelled, and it seemed to startle

him. His hands started to make their way behind his back at an almost parade rest.

"Stop. Don't do that," I said, putting my hand out.

"Oh, my apologies, Doc," he'd say. He cracked a smile but kept his head down, almost too nervous to look up.

"It's just, ya know…," he'd then start to say, but then trailed off.

"We've all been there, trust me. It'll get better soon," I said, trying to be optimistic. I could see that he was agreeing with me, nodding his hanging head and starting to kick at the gravel.

"Got any plans tonight?" I asked.

"Not really," he'd slowly start to say. "I was going to try and see what the PX had. I haven't had the opportunity to venture out yet. It's sort of been busy."

"Yeah, I completely understand…," and it was quiet for several moments. He started to turn towards his room again.

"Alright Doc, I'll see you on Monday."

"Do you wanna order some pizza?" I quickly asked.

He looked up at me and smiled, "That'd be cool."

We crossed the desert in a long caravan of seven-tons. These types of seven-tons were a bit different. They actually had a

Just Glow

roof. But we still sat in the back with no seatbelts. Although with only one bench, at least the sun wasn't given the chance to roast us for the two-hour drive. The loud hum and the occasional bump usually put me to sleep but for some reason, this one felt *different*. I was restless. Wide eyed. I looked down the line at the others but no one else was speaking. Everyone stared at the desert. *Were they just like me?*

As we got closer to the city, I could feel a dark sense of an unknowing and this time, white knuckled, I gripped the vertical handle of my M16. I nervously raised it up and blew the grains of sand on the ACOG lens. I tried to slow my breathing down, but I couldn't help the overwhelming feeling of something happening. IED. Ambush. The wide-open desert was way too quiet. A calm before the storm.

The endless sea of sand slowly turned into small houses, built of brick and stone. The dirt road developed into actual paved roads and by the looks of it, Haqlaniyah appeared to be a suburban town.

I sat in the back of the line, closest to the exit and watched the last truck trail behind. We were now in the city, and it dawned on me. A few minutes ago, there seemed to be people outside of their houses watching us. Hands at their hips or over their brows to cover their eyes from the sun, but now I noticed it to be different. There was no one in sight. Like a ghost town with only us on the road. It was an eerie feeling, but the roaring sound of the truck blocked it out. Or tried to, at least.

"Last stretch of road here, Boys! Almost there!" Sergeant yelled out from the front of the line. He was looking back at all of us, his helmet tightly secured and his Oakley sunglasses on.

Augusto C. Cespedes, Jr.

As we neared the base, I glanced back at the open desert that we had just passed, how much of a difference this all was from Afghanistan. I stared at the last seven-ton and wondered, "First day, here goes no-...."

BOOM. Like a giant firework uprooting from the street, a cloud of smoke, parts of rock and several sparks lit up the front end of the last truck causing it to hastily veer left and right. Out of instinct, I ducked at the sound of it. A deep crack of thunder.

"HOLY!" The sound of the seven-ton drowned out the sound of the explosion, but the image stuck.

And the message was clear. The enemy was waiting.

Expecting us.

Some Marines yelled in excitement to numb the fear. Some sat silent. Others just watched. I was one that watched, and I gulped. Hard.

"BARELY THE FIRST DAY, GENTS! Now that's what I call a warm welcome!" Sergeant yelled out, his fist in the air. The truck luckily stayed behind us, and the smoke had slowly gotten smaller as we drove faster towards the base.

I knew we neared the base because we started to slow down, and the truck began to zigzag itself through the first gate. Heavily fortified with concertina wire and high walls of Hesco barriers and plywood, our base stood out of place from its surroundings. I looked towards the right and saw a heavy piece of glass covering what appeared to be a post,

Just Glow

and I noticed there was someone behind it. Then I noticed other posts that circled the base.

The trucks came to a halt and once we reached the top, it was all there. Our new home.

"Welp," Sergeant said, jumping down from the truck, "so much for a Day One." He spat on the ground, adjusted his gear, swung his rifle around to his back and walked towards the others to help get the packs off the truck.

I jumped down and glanced at one of the Marines from the other unit and immediately noticed how he looked. Severely disheveled, his eyes zombie-like and his face and uniform caked with sweat, dust and dried blood.

He walked towards me and then raised his eyes. In an instant, I sensed he had noticed my clean uniform because it was the crack of his mouth that formed a smile, and I heard him snort. It wasn't a smile of happiness, but more of sympathy.

I didn't know what to make of it, but the smile stayed and then, with what seemed to be of increased effort, shook his head and said, "Good luck, Bro." I stood there and stared blankly, wondering what that meant in a time of war.

Augusto C. Cespedes, Jr.

From the diaphragm, Staff Sergeant yelled, "First Platoon! Gather 'round! Move!"

Without hesitation, we all circled him. The straggling Juniors were pulled from their flak jackets by the Seniors if they didn't move fast enough.

"We're back here, on this side of the base," he pointed up to the left. "Get situated and when the sun sets, we're going out."

In unison, low and quick, everyone said "Rah." The clinking of weapons and gear sounded as everyone walked up the small hill into our barracks, which was a heavily fortified concrete building. The metal door, rusty and obviously out of alignment, was partially opened.

"Hellooooo…?" Corporal said jokingly, as he knew no one was in there. His voice echoed through the cold, damp space.

I opened the door a little more to see what was inside, and it was wall to wall concrete, and no natural light.

It was a large common area with three separate smaller areas. Each smaller room had four or five bunk beds, with bare mattresses smeared with stains. The smell of wet rock and an unfamiliar odor sifted through the air.

"I got bottom bunk!" someone yelled, running through the others. His things trailed behind him as his excitement seem to overtake.

"Okay, well, I get the next bottom bunk!" Another

Just Glow

Marine said playfully. Like watching two small kids enter a furniture store and seeing the floor display, they both jumped onto what they've claimed. I sat and observed it. It didn't bother them, the smell, the look of the rooms. It was home.

The day had quickly turned to nightfall, and it was time for our first night patrol. It was told to us that second platoon had already received small arms fire and we were to assess the situation.

Scattered, echoing sounds of rearranged gear and the crunching and crackling of Velcro were heard throughout the concrete walls and as the sun went down, no one seemed to speak. I could feel the thick feeling of nervousness floating stagnant in the musty air. I neatly folded and placed two tourniquets into each cargo pocket and I reached for my side. Nothing. No sidearm. I didn't have the M9 anymore. I glanced at the M16, an assault rifle that was registered to me as it was propped up against my rack. The black, long rifle intimidated me, but I couldn't let it get to me. I had to understand that this was to protect me, not hurt me. The Marines held it with ease, slung on their chests or back and mine was leaning by itself. Untouched.

"Ready, Doc?" A Marine grabbed me from around the neck. He was one of the Marines that went to Afghanistan with me, now a Senior.

"Got no choice, right?" I said, nervously smiling. I was glad I was wearing my flak jacket because I swore I could feel my heart beating out of my chest.

Augusto C. Cespedes, Jr.

"Let's go, Gents!" Sergeant said, clapping. The quick connection of the palms of his hands echoed loudly through cold concrete as we, one by one, exited through the half bent, rusty metal door.

The smell in the air was distinct. When I took a deep breath in, it was sadly familiar. Almost like charred meat. I had a feeling it was something else but was afraid to ask. But I couldn't let it linger in my mind during our first patrol.

"What is that smell?" I asked, sniffing in the air.

"Doc, you don't remember that smell?!" Corporal asked. "Gotta get rid of our shit some way," he continued, his laugh following him down the dusty berm.

At the end of the berm were the clearing barrels, the only area where you can safely discharge your weapon or unload it.

"Let's rock and roll, Boys," Sergeant said. But no one said anything. We all stared in the same direction, focusing on making sure we had a round in the chamber before leaving the clearing barrels.

"Golf Base, Golf Base, this is First Platoon," the Marine with the radio had said, the handset connecting to his mouth. The static blared, following with high pitched sounds and finally, a voice was heard on the other end.

"This is Golf Base. Send it," it said.

"Roger. Permission to go outside the wire. Over."

Prolonged static. We all looked at each other, wondering

Just Glow

what the other one was thinking. Fear of death or actually accepting it.

"Roger that. Permission granted."

With a gloved hand, Sergeant pulled the concertina wire to the right and motioned for us to move through. The scraping of our boots in the sand and rocks echoed loudly.

"Luckie," Sergeant said in a loud whisper, "you take rear and keep eyes on that," he then said, pointing his forefinger and middle finger at his eyes and then up to the sky.

I followed the trail of where he was pointing. About a hundred yards away, a darkened silhouette slowly came into focus and then I noticed what it was. Like an old clock tower, it appeared abandoned; alone and mysteriously desolate. The first beams of the moon cast its light through the misshapen holes of its structure. As we all stood there at the wire, it was almost like it was staring right at us. Hovering. Waiting.

I turned my eyes towards Luckie and with locked eyes, he held the muzzle of his rifle steady and pointed straight towards it.

"Already there, Sergeant," he said.

Lance Corporal Luckie, a 19-year-old from Ohio, was one of the squad's riflemen. He was laid back, calm, collected and never yelled out or even seem upset.

He kept his rifle pointed at the tower as we all shuffled past him, patting him on the shoulder as a sign of respect. Or trust. The last Marine lightly squeezed his shoulder to let him know he was the last one out. Luckie then looked towards the base and pulled the wire shut, dragging it to the other side.

After several seconds, we all were outside of the wire.

Maybe it was sleep deprivation. Nervousness. Fear. Or all of it. But the first several steps outside of the wire were heavy. Uncomfortable. Heavier than Afghanistan. Heavier than I could have ever imagined.

With my helmet on, I took a few deep breaths and distanced myself away from the group, hearing my every breath. Each exhaled breath intensified and like a beached conch shell, the tunneled sounds of the background crawled in and around the hollow walls of my helmet. After every heavy step, I caught myself flinching, squinting at each and every connection to the ground and all I could think about was the anti-personnel mine that almost hit us on the way in. I blinked and then swallowed hard, hoping it would already end.

Sergeant pointed to a few of the Marines and like muscle memory, they dispersed off the road and joined the shadows.

There was something about the way the moon lit the streets. Its midnight beams laid across the pavement like haunting sheets of ice creating a ghostly, iridescent shimmer. Different colors of low, luminous lights shined down above the small shops as their doors were closed for the night. But the light of the moon, that mysterious light of the rising moon, was strong.

No one said a word. The silence was so loud that I could

Just Glow

almost hear that small ringing in my ears. It was just the rustling of gear. Dogs barking in the distance knowing there were visitors in town. Pebbles on the ground skipping across the road or the crunching of boots on gravel as we kept walking.

We stayed within the shadows throughout the patrol. A constant run, stop, and kneel. Wait several seconds and repeat. Again. And again. Then we took a right.

Okay, this is not Afghanistan anymore. I wanted to laugh, even in silent, but my body's attempt to swallow hard and the loud noises of my own breathing kept me from that gesture.

After several more yards, another right. The more I ran to stop and kneel, the sweat uncontrollably dripped, soaking my chin strap. The now familiar hollowed sounds of the background noise and my breaths were all I heard as I constantly rethought and prayed that nothing was to happen to us. Not this time. Not on our first night outside the wire.

I could sense we were nearing the end of the patrol as we'd circled the clock tower and now on its left side. Nervous about the rear, I checked the last few Marines and noticed the back of the last Marine's helmet. It was Luckie. Slowly floating up and down like a bird on a gentle wave, he calmly walked backwards, never turning around. And at that instant, my breathing slowed. I found myself walking backwards for a few seconds, but I turned around, and could see the beginning of the wire.

"We live another day," Sergeant said in a normal tone of voice. I raised my eyes and noticed a Marine at one of the posts, motioning a hand salute.

"Golf Base, Golf Base," the Marine with the radio had said.

"Roger, send it," it said again.

"This is First Platoon. Permission to enter the wire."

I looked back once more at Luckie, who still had his back towards the rest of us. Still slowly scanning.

"Roger. Permission to enter the wire."

Man… to hear that transmission again.

Daily Routines

Iraq was a different beast. Unlike Afghanistan, it didn't have forests or huge mountains to scale. The enemy didn't hide in small villages of straw huts. We didn't have to ride in armored trucks for hours on end praying we wouldn't hit a roadside bomb or worry about how many bottles of water to bring for a two-week operation.

It was worse.

Like a disturbing, endless labyrinth, the city's walls stood tall, never revealing what was on the other side. But it didn't matter. We still walked and we still patrolled. And every single day, it felt like we were fighting a war against ghosts, an enemy that seemed to not exist. But it didn't take long to realize that the enemy hid within the innocent.

Just Glow

Before every turn of a corner was a question to yourself of "what will happen to me?" I'd raise my rifle with confidence and fearfulness and when nothing happened, that simple thought would dissipate and repeat itself over and over, again and again until we were back in the wire.

"Keep your eyes peeled, Gents," Sergeant would calmly yell out as we opened the gate to the outside world. Everything was fair game once we stepped onto the other side. I always looked at it like this magical portal. The soft rustling of sand and gravel would make the only noise as we steadily walked out into the city.

Our base was an abandoned school located across from a bridge and west of the Euphrates. Fortified with several outposts, sandbags, plywood and concertina wire, it was still considered home.

And day in and day out, the patrols went on. And soon enough, the things that made us scared became repetitious. Like a sick, habitual routine.

"...Walk up to the wire, pull charging handle, check chamber for the round and set lever to semi..."

But little did we know, the routine was a dark reminder that we were still alive.

"I don't wanna knowwww," LCPL Dale would sing out. Out of tune and completely tone deaf but still belted it out. We sat against a wall in one of the rooms inside a house, the floor riddled with dust, small pieces of stone and figs. Because of the lack of furniture, our voices easily echoed. Shifting our weight every now and then, the sounds of rustled gear bounced off of the cement walls.

"Oh man, bangerrrr," another one would say. And a few of us would smile, one singing the guitar part, another tapping their fingers on the floor.

"What the hell are you even singing?" Sergeant said, laughing. "You children these days man, y'all gotta listen to Zeppelin or AC/DC."

They both looked at each other and then at Sergeant and laughed simultaneously.

We couldn't bring music players on patrol, but no one told us we couldn't sing songs. It didn't matter what time it was, if someone brought up a song with a catchy tune and it sparked even the slightest bit of nostalgia, it was a good day.

To the Bone

I cannot recall the exact moment I started biting the nails and skin of my fingers, but it started from one thread of skin that hung off of one fingernail.

The tiniest piece of skin.

Just Glow

I didn't like the idea. In fact, I was grossed out by it. It was a disgusting, horrible habit.

I must have been eight or nine years old sitting in class, legs crossed calling it Indian Style, and like a piece of thread, I picked it off of my index finger. A slightly hardened thimble of skin.

But the satisfaction was there.

"Just this…one…little…thing…" I whispered.

Quick fix. *Skin present, boop, skin gone.* And I went about my day.

But it kept going. I became more observant. I found a gross hobby that I only knew of.

One little thing became a few more. As the months went on, I would notice other little threads of skin at the edges of my nails, begging to be plucked off.

"Well, I HAVE to take this one off…" I rationalized, "it just looks weird."

And the more times I noticed them, the excuses became easier. The reasons to pick at them became a habit.

"Stop that, JR," my mom would say to me, clicking her tongue in disgust, "you don't know where your hands've been." She'd swipe her hand across my face, the scent of her perfume wafting in the air.

At one point when she noticed me biting my fingers on

more than multiple occasions, she opened the refrigerator and grabbed the bottle of hot sauce.

"Give me your hands right now," she demanded. I could see her mouth forming into pursed lips. She took my hands, untwisted the cap from the bottle and held my fingers over the sink like a raw vegetable.

"Try biting your fingers with this," she said and shook the bottle in a vertical motion. The red fluid covered my fingers, splattered like blood on my skin and the steel sink. The stench of the sauce created this prickly sensation on my forehead.

The powerful smell of the hot sauce instantly repelled me, causing me to turn away.

"Go sit down now," she'd say, pointing towards the kitchen table.

Eventually I came to the realization of my access to soap and water and then grew a love for the taste of hot sauce.

In 1996, my family and I took a trip to the Philippines to visit my mom's side of her family and to see where she grew up and went to school.

My habit of biting my fingers was to the point where my right thumb had two different tones of skin to it and my mom would say things like "You're gonna look like Michael Jackson."

One morning, my mom told me she invited someone to come do manicures and when they showed up, pointed to me to start on my hands first.

Just Glow

"You have no say in this, JR," she'd say, forcibly pushing my shoulders down to sit on a plastic white chair.

The woman, who did not speak or understand English, glanced at my hands and her eyes widened in utter disbelief. She licked her lip once, bit it and said something in her native tongue. My mom laughed and responded back to her in the same language. My eyes were like ping pong balls, bouncing back and forth to each of their responses.

I opened my mouth and raised my finger, but my mom already knew what I was going to say.

"She says you've created an evil habit, and she has never seen anything like it," my mom said, "but she will pray for you."

At almost 11 years old, I didn't really know how to take that. But after a few minutes, she started to clean.

Each fingernail was cleaned up like I had never seen before. A sharp tool repeatedly scraped over my nail, pushing my cuticle back, exposing the nail and revealing a new shininess to it.

Let's just say, after one hour of this, my nails were brand new. What they were supposed to look like.

"See, Jay," my mom would say, "isn't that better? Now stop."

It took sheer willpower to not touch them. To not start biting them again.

Sure, it was nice to look at them. Clean. Refreshed.

For some time, I admired the fact that from all of the times I put my teeth on them, that they *could* look brand new. But the more I waited, the more I wanted them back to how they were before; tattered and worn.

So, after several weeks of patiently waiting, I went back to the disgusting habit.

One piece of torn skin turned into the whole side of my finger chewed. Bleeding.

They were like little projects. One finger had this many marks and this one with this many. And I kept track like a logbook. And this just went on for years. YEARS.

Out to dinner. School. Soccer. Before bed. It was a constant, sick habit I couldn't kick.

But my cutoff was bleeding.

"Ah, shit," I would yell, first staring at what I had done, shaking it, and then starting to put pressure on it. But I would just go to the next finger. I had nine more fingers.

"Dude," my friend would say, observing me across the table of the lunch room, "why are you chewing on your fingers?"

I curled my fingers to make balls of fists, putting them under the table and smiled. I didn't have a response.

"Ya…I dunno. I've done it for so long," I would start to say, "must be a nervous habit." Embarrassed, I looked away

Just Glow

towards the clock, wondering how much time was left of the lunch period.

I absolutely hated the summers, especially anything involving water. The pool parties, nights in the hot tub.

"Can't get my hands wet," I thought, walking through the house of my friend's house.

"Everyone's in the back! Drinks are in the fridge! Help yourself!"

I carefully examined the hot tub, seeing where the part where I could sit and only have my legs in the water. There was nothing more embarrassing than having your hands in water for a few minutes, softening the skin, pruning and turning it white and exposing every imperfection of your fingers. It was disgusting. A shameful habit that I hid from everyone, hoping no one really noticed.

But when I endured my first few patrols in Iraq with the squad…everything, the disgusting, horrible habit I had created, just stopped.

Everything. I glanced at my fingers, but with no desire to do anything. For once, in a long time, my fingers were able to heal to what they were supposed to look like. Not bitten. Not chewed.

And I never understood it. The most stressful environment I would ever experience caused me to stop the only coping mechanism I ever knew.

Augusto C. Cespedes, Jr.

Perfect Vision

It's why we hate the sound of bubble wrap. Black cats. M60s. Fireworks that mimic someone shooting at you from a distance. Once you go through it, your body never forgets it.

"Guys! Contact front! Rooftop! Rooftop!" someone yelled, his mouth pointed towards the sky as his back was against the berm. His voice cracked like a juvenile boy as the opposing rounds zipped by our heads.

"Get down! Save your rounds!" Corporal yelled out, his back against the cement roadblock. His voice seemed calm, but the more he backed up against the roadblock, the more his boots slid on the loose gravel of Boardwalk.

I couldn't help myself but mimic his movements, falling to the ground. The overpowered adrenaline that instantly erupted had spilt itself over me. I started to mumble to myself, trying to remember which responsibilities were of me.

Heavily breathing and now in an awkward position, I patted both of my cargo pockets, which were stuffed with neatly folded tourniquets. My body was almost flat on the ground, my head perked up like I was trying to stay above water. The lighter, smaller pack that I had with me, which was an upgrade from the Vietnam-era med pack I carried in Afghanistan, was now covered in fresh dirt after throwing myself onto the road.

"SAWs! Suppress! Suppress!" Corporal's voice was now at its loudest, with the exhaled air from his mouth

Just Glow

discharging balls of saliva that reeked of snuff and cigarette smoke.

Once I had regained my composure, I started to focus on the pebbles on the ground, the loose gravel that scattered all over the road. Sharp-edged rocks.

"Wait…" I thought, squinting, "sharp…lines…?"

I gasped.

"Ha! Holy shit!" I said out loud, feeling like I was smiling from ear to ear. My eyes were rapidly blinking, amazed at the sight of it.

As guns started to fire off, Corporal ducked his head even more, but yelled out. "What, Doc?! What's wrong?!!"

And it took me back.

"Ok…" the doctor began to say as the squeaking of the office chair had trailed off, "the drops that I'm going to give you are numbing drops. Going to give you a few seconds and then let me know when you're ready." The surgeon, a balding white man with a face that hadn't seen a razor in a few days, towered over me as his assistants were on both sides of him, smiling cheerfully.

The ones who were going to Iraq had priority for eye surgery. It was sort of nice knowing that we'd been put at the top of the list, but it was almost like an act of sympathy. We were getting our eyes fixed before we were in the shit.

With my feet up and lying back, I tried to not focus so much on their facial expressions. They seemed happy. Overly happy. Their smiles were excessive, yellowish white teeth gleaming from lipstick covered lips, but it didn't match their eyes; they appeared like they were sad for me.

I blinked a few more times, and once I had sensed I was ready, I mumbled, "Ok, I'm good."

The doctor brought over a small plastic device with a pinpoint tip and brought it close to my right eye. I felt myself tense, trying to back my head away from it, but it only met the soft, leather cushion of the head rest. I didn't blink.

"Feel that?" He asked, backing it away from my face. His assistants looked at him and then at me.

"No," I replied, responding in a nervous manner and keeping my head still like it had mattered. The familiar squeaking of the procedure chairs rang again, and I kept my eyes on the ceiling.

"Well alright, let's proceed, Folks," the doctor said, clapping his hands together.

"Mister...." he trailed off, "What do you go by?" He glanced from me to look at my paper record located on the table.

"Cespedes? Navy. Marines. Don't they call y'all Doc?" He smiled, his half shaved face now wrinkled.

"See that clock?" He asked turning around and pointing to it. It was a clock that belonged in a school cafeteria. A plain black border, a white face with black hands. It read 9:45.

To me it was a blur, so I just said, "Barely, yeah."

"Oh ya," he laughed. "Probably blurry for you. Well, remember

Just Glow

how it looks now. I'll ask you to look at it when we're done here." He was organizing his equipment as he talked, causing sounds that started to make me nervous.

"Has your vision always been poor?" he asked me.

"From what I remember," I admitted, "ever since I was eight, I..."

"Well," he continued to say, "your life is about to change."

I kept staring at the series of lights and lenses that pointed towards my face, and I felt my mouth curl.

"Coach...?" I said out loud, squinting as if it would make my vision better, "Can we wear our other jersey?" My eyes only saw blobs of color; green colors for the grass, white uniforms that seemed to move in the air but, of course, I knew they were people.

I immediately thought of the day that I couldn't find the designer glasses my parents had gotten for me. I touched every potential surface that it could have laid on. Bed. Dresser. Nightstand. Desk. My head spun and the blurred vision had caused me to feel exhausted.

I needed a place to sit after trying to find them for what seemed like an hour.

Noticing my sister's old doll chair that was made of dark wood that sat against our poorly painted popcorn textured wall that we'd peel off on nights when we were bored, I sat down and suddenly felt something hard, like metal, pierce the cheek of my buttock.

Augusto C. Cespedes, Jr.

I didn't move. I practically froze and paused. Trembling. I was mid squat. Surprised. Scared. Blind.

"Mom's gonna kill you, Dummy," my sister said, scolding me. With no glasses, I wouldn't have been able to dodge the "chinelas" (aka any shoe in close proximity) that she was gonna throw at me and most likely run into the popcorn textured wall.

"Think I'm ready," I said, bringing my mind back to the exam chair.

He clasped his hands together again. "Let 'er rip, Ladies," *he announced.*

It smelled like burnt hair. The machine-like sounds were of an MRI — Clicking. Bolting.

I couldn't feel anything, but in my periphery, it was the trail of smoke that rose from my face that made me hold my breath.

"Are you…burning my eyes???" I thought, but I felt myself only mouthing the words.

"How ya doin, Cespedes?" *he'd ask me. It felt like hours, but it was only about 15 minutes.*

"I mean," I began to say, clearing my throat, "other than ignoring the fact that I see Indian in the Cupboard teepee smoke coming out of my eyes, I'm just peachy."

Seeming like it was a minor problem, he replied, "Bah, that's just a little burnin'."

And it was just a few more minutes that he said, "Aaaand we're

Just Glow

all done here!" The sounds that he and his assistants had made were masked by my release of inhaled air that I felt like I had kept in for the last 20 seconds.

"Well...? Remember that clock I told you about? Sit up and take a look," he said, patting me on the right shoulder.

I sat up and after a few hardened blinks of my eyes, I'd notice the sharp, slender hands of the clock. Black, thin sticks that now pointed to 10:10. Instinctively, I raised my right hand and using my thumb and index, motioned to "fix" my glasses, but I realized I wasn't wearing any.

"That's so funny," he chuckled. "Everyone does that, and I laugh every time."

But I couldn't even believe it. All of these years, and I finally could see without glasses. Embarrassed, I put my hand down but kept my eyes on the clock, completely mesmerized by its fine details.

"You've got a whole life ahead of you, Buddy." He began to say, his voice more upbeat now. His assistants couldn't help themselves but smile as they took off their gloves and started to clean up the area. They didn't have to say anything. I knew what they were thinking.

So I just stared off, still looking at the clock, something I took as a piece of validation. Its slender second hand not stopping.

I heard myself let out a deep sigh, fully knowing that I had to go to war to get perfect vision.

Heavy, cyclic sounds of machine guns fired off as my heavy blinking caused the harsh transition to reality.

"Dude!" I yelled, simultaneous ducking from the sounds of gunfire, "I HAVE PERFECT VISION!"

He lowered his head, looked at me with the most confused face and yelled, "What?!"

I tried to explain to him what I'd noticed on the ground — the sharp details of the rocks — but he didn't relate.

He instead just yanked hard on my flak jacket and yelled, "Y'all Navy Docs are a different breed! Come on, Doc! We gotta go!"

Focusing on his lips to read what he was saying, it was the edges of his mouth that kept me staring. A cheesy film spread itself apart from his lips.

He was dehydrated.

It was hot.

He needed to drink more. I should tell him to drink more.

But the sound of gunfire engulfed the muffled sound of my slow motioned daze and only grew louder as he snapped me out of my observation.

"DOC!" now yelling in my face, "MOVE!"

I shook off the debris that had fallen on me from the berm and started to situate myself to where my eyes were now facing forward towards the enemy.

Just Glow

Mouth open. Heavy breathing. I felt my heart beating against the walls of my helmet.

"Come onnnnnn..." I'd said, grumbling under my breath, feeling a rattling sensation in the back of my throat.

It was only a few weeks since we've landed in Iraq.

"Pop smoke! Pop smoke!" someone to the right of me yelled. It was a Junior, one of the riflemen.

I wanted to wipe my eyes, but I was afraid of getting sand in them. Then I wouldn't be able to see.

We're probably moving. God, I hope we're moving.

Once the can hit the ground, it hissed out a jet of smoke and only after a few seconds, developed a smoke screen.

"Mooove! Moooove!" Corporal bravely raised his head and moved his hand repeatedly in an "up and over" motion.

It was now or never.

I muscled up off the berm and with my head down, ran for cover towards one of the houses that sat across from the palm groves.

Please don't shoot me, please don't shoot me, please don't shoot me... I had to say it at least more than once — like it was going to matter, unconsciously in a melodic manner to the sounds of my boots quickly hitting the ground.

Augusto C. Cespedes, Jr.

No one really knew what it felt like to be shot, but when we did talk about it, it was never a serious conversation.

"Hot lead burning through your flesh," one would say, before taking a long drag of his cigarette.

"Just let it happen quick so I can go to Germany," another would joke.

At first, it wasn't all fun and games. Or even the slightest of a light subject. Someone would outwardly question, "What the hell is wrong with you?!" But the more we spoke about it, the less it became a threat and more of a chance to leave the country, and honestly, Germany didn't sound too bad.

Germany was known to us as this magical place where the injured would go to recover from being wounded. Clean, white hospital sheets, hot food, and all the ice cream you could ever eat. Or that's what we dreamed of.

"If I was gonna get shot, I'd only want it to be a flesh wound, through and through," a Senior Marine would say, standing tall like he had the thought in his head for a while.

I never gave my "if I was ever shot" comment, but a simple flesh wound would probably be the way to go.

I reached for the side of the house as if I was a swimmer at his last few feet to the finish-line. My fingertips felt it first and in an instant, my shoulder checked off of the wall with a hard thump. I felt the unforgiving impact of hardened stone, but it was the adrenaline that took over the pain.

Just Glow

I tried to slow down my breathing, resting the back of my helmet to the concrete wall. I started to check myself.

No blood, no wounds. No blood, no wounds. I was patting down my arms and legs like a nervous wreck. The phrase was something that was taught to us in Field Medical Service School.

I didn't feel any burning of my flesh. No trail of blood that I had left behind me. Seconds later, I started to feel my chest hit my flak jacket less.

I made it.

Swallowed hard.

Deep breaths.

Deep breaths.

Corporal suddenly came out of the smoke screen and with no regard to the house's hardened wall, hit it with a hard thump, letting the armored plate absorb the impact.

"You good, Doc??!" he said, his head in a similar position as mine, pinned against the wall.

"Two weeks?!" My eyes bulged as I asked the question. "We're only at two weeks?!"

But he just laughed at me, his head still against the wall.

I adjusted my eyes and again noticed the sharp edges on what was in front of me. Words in Arabic that had spread across the walls of shops. Crisp lines that had increased its sharpness as I kept blinking.

"Perfect vision," I said to myself, "Perfect vision…" my breathing now almost feeling normal.

The days were long. Well, they felt long.

Jumbled together it seemed like.

We'd go outside the wire, thinking it would only be a few hours and it'd turned into several hours to even a few days.

"When was the last time we had steak and lobster?" someone would ask and during the most random time, too. Nightfall, middle of the night. It didn't matter what time of day it was, the question made our mouths water.

The room we stayed in had no windows, so you'd easily lose the time of day.

"Anyone awake?" I'd loudly whisper, staring at the only light that was under the metal door, a thin sliver of an orange yellow glow that bled itself onto the concrete floor.

Just Glow

I hated looking at my watch, as it only reminded me of how slow time was moving, but I glanced at it at times like those.

But it was really a holiday that would give us any sense of time.

Leadership made attempts to try and make the base "festive." During Halloween, they would place spiderwebs that strung across the small, dusty hallways leading to the wooden picnic tables we ate at. You're finally sitting down for a hot meal and notice a new item on the table, a paper centerpiece — a cartoon figure of a ghost or monster that watched you eat.

"Oh shit," you'd think, "Halloween already?"

How 'bout that.

Coffee

"Cespedes, you're up tonight for watch!"

He had his back turned to me with the watch list inches from his face.

Watch was something that was introduced to you during basic training.

It was a responsibility that everyone had.

Augusto C. Cespedes, Jr.

And it was simple.

There was a rover watch and a security watch.

Rovers walked around to make sure there wasn't anything out of place, checked the thermostat and was lucky enough to keep moving so they wouldn't fall asleep.

Bottom line: You DEFINITELY wanted to be a rover watch.

But security watch, ha!

Security watch was a bit different.

No one wanted it because while everyone was asleep, you stood in one spot, at attention and stared at a red light that hung at the ceiling for two straight hours.

"Lemme see that," I said out loud, walking towards him. I snatched the list from him and looked at it.

"Cespedes, Security - 0230 HRS."

I swore I felt like Marty Mcfly when he watched Doc fall to the ground.

"Noooooooo!" went through my mind.

They all looked at me but didn't seem to care. Maybe because we all had to do it.

…0215 HRS…

"Cespedes," the rover whispered, "you're up."

Just Glow

My mattress audibly crinkled like a piece of paper, rolling over to the sound of his voice.

"Hmm...?"

"It's 0220. You're up for watch." Even in a whisper, his voice sounded pleasant, but it was likely because he was the one that was done.

"I'm up," I said, "I'm up."

He didn't say anything, just the red glow of his flashlight came off of my mattress and spilled across the floor.

Once I got ready, I stood in front of the security watch and in a low, sarcastic voice said, "You are relieved."

I could see his teeth as he snarled at me. "Enjoy."

I stood there under the red light and listened to the rattling hum of the air conditioner.

I tried to remind myself not to lock my knees. "This is gonna be a long 2 hours..."

I felt my form start to slack but remembered that any of the Petty Officers could barge in any time of the night just to "check on things."

"Don't think we won't come in at 0300 to make sure you numbskulls are doin' the right thing." The voice of Muscles rang in my head. His gap-toothed smile was all I could see.

I stood in the dark but as I looked closer, through the

pretend port hole of the front door and across the hallway, there stood the security watch for the other division in the other room. Doing the same exact thing I was doing.

Standing.

Alone.

Under a red light.

So, me being a kid at heart, found myself puffing out my cheeks, bulging out my eyes and bending my knees to lower myself down.

I was seeing if the other security watch would catch on to notice I was acting like I was underwater.

I did this for about 5-10 seconds and finally I could see he was glancing at me. But he wasn't smiling. Not even the slightest bit.

"Oh shit, I'm doomed," I thought, "he's probably one of those good recruits."

I was trying to think of an excuse as to why I was doing what I was doing.

"Petty Officer, I was doing my breathing exercises. My apologies," I would try to think to say.

So I stopped, thinking that he was going to rat on me and placed my most serious expression on my face. Completely embarrassed.

There was an awkward moment to where we both

Just Glow

looked at each other and then, still with the most serious expression on his face, started to slowly disappear from the porthole.

"Wha...what...is he doing...?"

He was gone.

I was definitely doomed. Done for.

I started to breathe a bit faster, reciting my "breathing exercise statement" when, with puffed out cheeks and bulging eyes, the security watch slowly rose back up and did the SAME EXACT thing I did before.

Probably my most fondest memory of standing watch.

But I soon found out that standing watch in a combat zone was not at all like that, let alone hearing the sweet, humming sound of an air conditioner.

You were on watch while your buddies put complete trust in you. They slept right next to you while the ashes from your slowly burning cigarette fell on them like snowflakes.

There was no time for jokes. And if there was, it was you just entertaining yourself.

"Jones, youuu're up for radio watch," Corporal said, almost imitating a game show host calling over a contestant.

Sleep deprived, dusty and sweaty, someone started to say, "Well," he started to say in a high pitched, female like commentator voice, "what does he win, Tom?!!"

Augusto C. Cespedes, Jr.

"A four-hour radio watch all by himseeeeeelf," he finished saying. There was a small, faded round of applause but everyone was too tired to even continue the joke.

During the Iraq deployment, we shared a COP, or Combat Outpost, with the Iraqi army. It was a concrete building built with small rooms and a small courtyard. The upside to staying at the COP was it got us away from the "higher ups" of the main base. Having to do tedious things like filling sandbags or burning shit (literally).

Jones, a PFC machine gunner that carried the M249 SAW, didn't laugh. But instead, out of respect and pure muscle memory, got out of his rack, calmly grabbed his weapon and cover and started to walk towards the radio room.

"Roger that," he said, almost forcing himself to make it audible.

I could tell that he was tired. More than the rest of us.

"Stop, stop...." I said aloud, putting my hand out. Everyone stopped what they were doing and looked at me.

"I'll do it."

"It's fine, Doc," Corporal started to say out loud so that everyone could hear, "Jones is used to it, right Jones...?" He looked at him and Jones just slowly moved his eyes towards him and said, "Yes, Corporal."

I couldn't look at Jones' face anymore.

Just Glow

"I said I can do it," I repeated myself, cutting right through the tension that was in the room.

I could feel Jones' eyes move like a swinging pendulum as he was anticipating someone to say something.

I'd never done radio watch at the COP (Combat Outpost) but I was imagining it no different than standing radio watch at the main base.

"Where's the radio?" I asked, walking towards the door.

"You've never stood watch here?" Corporal asked.

"Never," I admitted.

His expression changed.

"Get enough sleep?" he asked with a grin.

"…why?" I was scared to ask.

"Pretty boring in there," he said, laying out his sleeping bag "you'll see. It's past the courtyard. Simmons is up after you."

I walked down the small hallway into the courtyard, and I could hear different volumes of conversation. All in Arabic or dialectics. The sounds of a sports commentator yelling, drowning in static. A strong smell of spices and smoke made its way towards my nose and just a few steps more, I suddenly found myself looking at the radio.

"Hey Doc," one of the Marines said, "you're relieving me?

Augusto C. Cespedes, Jr.

I yawned and said, "Doin' Jones a favor." I felt my eyes bulging out that I yawned.

No way I'm tired, can't be.

The radio was a bit smaller than the main base radio. It sat on a rickety wooden desk in a room with four walls of concrete. Pierced with several black wires and painted forest green, it intermittently made a "beeping" sound. Next to it was an opened MRE.

"Ever been on radio watch?" he asked, stepping on the last of his cigarette.

"Ya, but only at the main base."

"Roger," he said, "it's pretty simple actually. Definitely not as busy as the main base. And it's the middle of the night so you'll be fine."

His face was scruffy, dirty blonde hair matted down and fixed in a way of a surfer but with days old oil and sweat. He reeked of smokeless tobacco.

"Ya, you're probably right," I agreed. I stared at the radio for several seconds as it made these intermittent beeping sounds with a few random transmissions and once it ended I put my finger in the air and said, "so one question, d-…"

I turned around to an empty doorway and the lingering smell of cigarette ash that was smeared black on the concrete floor.

Just Glow

He had already left.

I walked around the room and started to inspect every crevice like I was to be there for years. I immediately noticed the many flattened cigarette butts that lined the part of the floor that met the wall. Half-filled water bottles filled with dark yellow urine or cans of dip spit neatly tucked under the table like they were saving it for next time.

"K3, K3, this is Golf Base, radio check over," the speaker said. I lunged over to the table, grabbed the black handset and put it to my mouth.

"This is K3, Lima Charlie over," I said.

"Roger, K3…" and it faded out.

It was silent.

The next hour or so I spent pacing the same, tired lines of the room. Almost like a dog who ran laps in the same spots of a backyard that made trail marks in the ground.

I began to feel it and I was feeling it fast. It was starting to set in. My eyes, heavy like thick, velvet curtains, were slowly lowering themselves.

I was getting tired.

The cheering sounds of the Iraqi army had stopped and it was only me, the scuffing of my boots and the faint sounds of the radio.

Damnit…should I, like, slap myself or something?

Augusto C. Cespedes, Jr.

It was tempting. I started to rub my hands together to warm them up before the big slap.

Then this subtle hissing came from the radio. Inaudible voices of what seemed to be a transmission.

Whooshing sounds. A long beep, then "….three…" it said.

I shook my face out and started to focus my eyes on the small, black holes of the receiver.

I leaned in to listen closer.

A familiar static, then, "K3, radio check, over…"

I grabbed the receiver and clutched it to make sure all of my words were spoken loud.

"Roger, this is K3. Lima Charlie."

"K3, this is Eagle Eye, break," he said and paused. ("Break" in radio transmissions means to briefly stand by for more information from the deliverer)

Who the hell is Eagle Eye? I took the receiver off of my face and stared at it.

"We're trying to get into contact with Golf Base but it appears they are too far, over."

At that moment, I felt obligated to pay more attention but could feel the sluggishness in my eyes.

I put the handset to my face.

Just Glow

"Roger, Eagle Eye. Will contact Golf Base and get back to you, over."

"Roger, K3. There are two individuals in the road we have been monitoring, possible tango. Please relay to Golf Base, over."

"Roger, Eagle Eye," I replied back, "stand by."

I felt nothing but my hot breath colliding with the receiver as I tried to gather my thoughts.

"Ok…" I said out loud. *It's 2am…it's only 2am…gotta call Golf Base.* I pressed a different button and held it down.

"Golf Base, Golf Base, this is K3, over," I said, finally with confidence.

I waited for a few seconds.

"Roger K3, this is Golf Base," it said, "send it."

I felt myself gulp hard and tried to gather the words.

"Eagle Eye is trying to get in contact with you but you are too far, break," I said, pausing because I had suddenly lost my train of thought. "So they contacted me to tell you there are two possible tangos in the area."

A few seconds passed by.

"Roger that K3, Eagle Eye has spotted two possible tangos. Relay all messages to Golf Base, how copy, over?"

Augusto C. Cespedes, Jr.

I responded, "Roger, Golf Base, Lima Charlie."

And just like that, the series of transmissions were over.

Dead silence.

The adrenaline had stuck around for a bit but it was like a slow glowing ember; I could feel my eyes were slowly burning out.

But it kept ringing in my head...

"Relay all messages to Golf Base..."

Then deeper.

"Relay...all...messages..."

Fading in and out.

"Golf Base..."

I stood up because I could feel my head start to bob.

My feet began to pace and all I could do was mumble, "No, no, no, no, no..."

Eagle Eye was depending on me. I was the only closest radio for them to contact so I couldn't get distracted or fade into some fleeting daydream.

How could I start to get sleepy now?!

My eyesight started to gravitate towards my nose, forcing my vision to go cross-eyed.

Just Glow

Shaking my head again, I turned around and circled back to the table, focusing on anything to keep my eyes from going cross-eyed.

Piss bottles. Spit cans. Cigarette butts.

"Tha'hell are you, Eagle Eye…" I mumbled, but loud enough that the radio would hear me.

Stashed in the corner of the table next to a cardboard box of batteries was an opened MRE (Meal Ready to Eat). The hefty, salmon colored plastic pouch was split open like someone took their teeth to it; jagged edges and stretched ends.

"Menu #8, Beef Patty" it said in bold letters.

Maybe there's something in here, even it was just a biscuit or some candy…

I stuck my hand in it like a kid trying to find the prize at the bottom of a cereal bag and felt for anything edible. Crunchy. Sweet.

Unlucky. It was just trash.

I slowly took my hand out of the pouch. Disappointed. Tired. Wanting nothing more than just having my head hit the pillow.

But at the corner of my eye, I had noticed the shiny metal can. I picked it up and, to my surprise, was half filled with coffee grounds.

Augusto C. Cespedes, Jr.

I asked myself out loud, "Why would coffee grounds be in here? Maybe there was a coffee maker in here at some point?"

But it didn't matter anyways because I didn't have water. Hell, I couldn't make coffee even if I wanted to.

And I definitely couldn't leave the room.

"Cespedes!!" Muscles would stare down at me like I was some small insect, "what's your fifth general order???!!!"

"To quit my post only when properly relieved, Petty Officer!"

Ya, I couldn't leave. So I just stared at the metal can, wondering why on earth it was there in the first place.

But I remembered something.

Ever since I was attached to the platoon, dipping tobacco was the thing.

Snuff. Long cut. Pouches. You name it, the Marines had it.

Sure, it was a disgusting habit. But when you're in the shit, knowing that any moment you could be dead, you don't really think about the consequences.

After all, it passed the time.

It ceased the nervous ticks.

It was as if the thumping of the can was like the one who rang the triangle at the front porch for dinner.

Just Glow

Hell, it brought everyone together.

"Whatchu got? Cope? Ooo, a fresh can, too!" Someone would say smiling, emptying out their water bottles to collect their spit.

And one by one, with only the tips of their fingers, would take a heaping pinch of the moistened black flakes and carefully stuff it into their bottom lip.

When I was around them, the smell was so strong, I always tried to guess what it compared to.

"Smells like burnt rubber but with some pancake syrup on the side," I'd joke with them, looking up to the sky with my finger on my chin.

"Soooo good, Doc," someone would say with a protruding lip.

I couldn't help but laugh to myself.

It was dumb. Borderline juvenile.

But as dumb as it was, I realized it gave me an idea.

I slid the can over the splintered surface of the desk and peeled back the plastic lid.

And just like anyone would, I stuck my nose in it and breathed in.

I can do this.

I reached in with my fingers like a small claw and grabbed a heaping amount of coffee grounds.

Augusto C. Cespedes, Jr.

Took a deep breath.

Where the hell is Eagle Eye?

I swallowed hard, opened my mouth and stuffed the dried coffee grounds inside my bottom lip.

Gritty was only the thing I could describe it as. I felt every sharp edge of crushed beans pushing against my lip.

It only took several seconds to feel the rush of adrenaline. Like a million little spiders crawling all over my face, I felt myself rapidly blink to adjust to the sensation.

I started to pace again, finding myself retracing the lines I had made the hour before but this time it was out of restlessness.

My body couldn't stop moving.

"K3," the radio hissed, "K3, this is Eagle Eye, over."

I stopped my line making and darted towards the radio.

"Heyyyy Eagle Eye, this is K3," I said, "send it!" I was a bit loud with it now.

"Roger," he said with what seemed like a whisper, "we're in position, break," and there was a pause.

I could feel my pulse bounding in my ears as I restlessly waited for the next transmission. My eyes felt like they were bulging.

Just Glow

"Two tangos are setting up in the road. Standby for coordinates."

At this point, I had to sit right by the radio. I couldn't let my ear off of the receiver, God forbid if I missed something important.

I realized at that moment, wide eyed and more alert than ever before, *that I was the messenger.*

"Roger, two tangos setting up in the road, standing by for coordinates."

"Tangos are west of the gas station, directly south of K3."

I looked down like I had something to write with but I didn't so I started to run it through my head, making sure I had it right and started my own transmission.

"Golf Base, Golf Base, this is K3," I said.

My right leg started to violently shake. Out of nervousness. Of caffeine adrenaline.

I waited a few seconds.

"K3, this is Golf Base, send it," it said.

"Rogerrrr," I started to say, "Eagle Eye in position, break..." I took a slow, deep breath, and suddenly felt confident.

"Eagle Eye west of the gas station, eyes on possible two

tangos in the road directly south of K3," I said with no hesitation.

"Roger, Lima Charlie. Will standby for further action."

Once the transmission was over, I ran almost every scenario in my head.

Just ordinary, innocent people, right?

But it's almost 3AM in the morning…can't be…

Ok, maybe not normal people. He said tangos.

I mean, they must know what they're doin'…they're scout snipers…

The silence was broken by the hissing of the radio again.

"K3, this is Eagle Eye," the voice had said.

"Roger, Eagle Eye, send it," I said, now locked in with bits of grounds flickering out of my mouth.

"Two individuals confirmed tangos. Weapons in possession digging in street for approximately 20 minutes. Requesting permission to engage."

My heavy jaw dropped and I stared at the radio's dusty knobs.

I immediately thought about what the Marine had told me.

"…it's the middle of the night so you'll be fine…"

Just Glow

"What a crock'uh shit, man," I muttered.

I sat tall in the rickety, wooden chair, trying not to overthink it and pressed the button.

"Roger, Eagle Eye. Two individuals confirmed tangos. Weapons in possession digging in street for approximately 20 minutes. Requesting permission to engage, over."

"Affirmative, K3. Standing by for orders."

This is it. I'm actually going to witness this as the messenger.

I pressed the handset again.

"Golf Base, this is K3, over," I said.

"Roger, K3, send it."

"Roger," I started to say, "Eagle Eye reporting two confirmed tangos. Weapons in possession digging in street for approximately 20 minutes. Requesting permission to engage, over…"

I let out a long sigh of relief, feeling so proud of myself that I wasn't overwhelmed or even stuttered despite the dried coffee grounds that were shoved into my lip.

"Affirmative, K3, Eagle Eye reporting two confirmed tangos. Weapons in possession digging in street for approximately 20 minutes. Requesting permission to engage, over."

"That's affirmative, Golf Base," I repeated.

Augusto C. Cespedes, Jr.

Hyped up, feeling obligated and now more awake than ever before, I waited for the next transmission.

The most important one.

This time, I didn't need to retrace the cracked pavement lines anymore or fix my eyes on the half full piss bottles or slimy spit cans.

It was me, a lip full of coffee grounds and the radio receiver.

"K3, this is Golf Base, over," the radio blared. I leaned over, feeling the pulse of my carotid arteries now in sync with my breathing.

"Roger, Golf Base. Send it." My palms felt wet as I waited for what they would say next.

"Eagle Eye is cleared to engage," it said. The voice on the other end sounded older, a man, not the same person I was previously speaking to.

I shuddered, gulped hard and simply said, "Affirmative, Golf Base."

At first I felt a sense of sympathy, as a part of me wanted to cancel the transmission all together.

Maybe they weren't actually terrorists, probably just guys in need of money for their family and —

"K3, this is Eagle Eye," the radio went off, "requesting status on order of Golf Base." The violent static of the

Just Glow

radio had drowned out the innocent, sympathetic thoughts my mind had created.

"…K3?" The radio said again.

I pressed the handset one last time.

"Eagle Eye, this is K3, Golf Base gives green light to engage."

I let go of the button that I had been pressing on for the past 3 hours and could feel the decreasing sensation of my pulse.

"Roger that, K3…" it said.

And it was done.

I sat there on the uneven chair and listened for anything else. But there was no other sound.

Just the dying surge of my increased pulse, the distaste of coffee grounds and the minutes that ticked away the rest of my radio watch.

"Well," someone said, barging in, "sorry I'm late." In sweat-caked cammies that appeared dusty, he ran into the doorframe like a student late for class.

"Anything good hap'nin?" He asked, thumping his snuff can and lugging a bag full of snacks that seemed to be from home onto the table.

My mind was still racing a mile a minute, trying its best to come down from what all had happened, but I just numbingly stared at the radio and then him and said, "it's the middle of the night so you'll be fine."

November 21st, 2006

I stared down at my desert boots that continued to mindlessly shuffle around the specks of sand on the dusty floor of the room.

The Briefing Room we called it, just outside of the radio room.

Anyone going out on patrol would do all of the preparation in that room.

Before going out in the open air towards the clearing barrels.

Before going outside the wire.

"Gents," his voice pierced through the dusty air of the Briefing Room, "it would be who of you to bring a backpack to this," Sergeant ordered, as we all huddled around him. The map he pointed to was poster sized, laminated and with several holes from tacks. It hung on the wall like the others on display.

"I'm not sure how long we're going to be out. Hopefully it's only a night or two, but just be prepared. Bring your whatever, girly, whatever snacks you call them, with you. I don't wanna hear your bitchin' out there that you're hungry, Rah?"

Just Glow

With a low, monotonous tone, we all responded the same "Rah" back.

Remembering what Sergeant had said, I packed at least three pairs of socks, a small travel size container of baby powder and a pack of baby wipes. If anything was to be kept clean and dry, it was your feet and your crotch.

We were to set up at a house that overlooked a part of the city and had the perfect view of Haqlaniyah's main road.

Referred to as Boardwalk, it was the biggest and one of the most dangerous streets in Haqlaniyah. Two roads, divided by a median with its curb painted in a black and white pattern, had the width to fit two lanes. From the palm groves or a vehicle or from a window on the city side, you could make out the debris that had blown to the side, covered by sand and eventually left behind. But from the third story window of the house, the view was, well, beautiful.

Augusto C. Cespedes, Jr.

The lush green of palm groves moved like a gentle wave in the ocean and from where we were, it didn't reveal the small imperfections of what we walked on. The wind that blew off of the Euphrates caused a ripple effect and in one motion, I noticed the spiked leaves appeared to have moved in unison and from how high up we were, it covered it all. The rubble. The patrols. The violence. The destruction. I saw what it used to be. "It used to be a vacation spot," I remembered someone mentioning to me, and I easily imagined it, remembering the things I've seen in the first weeks of being in the country. Rusted lounge chairs at intersections of the city that faced the river, merchant carts deserted in the streets and left behind. And the main strip, Boardwalk, lined with shops, now closed shut. It was a ghost town.

No one ever actually walked down Boardwalk. Well, never during the day I should say.

Just Glow

And there were good reasons for it. You were fully exposed.

On the west side of the four-lane road was the city. Houses and shops armed with high concrete walls, equipped with thickened metal gates and towering windows. On the other side was the Palm Groves, a heavy area of brush and trees that covered the uneven land that once was used for farming that lined the Euphrates River. If anyone ever walked on Boardwalk, you were asking for a fight.

It was a steady incline of uneven rock and gravel as we tried to stay as alert as possible getting to the house. After the intermittent forward to sideways and backwards walking, it took roughly an hour to get both squads up to the entrance of the house.

I dropped my pack on the concrete slab floor and instinctively glanced at my watch. One by one, the Marines started to come into the house and within minutes, Marines were already taking their spots for overnight watch.

2159 HRS.

Augusto C. Cespedes, Jr.

"Battle Buddies! Pick one," I heard from across the room.

"Pick a buddy, Gents," Sergeant yelled out. We all glanced at him and started to look around. I started to walk towards the stairs but was interrupted by Sergeant's arm, running across my flak jacket.

"Doc, you and Morris should stay together, especially if someone needs you, ya know? You can be contacted with Morris having the radio. Cool?" he said, patting me on the helmet. The hollowing sound lingered on as I looked at Morris and slowly cracked a smile.

But he didn't. And I knew why.

We both looked at each other and knew exactly what each other was thinking; why I yelled at him.

Thursday. Finally Thursday.

"I'll meet you after formation," I shouted to one of the other Corpsmen. My hands formed a cone and my voice bounced off the walls to the end of the walkway. I had always enjoyed leaving the BAS as its surrounding hallways created this powerful gust of wind. I jokingly pivoted my foot against the concrete, its caked-on dirt pasted on the surface, making a scratching sound. Just a few more steps around the corner, the faint but distinctive sounds of Marines were near the area of formation.

"One more day of the bull crap..." I thought to myself as my boots ended on concrete and felt the soft surface of the grass. I picked up my pace a little bit more as I saw the hopping birds again, making them

Just Glow

hop faster as I let the high weeds slap off my boots. It was the wind from the mountains that swooped down to the bay that made even a Thursday afternoon feel like it was the weekend.

My eyes stopped chasing the hopping birds to a group of Marines with their backs towards me. There were a few smiles, some more of "Well, we're screwed," and some happy to see me but one was on top of the other and it gave me the urge to stop it.

"What the hell is going on here?" I yelled out, making sure it was my deepest voice. From the gut. I was a Senior now, so I had to show it. Most of them turned around and I noticed they were all the new Juniors.

As I got closer to the Marines who were wrestling, I noticed it was a Junior named Daniel Morris who was on top of the other, pinning him down. I clenched my teeth and could feel my muscles tense.

"Get OFF," I said. With my right hand, I forcibly pulled on Morris' shoulder, grasping his clavicle in which it immediately brought him to the ground, his back hitting the dirt. The idea of it all came over me like boulders off a cliff and I ended up towering over him, with angered eyes and both of my hands grabbing the collar of his uniform. As I loosened my grip on his blouse, I noticed colored print on his olive undershirt. We were only supposed to wear military undershirts, olive colored. With both hands, I unbuttoned the 2nd and 3rd buttons and saw it. It was an olive drab Hawaiian shirt with a hand making the "Shaka." The print was about two to three inches from his collar. My nostrils flared, and I grabbed his blouse again, now tighter.

"You think that's okay?!!" I said, my eyes enraged and my lips pursed. I could feel the tension in my forearms as we looked at each other. Everyone stood around, shocked at how I had reacted but they knew me as their Senior Corpsman so no one did anything but watch what was to happen next.

Augusto C. Cespedes, Jr.

Embarrassed in front of his peers, he, in a low and sarcastic tone said, "No, Doc."

It grew silent.

With locked eyes it was like a battle between who would say something first. I knew Morris wouldn't say anything, but I could see, deep into his eyes, he had inappropriate words to say.

I immediately regretted what I did, but I couldn't go back on it. I was a Senior Corpsman and I had to make sure those Juniors knew who I was.

I stepped off of Morris and immediately turned my back, hiding my expression of regret.

"Doc…?" Morris scoffed, looked down, and rumbled through his backpack. I could sense the memory of our last interaction in his voice was as fresh as the one in my own head.

"Guess we're battle buddies…" I said, my words trailing off to the sounds of fastened buckles and straps.

"Yup…that's what he said…" Morris fired back. He stopped what he was doing for a second but then continued to look through his backpack. His voice was gentle, more airy than most, but with a subtle hint of sarcasm.

The slab of the hallway floor was freezing cold, so I grabbed the end of the carpet runner, a material much like a thicker

Just Glow

potato sack, pulled it to the wall and slowly sat down. The hardness and heavy weight of my flak jacket smeared the wall on its way down to the floor. Away from windows and our backs against the wall, we felt like it was a good spot for the night.

The faint and distant sound of a voice on a loudspeaker crept in the openings of the house. Isha. It was the last prayer call.

I glanced at my watch. 2050 HRS.

As I looked up from my watch, Morris, in all his gear, slid down next to me, but kept his eyes forward.

It was awkward. I didn't know him, and we were to spend the next however many months as Battle Buddies. I had to speak up.

"Hey, about that time…" I started to say. We both kept our eyes at the staircase in front of us.

"I understand, Doc," he interrupted. The tone of his voice changed. It was sympathetic. Forgiving.

That was when I turned to look at him. His eyes, soft shades of blue, had reflected off the hallway light. When he blinked a few times, the light had revealed his long, brown eye lashes.

"I was probably stressed about leaving the country again. I dunno," I admitted. "It's hard leaving it all behind. Not knowing if you're gonna be back to it all again." The thought of it made my stomach turn.

Augusto C. Cespedes, Jr.

"Welp," he softly said, "we're here now." He couldn't help but smile. "We all have each other now."

Morris looked around, and then said, "I think we can take our helmets off." He unbuckled it from under his chin and sighed, as if it was constricting his neck. I had to look around in order to follow him. I unbuckled it, and the hollowing sound had dissipated.

I smiled. "Where are you from?" I asked him. We both now turned to each other. We attempted to talk in a low whisper as it was late, and the house was still occupied by a family.

"Good 'ole Virginia," he said. I couldn't tell if he was serious or sarcastic. "Really nothin' much where I live except a bunch of old people like my Gramma Johnny and..." he stopped.

My jaw dropped and he suddenly laughed.

"I'm kidding, Doc," he said, putting his hand out. "No, but seriously, my Gramma Johnny's gettin' older and it's a small town."

And that was the icebreaker. We realized we had so much in common.

We talked about how he played trumpet in the marching band and how I played the clarinet. We talked about our celebrity crushes, his being Jennifer Aniston and mine Sarah Michelle Gellar and who has liked theirs the longest. We laughed about how we both used to fry French fries in the fryers and smelled like cooking oil driving home.

Just Glow

He didn't have an accent, but I felt like the more sarcastic he was, the more of a twang that came out of him. Even in the last hours of the night sitting on the concrete slab, it made both of us laugh and it was a back and forth of "shhh'ing" each other to keep quiet.

And it was then we had forgotten where we were. Sitting in the middle of a hallway at almost midnight with a single bulb giving off the only source of light. But… we had to get used to it.

That was the thing about fighting in a war. It created a constant battle in your own head and whatever amount of homesickness or loneliness you were to feel, you yearned for that next dirty joke, comment or forgotten story to simply push it away, only for it to just haunt you all over again.

"Alright Doc," Morris whispered loudly. "I'll take first watch. You get some shuteye, ya hear?" The sarcasm from his voice was still enough for a smile back but had faded as our conversation slowly ended.

With my eyes still closed, I slowly woke up to quick, fast sounds of a zipper opening and closing.

"We're packing up already? Couldn't be," I thought, my eyes still closed. I was afraid to open them as I felt like I'd only slept for 45 minutes.

The innocent whisper of a child's voice caused me to crack one eye open, trying not to move from my spot on the ground.

Augusto C. Cespedes, Jr.

The light had been turned on and standing by the staircase was a small boy who, at least under the age of seven, placed something in his backpack. With only my left eye open, I could see it to be a few notebooks.

But then he just stopped. He slowly turned his body and within a few seconds, was turned towards us.

In my periphery, I'd sensed that Morris was still half asleep, his head nodding up and down in a dysfunctional rhythmic pattern while I sat there, just watching the boy.

I thought my eyes were not noticeably open, so I kept them cracked just enough to see.

Then his eyes met mine and we just... stared.

Ever since we started foot patrols, we were always nervous about the presence of people. With the insurgents hiding amongst the innocent, it was hard to not look at everyone as the ones who wanted us dead. And after only a few months, everything was seen as a potential threat.

The insurgents were clever. They would pay the innocent money to do harm to us.

Before stepping outside of the wire, we reminded each other to never have our backs against an alleyway, as kids rode bikes with baskets that held grenades. If someone was walking against a wall, a buddy would keep their eyes on them. If something was tossed over the wall, they would at least have a chance to run from it.

When we walked down the street, no one acknowledged us. And for good reason, too. We were in full gear, our

Just Glow

fingers were light on the trigger and we walked on high alert. But they sure did stare…and they stared hard.

They leaned on the walls of the alleyways or shops and carefully watched us, their eyes following our every move as we passed them on the road. Faces like stone. An unknown judgement that laid beneath their skin.

But it was under the gear and behind the weapon, as a young serviceman, a fear I've never felt before. I couldn't shake it off. I constantly thought about my childhood. My parents. My sister. My friends. I wanted to go home. But more so, I wanted to make it home. My eyes were on high alert, barely blinking and on the mode of constant scanning. It was draining. But there wasn't a choice. This was home.

"Please, God…" I would mumble, making sure it was only under my breath and gave myself enough room from the Marines so they wouldn't hear it.

For some reason I felt like if it was more audible, there was a better chance of God actually acknowledging it. But from the outside, I made certain that I kept my face a stone wall. Expressionless. I didn't want anyone to think I had a weakness. We all didn't.

"Morris," I whispered, simultaneously tapping him on his leg. I tried to not move my lips as I kept my eyes on the boy.

It took a few more taps to get Morris to open his eyes and it was only after the last forceful tap, he finally looked at me.

"Hmm…?" he hummed at a low tone.

Augusto C. Cespedes, Jr.

With my lips partially closed, I mumbled, "Look."

The small boy seemed to not be phased. It felt like we had stared for minutes as he stood under the yellow tinted light, like a deer staring off at the hunter who admired it rather than wanting to harm it.

I couldn't tell what Morris was thinking but I just kept asking myself, *Why aren't you walking away? What are you about to do?*

His torso now facing towards us, he started to smile. In that instant, I glanced at Morris who was smiling back. His brown hair was in a tossed, bed head manner and his eyes were squinting at the boy, almost mocking him. I felt glazed over, enjoying the innocent interaction until I realized where we were.

No helmet. No flak jacket and still sitting on the cold, hard floor. Deprived from sleep, I forgot we had taken it all off. A part of me wanted to quickly move to put it all back on but I felt it being hopeless. The boy had already seen us exposed.

But he continued to put his backpack on, like we were just visitors. Spectators. Harmless.

Rustling sounds of hardened cloth caught my attention and I noticed that it was Morris. He was rummaging through his backpack and in seconds was a high-pitched grinding sound heard at my right ear.

He looked at me and with a look of accusation said,

Just Glow

"What?" He smiled. "Gotta take a picture..." and continued to wind the disposable camera until it clicked.

I silently mouthed a laugh, covering my mouth as to not make a noise. I felt like we were kids again, enjoying the small moment of innocence. And the boy, still standing there now seeming more comfortable than he had ever been, had the biggest smile on his face. But it wasn't more than a few seconds later, he left the room and the harsh reality of war had continued on.

The numbing sounds of sliding gear and weapons being picked up created the unwanted feeling of getting up. The sun, a slow ember rising from the East, started to wrap itself around the corners of the room. The familiar smell of cigarette smoke and the thumping of smokeless tobacco cans replaced freshly brewed coffee and the scent of breakfast.

"Wakey, wakey, eggs and bakey," one of the Juniors had said, peering around the corner. His voice was raspy like he had to clear his throat. His face still appeared like it was in need of more sleep, but he didn't have a choice. We all didn't.

Augusto C. Cespedes, Jr.

The day was different. It felt different. It was a perfect day, a cloudless sky like unmatched baby blue eyes but time itself felt heavy. No matter how many times I'd checked my watch, the hands seemed like they quivered at a darkened standstill.

But the jokes still spewed out. The smell of cigarette smoke slowly climbed up the unfinished stairs to where we had stood; a mesmerizing view of an area of Haqlaniyah, Boardwalk and the Euphrates. From where we were, the small convoy of military vehicles appeared like toy cars, slowly moving on the two-lane road. We all took turns looking out from the third story window, each wanting a chance to see the city from that point of view.

"Ok it's my turn! You've had enough time," someone jokingly said. His arm was across another Marine's chest, playfully hitting his flak jacket like the arm of a malfunctioning garage gate, inching his way towards the edge of the window.

"I barely was up here, shut up," the other said.

"Enough, children. There's room for both of you anklebiters," Sergeant said, keeping his eyes on the road. For several seconds we all were able to take in the view. I felt the wind gently brush on my face as I sat at the sill, my arm leaning hard on the frame.

I was mid breath and that was when it appeared; a bright ball of fire lit the road, and we couldn't see the convoy anymore.

Just Glow

That moment, it validated that the speed of light was faster than the speed of sound.

Time had stood still.

The day felt different. I thought back from the early morning.

Seconds later, a large wave of tremendous impact erupted. The sound and devastating force of the bomb had caused us to fall, like dominoes, off the window frame.

The ground violently shook. The unfinished walls and floor vibrated, bringing the loose dirt and rock from their resting place and showered the room with a cloud of dust.

Like thin, weakened toothpicks attempting to stand upright, we tried to regain footing.

"Oh God," Sergeant yelled. He immediately scrambled for the radio, getting up from the floor. He was the first to stick his head out of the window, looking to see the aftermath of the fireball.

A few of us had gotten up and held onto the sill, while others just sat there, scared to see the aftermath. Speechless. Mentally unable to see through the window.

The explosion was now an enormous mushroom cloud of black smoke, at least five times larger than the wreck. The noises from the city had suddenly halted and not a single bird was in the sky.

Faint, high-pitched static sounds were coming from the

radio and Sergeant pressed it against his chest, the antenna over his shoulder like a rifle.

We quietly waited together in an unintentional huddle like we knew the next transmission was someone. Anyone.

And it clicked.

"Golf Base," the voice had said. It was a haunting, distressing tone. The fluctuating sounds of frequency waves engulfed the sound of his voice, but we were able to make out what he'd said.

"This is QRF," he continued to say, forcing the words out of his mouth, "We've got KIAs, break…" and the thought of his finger releasing the button to speak affected us as a whole. We kept looking at the explosion site, now engulfed in flames. With heavy breathing, waited for the next transmission.

"Golf Base…" it clicked again.

"Roger, QRF. Send it," the other voice had responded. I felt like it was one of the younger Marines, and I had imagined them wondering the same: who it was and was it their friend, but trying so hard to stay professional over the radio.

"Charlie…Alpha…KIA, break," and then stopped.

"Goddamnit!!!" someone yelled, followed with a loud thump that echoed in the space. Across the room I heard a few Marines exchange words and start making their way to the sound of the radio.

"Juliet…Delta…KIA, break," he continued. His

Just Glow

increased loud breaths that spilled over the radio were felt more as Sergeant slowly turned up the volume knob. Because of the wind, the smell of the explosion started to make its way to us. A stench of burning rubber.

"Hotel...Whiskey...KIA." And it clicked.

Oh no.

Heath.

After holding so much tension to listen to the radio, we'd finally let go. It fell silent. The quiet was at a roaring standstill.

Some had leaned against the wall, and it was the sound of a lighter within seconds.

Scuffled sounds of boots. Rustling of gear.

The world, in that instant, grew heavy and the only sound that lingered were the barking dogs that ran astray. It was like they knew what had happened.

I picked up my head, took a breath in and started to walk downstairs.

"Mistuh! Mistuh!" a voice had called out. I picked my head up to make sure I wasn't going to run into anyone, and I'd noticed it was the small boy. He must have gotten home from school.

"Play?" he then asked, smiling. He sat on the floor with his legs crossed, in front of a set of wooden cars laid out on the cold concrete floor. A few cars had sides that were broken off, areas where the paint was chipped.

Danny looked at me and tried to smile but it ended with him pursing his lips, an attempt to keep his emotions inside.

"Ok, Buddy," I said, taking a breath. He smiled at me the way he did in the morning. When the day felt different.

The Hawaiian Night

"Man, come on! We're gonna be late," one of the younger Marines had said, motioning me to catch up. We walked the usual alleyway that made its way to the back of the strip club.

"Are we really going to this tonight?" I asked.

"Doc," he calmly said, exhaling the cigarette smoke from his mouth, "We're gonna be in the desert in like, uh, four months. I'm seeing my fair share of action before then," he said, confidently, his head held high.

The alleyway, made of poorly constructed stone, sat below a series of yellow and white luminescent bulbs, some swarmed with insects. Small puddles of water, some escaping the shadows, were met with the intermittent drops of air conditioners that were placed in the windows. As I walked by, different pitches of a low hum blew out warm air, hitting my face as it rattled to cool the other side.

Just Glow

"There they are," he mumbled loudly, now smiling. He started to pick up his pace, now several feet in front of me.

"What up, Fools?!" He yelled out, raising his hands up in the air, almost hitting one of the air conditioner units.

"You ready??!!" He went from calmly walking to an ecstatic gallop as he got to the others, who sat on the wooden bench outside of the strip club.

"Yup, been waiting forever! Even my GRAND-MOTHER moves faster than you," one Marine jokingly commented, now standing up from the bench and stretching. The other guys laughed, some under their breath but still sitting on the bench.

The small area at the end of the alleyway was covered in molding brick and with the group that sat there, it started to smell of cigarette smoke. The smell of menthol and smokeless tobacco had traveled to my nose as some of them had an empty bottle to spit in.

"Oh snap, you brought Doc!" One of the Marines stood up. He was dressed in jeans and a long sleeve shirt with black skateboard shoes and a backwards cap. Walking up to me, he put out his hand and we shook hands.

"You ready to party, Doc?" He asked. I looked at the bench of Marines that all waited patiently and in the shadow was a figure motioning his hands in the air in a dance type rhythm. I tried to make out who it was. Then a jab to my shoulder disrupted my focus.

"Ya, maaaan…" I said, breathing out my response in hesitancy. I really didn't want to spend my hard-earned money throwing singles at strange women but I also could see why they wanted to do it.

Eight-month deployment. Third world country. No physical contact or even the sight of women. I had to support the cause.

Everyone started to stand up, stretch and walk to throw away their bottles of spit or put out their cigarettes.

As most of them made their way to the entrance, someone had spoken out from the shadows of the alleyway.

"I think I'm gonna skip out, Guys..." he said.

His tone was weak, hesitant, and almost at a mumble. And the comments just came out.

"...What?"

"Dude, seriously?"

"We drove you all the way here!"

"Don't be such a bitch, Warner!"

But he just stood there in the darkened side of the alleyway. The humming from the air conditioners had stopped, like they had halted for the others to hear him speak.

"I...should have never come. The strip club just isn't for me. I'm sorry." He looked down, embarrassed of what he had said.

"Psh! "Your loss, Man! I'm goin' in. Let's go," he said

Just Glow

and lifted his arm in a "clothesline" fashion, motioning me towards the entrance.

But I resisted and kept my eyes towards the shadows. His arm brushed off me, sensing that I wasn't walking.

"Let's go, Doc. The women might need medical attention," he said, chuckling at his own joke. He started walking and attempted to pull the others with him.

But I couldn't move. Something felt different.

"I'm gonna hang back, too," I'd decided.

"WHAT??" One of the Marines had blurted out, "Now you both aren't making sense." He then turned towards me to acknowledge my response.

"Listen, Doc," he began to say, his hand now in the shape of a knife. "I came here with you to enjoy our last months of freedom," he started to say, "and you're runnin' off to go, I dunno, waste your night." He abruptly stopped talking as if he had said it in one giant breath.

I looked him in the eyes and could see the disappointment. But it was in that moment I'd thought back to that Friday formation in the blistering sun, seeing Heath walking towards his room.

"Not wasting my night," I immediately replied back, my head held high. "We'll take a cab back to base." I turned around towards the entrance of the alleyway, and saw Heath still in the darker corner, avoiding confrontation.

"DOC! Come on, Bro. Are you serious?!"

Augusto C. Cespedes, Jr.

I turned around, hiding my smile.

"I'm sure the women will be fine without me," I blurted out, my head slightly turned towards them.

"I'm actually hungry," I said, in a different tone now, like I'd forgotten the whole conversation. I looked into the shadow and saw Heath slowly come out into the light, walking towards me.

"Me too, Doc," he said. His glasses caught a glare from the flickering bulbs that dangled above.

"Fine, enjoy your date night! Pretty cute, Doc. I wouldn't expect anything less from a Navy Boy," he said, laughing, his attempt of making me feel bad.

"You've got that right, and don't forget it!" I shouted and laughed. I was already walking past the air conditioners now. Their weak motors started up like old antique cars to blow its cold air. The warm, unpleasant air from the units blew into my face as I continued to walk towards the street.

"Just you and me, Bro," I said with just a few steps before walking onto the Waikiki strip. Even the pavement was different. From moldy, darkened broken stone to a well-kept sidewalk surrounded by flowers, we'd left the alleyway onto the main road. It was night and day. Tiki Torches lined the sidewalks with some pathways that led to five-star restaurants. It was the area of tourists. For tourists.

As we walked away from the alleyway, I couldn't help but overhear the conversations of people.

Just Glow

"I am so excited, Mom! This is the best vacation ever!"

"Can't wait to surf and swim with the dolphins! Ooo! But first, dinner!" The family would all cheer.

This was their vacation, and they'd have the best time of their lives. With their family —friends.

Their time on the island would only last a week or two, sure, but they'd be able to go home. Together. Out of innocence, I imagined I was there with them — like I was a part of their family. Smiling, laughing and looking forward to the plans they've made and not having a worry in the world.

And it was then that time had stood still.

Like a snowy winter's night, I felt alone outside watching them through a frosted windowpane. Slow moving particles of pearly white flurries floated in the air as I gazed on in a blissful daydream.

Buried deep in thought, I almost ran into a tiki torch that sat at the end of the beautifully paved sidewalk.

"Doc, watch out!" Heath yelled out, putting his hand in between me and the flame. I shook my head like a wet dog, sensing the warmth of the burning kerosene.

I found myself being forced back to reality.

"You okay, Doc?" Heath asked, concerned. "Thought I lost ya."

I stared blankly at the area where the family was, but they had already disappeared into the sea of other tourists.

Augusto C. Cespedes, Jr.

My foot felt the edge of the sidewalk like a climber to a cliff and the rubber of my shoe quickly backed away. I unconsciously smiled, knowing it was good to hear from him — but deep down, I hated to hear it.

The cracking of his voice was only but a sheer reminder that we were leaving for Iraq in just a few months.

"Can't believe we're on this island, Man! This is crazy!" We'd always say to each other driving down the H3 as we passed the lush green mountains — a beautiful stretch of highway with nothing but spectacular views of Oahu. But it was late 2004 at that time, not even close to our first deployment to Afghanistan — now, just months away from Iraq, it was different.

To us servicemen, no matter if we were there every weekend, it just never hit the same. It was always unsettling as if there was a time limit. Clocks of every size and shape, with ticking hands that forcibly struck its way clockwise into the hollowed curvature of my ears.

The Hawaiian statues that stood tall in the town started to appear as hourglasses filled with dry sand that slowly trickled down and my fearful mind of naivety couldn't get past it.

"Hey Doc?" Heath said, looking at the row of restaurants. Dressed in frayed cargo shorts and a gray shirt with the letters "USMC" in black on the chest, he smirked at the sign of one of the restaurants.

"BUSINESS CASUAL ATTIRE ONLY," it said.

Just Glow

"Ahh," he said annoyed, "I don't think we can go here." Disappointed, he turned to me and waited for an answer. I could barely make out the black frames of his glasses, but I noticed the curvature of his eyebrows that signaled him as upset.

Heath loved and held high respect for the Japanese culture and the cuisine was at the top of his list — sushi.

"Where to now, Doc?"

It was getting late. The crowds that had covered the sidewalks had now lessened to families here and there. Vendors that were outside of their shops turned in for the night, folding their signs that had been sitting out for hours. We both didn't speak about it, but we knew it was counting down to one of our last Saturday nights.

Looking around, I'd noticed Chili's not more than 60 yards away.

"I mean, I'm hungry," I said, rubbing my belly. "Let's just go there," pointing to the main entrance.

Walking inside, the vibe of the island quickly dissipated. The smell of tortilla chips and a freshly mopped floor made its way to us — without warning, nestling into our nares.

I unintentionally scanned the room, initially admiring how empty it was but then quickly felt ashamed at what we were doing in such an empty place.

A muffled voice in the distance.

Only a few sat at the bar. With noticeably bad postures

they watched the baseball game and a random television screen displaying numbers like the stock market, random bouts of data in green that zipped by from right to left and a guy yelling "Ya think the economy is liking this? Huh?!!" I smiled to myself, making fun of his bulging eyes as he stared at the camera like he was looking at me.

"How many?"

The muffled voice wormed its way out of a hole and suddenly, it slowly became clear.

"Hello?"

I blinked hard and shook my head, thinking that would help.

"Oh my god, I'm so sorry. Two, please."

The young hostess quickly pushed the laminated menus, still wet from the overused dish towel used to wipe it with, to her chest and said, "Okay, follow me."

The dining room was noticeably dim like it was too late to be there, but I turned my head quickly to confirm we weren't the only ones sitting down. Though spread out across the dining room, several parties were seen sitting with some even looking at me oddly as I scanned the room.

"Ok, here we are," the hostess said and placed the menus on the table. "Enjoy."

"Whatcha gonna get, Warner?"

I unintentionally slouched over the table with my fore-

Just Glow

arms casually resting at the edges, feeling the slow creation of indentation into my skin. But I then noticed Heath, sitting up straight with his hands held together looking towards the light.

"I really like what this restaurant chain has done in their renovations," he said in a genuine tone. He smiled as the glare from the light bounced off his glasses revealing two identical balls of light. "Nice," he added, nodding his head.

I couldn't help but raise my eyes.

I studied the small intricacies of lights — like a series of bright stars. A simple, yet perfect alignment that oddly seemed to pull me in.

The glow of lights had gotten bigger and started to burn my eyes, forcing myself to look away. But I couldn't.

"Jay??"

"Hello??"

"Jay, what do you want to eat? Hurry! She's coming over now," a woman's voice blurred out.

The high-pitched clinking of utensils meeting plates battled with the noise from conversations.

The shade of light had eased off my eyes, but I'd noticed I was further away from it.

"Pay attention, please??"

I nodded but only out of instinct and looked down to a few crayons

Augusto C. Cespedes, Jr.

and a kids menu riddled with colored lines. Without hesitation, I picked up a blue crayon and started to color in the logo, carefully shading in the block letters. But as I started to glide the crayon over and over, it became noticeably uneven, the crayon rhythmically hitting a dip that created a distinct line.

I readjusted my eyes, upset at what had happened and looked straight ahead. A dark-haired woman sat across from me.

"Mom...?"

She clicked her tongue and put her hand in front of my face.

"He will have chicken tenders," my mom said. The slight accent in her voice was overcome by the annoyance, as she gathered the menus and handed it to the waitress.

The table felt bigger — its wooden edge at my chest. I immediately recognized my sister who was next to me and my dad, who was staring off into space.

"I'm so hungry I could eat a horse!" my sister said out loud, who was also coloring in the menu.

"Hahaha..."

An erupted, deep, bellowed laugh rang in sync after what my sister had said — like as if that person reacted to my sister's joke. But it felt distant, the rhythmic sounds of a man's voice that climbed over a few tables. Like a wooden toy soldier, I stood erect, the edge of the table brushing my stomach as I turned my eyes over to where it came from.

"Congratulations, Marine," an older man said, who sat across from a much younger man dressed in a camouflage uniform. The older gentleman, who appeared scruffy and hunched over, wore a black hat

Just Glow

with a symbol colored in gold and white. His beard was a gray colored nest with slender locks of white, followed down to the middle of his chest.

"Thanks, Grandpa," the younger man replied, "it was okay. Better than I expected actually," he said, which resulted in a forced, cracked smile. "Just want to enjoy my time home before I have to go overseas again." A dramatic inspiration ensued the smile and he finally let out a deep sigh.

Confused but curious, I just stood there, unconsciously swaying, letting the cushion of the booth intermittently bounce off my legs as I attempted to understand their conversation. The verbiage was completely foreign to my ears but as I carefully studied the mannerisms of the younger man, I immediately sensed an intense emotion that was hard for me to understand. I couldn't put the feeling into words but it caused me to sink back onto the chair.

I knew sadness.

"Doc, what you gonna get?" A boy's voice followed by a pause.

"Doc?"

I blinked hard and after a few seconds, my eyes readjusted and it was Heath across from me. The table — its edge now above my belt — appeared empty except for the napkin-wrapped utensils that had spread across.

"It all looks good to me," I said, jokingly, "Sorry they don't have sushi here, Bro," I apologized, skimming the menu over and over as if to make sure they actually didn't have sushi.

Augusto C. Cespedes, Jr.

"It's alright, Doc. They do have entrees of fish so I will just look at that," he replied, his head buried in the menu.

"I guess I'll get a burger. Can't go wrong, ya know?" I said, dropping the menu on the table like a single domino. The damp, laminated menu stuck to the table like fresh plaster.

"And what would you boys like to drink tonight?" the waitress asked, a Caucasian, middle-aged female who didn't seem to be a local — more of from the Midwest.

Heath lowered his menu but only to his chin that exposed his mouth.

"Just a pop, please."

"A wha?" Her face squinted causing her eyebrows to wrinkle.

His eyes lowered, "Coke, please."

"Ahh," she said, writing on her pad. "And for you, young man?"

"Umm..." I said, feeling rushed. I thought about it being one of our last Saturdays on the island and before we knew it, we'd be in the never-ending transit to our deployment.

That was when I glanced at Heath. The small lenses of his glasses created a luminous glare that covered his eyes, revealing the small imperfections of each piece of glass — smudged, lightly scratched and bright. I opened my mouth to answer the waitress, but I noticed his expression, halting my response. I looked beyond his eyes and sank into my chair. It was a reminder that we were far from home.

"Make that two," I said.

High-pitched, ear-piercing laughter traveled quickly to our table and I, out of instinct, ducked my head. I disliked it, the sounds of kids enjoying their night, not having to care about anything but what to eat during their vacation. As the waitress walked away, it sadly turned one of our last nights out on the town into listening to children.

"Oh nooo! Haha!" The clatter of silverware and the slapping of palms to the table disrupted our barely functioning conversation.

"Tic tac toe, three in a row!" one of the kids cheered in the booth.

"You okay, Doc?" Heath asked. He'd noticed I looked restless, darting my eyes in every direction.

"Yeah, I'm okay," I replied, the bottoms of my forearms hitting the edges of the table, "I just can't believe we're leaving for deployment. Time is flying. I feel like we can barely catch a break," I said.

"Yep," Heath agreed.

"How do you feel about it all? Leaving and everything...?" I asked, pausing to hear him speak.

He gently laid the menu down and calmly said, "I would say pretty good. I feel like the training we received was almost like the real thing. I'm sure we'll be nervous at first, but I think the more we do it, we will be okay."

"It…" I repeated.

Heath straightened out his glasses, squinting. "Yeah, you know, patrols in the city, the operations…"

I felt both of us sigh.

Several seconds passed and he took his lips off his straw.

"We'll be okay, Doc."

The instant memories of Afghanistan flashed through my mind, but they ceased before I lost myself in them. I knew it was going to be different. We had only heard stories of Iraq.

Before I could completely snap myself out of the daydream, a rush of wind blew past us as a few of the kids ran down the aisle of tables.

"Geez, they need to get a handle on their own kids," I said out loud, standing up. I felt my nares flared at the sight of it. I was hoping someone had heard my complaint, but no one said anything and the kids just laughed by the window of one of the empty tables.

"Doc, they're just kids. They don't know any better," he said.

As I stood and scanned the area for the kids making another round, I knew Heath was right.

Just Glow

I felt the hardened, worn edges of the chair begin to indent itself onto the backs of my legs as I stood there and unconsciously swayed.

And I waited. My older self wanted to say something again, but it was what Heath had said that changed my stance. I looked beyond the loud, erupting laughter as they ran around the restaurant, the scuffing of rubber soled shoes on the floor and I gently sat back down.

I pursed my chapped lips to the plastic straw and took one small sip of the cola, anticipating the next moment the kids would run past.

Augusto C. Cespedes, Jr.

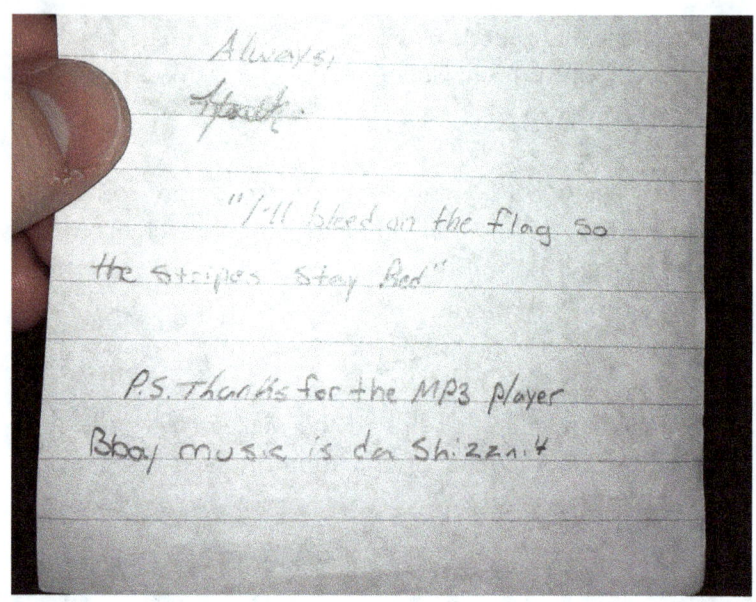

Chapter 11
Valentine's Day

"OH LUCY, I'M HOME!" one of the Juniors had sarcastically yelled while kicking open the heavily weighted entrance door to the common area.

His voice, raspy yet slightly high-pitched, traveled through the damp, concrete space.

An exaggerated tone. Exhausted.

The shuffling of his sand dusted boots made their way over to his bed and he dramatically ripped off his gear at the foot of his rack. Like a chain reaction, one by one, the crisp, crackling sound of Velcro from our flak jackets seemed to linger as more of us entered the stone enclosed room.

"Someone turn on some damn music," one of the other Juniors yelled out, his flak jacket falling to the cement floor. Sweaty and dusty, he plopped himself on his sheetless, worn out mattress like a lifeless, rag doll.

The white distinct lines of salt on his back colored his uniform with different shades of its digital pattern.

Augusto C. Cespedes, Jr.

I was the last one to enter through the doorway, my med pack bouncing off the metal door. I stuck my hand in my right cargo pocket and pulled out the unused tourniquets.

"Are ya ready, Kids??!" A familiar voice of a man sounding like a pirate made me laugh inside.

"Oh no," I whispered to myself, exhausted but smiling from what was going to happen next.

How are these guys with this type of energy….?

0510. My heavily scratched watch glowed brightly under the dim lightbulb that hung above the cracked, concrete ceiling.

"Tink, tink…" the sound of the bulb made as the switch, a small beaded chain, hit the snow painted glass of the lightbulb.

It swayed like a heavy, weighted pendulum as the Marines tapped it as if it was a way of saying, "Made it."

"Tink, tink…"

Back.

"Tink, tink…"

Alive.

I shook my head once and a few of the Marines started to gather their arms around each other like it was last call at the local bar.

Just Glow

They were singing the introduction of the show SpongeBob SquarePants.

"Oh no," I mumbled. Exhausted, I had remembered how long we'd been out on patrol for. But I just shook my head as I made my way towards my rack. With all my gear still on, I sat down, feeling the warmth of the sheet-less mattress weighing down under my sweat soaked uniform.

I sat and watched them dance. In a sense, I felt like a designated driver that watched their friends finish their last drink before heading home. In a drunken stupor being loud and obnoxious, but in that moment was this weird glimpse of happiness.

I just sat there, my rack squeaking as I repositioned myself to enjoy those moments, too tired to take off my gear.

"Absorbent and yellow and porous is he!"

With the last bit of energy, I pulled on the strap of my med pack, lifted it over my head and laid the pack on the mattress. Using the tips of my fingers digging into its seam, I pulled apart my flak jacket that produced a high-pitched crunching sound. And once it opened, I felt an instant relief. The heat and pressure from the sapi plates of the flak jacket that pressed against my body for hours was finally released. I could feel my diaphragm push itself down, and my chest finally rose its highest to breathe the damp air of the room.

"SpongeBob Square Paaaaaants!"

I half turned into the mattress that sat against an

unpainted, whitewashed wall and just a foot above my face was a floating shelf.

Throughout the first few weeks of being in Iraq, we each slowly tried to make our own area, well…ours. And when I mean area, I mean the mattress and the wall it leaned up against.

Photos sent from home that made some of us leave the room. Or we'd simply turn away so the others couldn't see our expressions.

Rosaries that hung like ornaments.

Pictures of our favorite actresses and models that were delicately ripped out from magazines that were sent to us.

When I received my first care package, a requested array of assorted items, I learned from my deployment to Afghanistan of what to ask for.

Jerky.

Trail mix.

Canned chili and soups.

Vienna sausage.

And moistened wipes. Also known as "baby wipes."

There was something special about a baby wipe.

Each wipe, neatly stacked and piled high in its plastic

Just Glow

packaging, maintained their moisture even several weeks later.

After missions lasting more than a few days, or even a patrol that has you dripping in sweat, the feeling of a cool baby wipe against your face was something magical.

You'd hold the wipe in your hand, subconsciously and low key jealous that your hand actually got a taste of that wipe first before any other part of your body. And with no hesitation, the cloth and skin met in an unforgettable connection that rang from your head to your toes.

Delightful. Glorious. The best reward.

And it was sadly one of those things you'd place at the top of your list of things you looked forward to before coming back into the wire.

I mean, it's just a baby wipe, right?

But it wasn't just a baby wipe. It was that small, delicate reminder, as it ran across your face, that you made it back.

All in perfect alignment, the packs of baby wipes sat on the shelf. Next to the cans of chili and soups.

Even if they hadn't moved in days.

Even if it was with my exhausted breath or my calloused fingertips, I had to touch them every time I came back from being outside the wire.

"Tink, tink…" the lightbulb would sound.

"We've got another week-long mission coming up," Sergeant would say to us as he made his way into the room.

"Packin' it up again, Gents," he'd started to say, "we're off for another one."

The One from Ohio

It felt like an ordinary patrol day. I liked the local patrols because we knew we would be home for hot chow and a decent night's sleep. But the night we left after dinner, we all were full, ready for bed and basically just over it.

"Captain wants us to do a perimeter patrol," Corporal yelled out. He was at the clearing barrels ahead of all of us, and appeared to be the only one who was in the mood to go out.

We tried not to use the same exact route this time, using different paths to patrol the perimeter. Squeezing through the alleyways, jumping over high walls. It was uncomfortable and I hated it, but if it kept us from being predictable, then so be it. That night, we decided to go to a different house.

Utilizing houses in urban warfare was common. For one, it got you out of the street. Out of harm's way. When it was hot as hell outside, you laid on the floor and felt the cool tile on the back of your head. When it was cold outside, you tried to find a house with a wood burning stove or a source of heat.

"Asalam alaykum," we'd say when we entered a house,

Just Glow

touching the chest portion of our flak jackets. And it was always to the man of the house. The greeting from them was always the same. Calm and usually friendly. We never asked where the women and children were as they were always tucked away in one room until we had left. Some people would offer us tea, sit on their couch, and even let us sleep in their house. There were also some that never left the room. They stood there, arms crossed waiting for us to leave and if there were more than a few of them, they'd take shifts until we left for another house.

0100 HRS. It was time to find a house to hide out in before we made our way back to base.

The lead Marine, or "point man," kicked the metal gate once, hard. Donkey kick hard. Turned around, knee to the chest, wound up for a nice one, hard. And hard enough that the sound echoed through the alleyway.

But we didn't have to worry about the noise. Didn't matter what time it was. We owned the streets. We were the ones with the weapons. The authority.

Another swift kick. And another.

"ARE YOU KIDDING ME?"

Silence. My mind felt like it was playing tricks on me.

"STOP IT!"

"JUST KNOCK ON THE FRONT DOOR!"

The silence was from straight shock. We were all stunned.

Augusto C. Cespedes, Jr.

It was a woman. A WOMAN. Yelling at us. In perfect English.

"Hello?" the point man stood there, waiting for his next order.

"Well??" she said. "Don't just stand there. I will open the front door."

In times of war, especially in the Middle East, women were not the ones who spoke out first.

Ever.

It was either the man of the house or the oldest son.

We never expected a woman to speak out to us, no matter the situation, and never ever did we think we'd hear a woman who sounded like an American.

One by one, we walked into the house, and I couldn't stop admiring how she sounded like one of us. It was like her voice took us all into a different realm. Not war. Not terror. Home.

"So why do you have to kick people's gates like that? And at this late hour in the night?" She sat down on the couch and poured a few cups of tea, setting them on the table.

Some of us were still a little stunned. Some of us didn't want to be complacent, so a few stood outside or kept looking out the window. But I felt like I could talk to this woman for hours. I felt welcomed. But I couldn't answer the question she was asking so I waited for Corporal to respond.

Just Glow

"We do it to alert the public that we're present." He was reaching for a cup of tea when she then spoke out.

"Bullshit. We know you're here. There's no need to do that."

Stunned again. My head felt like a ping pong ball, going back and forth as they each spoke.

He readjusted his gear, took a deep breath in and said, "I understand what you're saying."

But for me, I was still very intrigued. I had so many questions.

"Why here? What the hell are you doing in Haqlaniyah, Iraq?"

But of course, I stumbled on my words, even stuttered a bit but eventually was able ask a question.

"W-w-wha- what are you doing here? You sound like you're from the US."

She leaned in from the couch and calmly said, "Well, I am. I'm from Ohio." Her smile was genuine. Exposed. We rarely got to see the women as they were always covered in burkas or hidden.

There were so many questions I had but felt like I couldn't ask in front of everyone.

Why here?

Augusto C. Cespedes, Jr.

Why in this city?

So I said the first thing that was on my mind.

"Aren't you scared?"

She leaned back into the couch and smiled. "This is my parents' house. I'm visiting them. It's harder for them to come to the US because of their health, so I just come to them. I've been doing it for years." She continued to hold her cup of tea and just said, "I'm used to it."

As she spoke, the feeling to hear her speak was unexplainable. Like we had stepped into another dimension and harm's way just — vanished.

We laughed and listened carefully to her voice and watched — enjoyed for some — her mannerisms. It had been way too long.

It seemed we had talked for only several minutes, but time had quickly passed. And time had passed so quickly that I lost track of time.

"Doc we gotta go. It's almost zero three."

A part of me didn't want to leave.

A part of me wanted to talk to her about her home in Ohio and the things that she grew up doing because hearing her speak was like a small little piece of home.

But I knew it was time.

I knew we had to leave.

Just Glow

"Doc, you and your guys take care of yourself," she'd said, "You'll be home soon enough."

We didn't admit it but we needed that. Being yelled at by an American woman. The talk. Five months in country and hearing an American woman's voice? It almost recharged us.

We walked back to base with a pep in our step, some of us still talking about the whole thing like it was the greatest sports game we'd ever seen.

Day One

Outside the wire. Day one. Midday.

The sun, the warmest it's been for February, was at its highest point.

Midday. It was unheard of.

We never left for a mission midday. Either it was well after nightfall or just before the sun cracked open the sky, but never midday.

And it was beautiful outside.

"Two more months of this shit and we're home free." It was one of the Junior Marines. He puffed on a cigarette like a cigar as we started to ascend up one of the familiar hills in town. The same hill we had seen since those first days in country.

But it felt different. Comfortable.

We walked into the house we had always passed by but never actually entered.

Enormous stone pillars that stood high before the front door and were planted on a front walkway. And I'd noticed this many times before.

Huge pillars. A wooden door. The house up the hill.

But this time we were greeted with a kindness that was not familiar. But no one complained about it. A breath of fresh air for once.

It was day one of a week-long operation.

"Let's get settled in, Gents," Sergeant announced. The blowing of cold air from an air conditioner attached to the wall soothed me like an exhausted toddler as I was still recovering from the hill climb.

"I got window!" someone said, a Junior rifleman who shuffled his way towards the curtained window. It was Morris. He pinned himself against the wall and only using his finger, moved a small portion of the curtain like he was moving a piece of hair from his girlfriend's eyes.

"Let's establish presence on perimeter and rooftop. We'll rotate posts every four. First patrol in a few hours," he said.

"First day," someone sighed. It was a half effort comment that made its way to my ear as he passed, our shoulders brushing against each other as we started to walk in different directions.

I hated this part.

The downtime had begun.

No one truly enjoyed the silence.

It was loud. Haunting.

Its deafening existence pulsated in the hollows of our helmet.

Maybe that's why we had to keep moving.

We constantly tapped the snuff can, moving it through our fingers like a well-oiled machine.

Hummed a familiar or even a made up tune just to drown it out.

Even the subtle crackling of a cigarette we'd yearned for.

But no one ever admitted it.

It was just known.

"Doc…" Morris loudly whispered, "if you could have anything to eat right now, what would it be?" He kept his eyes on the window, his two fingers on the edge of the curtain.

I loved and hated this question.

Augusto C. Cespedes, Jr.

It was simple yet powerful enough to take you to a magical place, careening your tastebuds through this endless universe of delicious food you've eaten.

The ones you took for granted.

Your answer was important. As if it was the final one in a game show and whatever you chose was going to drop out of a chute right in front of you.

Something sweet? Maybe, but it can't be overpowering, though.

Spicy? No, no…wasn't feelin' it.

Different cuisines and dishes were coming to mind like they were on this conveyor belt that moved right to left.

"Doc? Well? What would you eat?"

It was like I had a hint of it before I'd said it, swallowing the increased saliva in my mouth like it was my first bite.

"Cinnamon Toast Crunch in cold milk."

He let go of the curtain, letting it lightly sway itself back to the window and then looked at me.

"Seriously?" He had a look of shock. Like I was going to say, "I'm kidding," but after waiting for several seconds, his expression changed to a serious one.

"You're serious," he then said.

Just Glow

"I have my reasons," I replied, feeling confident now.

I imagined sitting at my kitchen table, my feet barely touching the tiled floor, listening to the repeated "tink, tink, tink" of the small squares hitting the ceramic white bowl.

"Good, Jay?" My mom would ask me. I could smell the scent of fresh laundry and a perfume that I'd always noticed every morning.

After a few seconds of the cereal hitting the bowl, I'd slowly raise my hand and say, "Thanks, Mom."

"You're welcome, Tungko," she'd reply, dragging out the last syllable of the word with a cracked smile. It was a term of endearment in her native language that she'd use a lot. When hugging me, kissing me goodnight or just when she was in a good mood.

"What does that mean, Mom? Tungko..." I'd say it out loud, pronouncing it in a way that made her laugh.

"My little boy. Tungko...that's all," she'd reply, putting her hand on my head and gently bringing it back, her fingers running through my thick, wavy hair. I wouldn't say anything. I just smiled and ate my breakfast.

"I'll take your word for it," Morris said, interrupting the thought I had transformed myself in.

"What 'bout you? What would you like to eat?" I asked. I'd noticed the sunlight shining through his eyes; a shade of blue that I hadn't noticed before.

"I don't know about food, but I could reeeaaaally go for a cappuccino from Sheetz right now," he snickered. He quickly glanced at me but then his eyes darted back to the window.

"Sheetz?!!" I said out loud but then quickly covered my mouth.

I gave it a few seconds before I whispered, "What's that?!"

"It's a small convenience store," he started to say but didn't look at me.

"Where I'm from, we didn't have much. A few stores here and there so we'd make our own fun with what we had, and Sheetz was just one of those places close to us," he'd said, his eyes still at the window, "my best friend and I would get cappuccinos before school. I always looked forward to them…" he trailed off as his finger periodically touched the curtain. It was as if he was stuck in the thought and didn't want to come back to this. This hell.

It went silent for several seconds as if something were seen from the window. His face appeared different. More serious. So I let the time pass.

Then he spoke out, again, in a loud whisper.

"What made you join?"

I also hated this question. But I couldn't leave him hangin'. I rearranged myself, feeling the heavy weight of my flak jacket.

"I wasn't a good kid before all of this," I started to say.

Just Glow

He took his eyes off the window and looked at me. I had his full attention.

"You?! My Doc? Not a good kid?!" His face now directed towards me, now wide eyed with a prominent shade of baby blue.

I almost started to laugh but I'd remembered where we were, so I felt my mouth just form a smile.

"Believe it," I then said.

"I had no direction. Nowhere to go…"

"I'd made some poor decisions…" I trailed off, swallowed hard and leaned my head on the wall.

My mind had brought me back to the recruiter in the mall. Then to the girl on the couch. How lifeless she looked.

To that empty, embarrassing feeling of time elapsing as I stood in the parking lot covered in a stench of marijuana.

To that moment my eyes met the shine of a holstered handgun as I held a silly picture fan I had stolen from the local department store.

"Come with me," I'd remember the police officer saying, his finger pulling over his blazer to show off the grip of the pistol. "Don't you dare run, Boy."

I shook off the thought, completely disturbed by the mental images.

"What about you?" I asked.

Augusto C. Cespedes, Jr.

Morris kept his eyes on the window like he was waiting for someone but then began to speak.

"After 9/11, seeing all of those people free falling out of the windows, it made me mad. I wanted nothing more than to take away their pain. I didn't know how to explain it. I just felt it. I wanted to defend my country. And I still do. But at that time, I didn't know what that looked like. But being here, now, I now know what I'm fighting for."

I repositioned my feet and stared hard at the dust on my boots.

"Ya...? What's that?" I asked.

He took his eyes off the window, the shade of baby blue now in my direction.

"You and me."

Our conversation was quickly interrupted, making both of us jump.

"Gear up! Let's move out! Morris! Where ya at?!" It was a voice that sounded like Sergeant.

"Moving, Sarn't!" We both pried ourselves off the walls and headed towards the stairs. When we reached the top, we turned to the right into the room with a few of the others.

"We got everyone here?" Sergeant spoke out, his hand cupping his mouth like a megaphone. A few grunts and low "Here" were heard that were as loud as the sound of gear and boots scuffing the floor.

Just Glow

"First patrol of the mission. Day one of seven. We're at the home stretch. We've got comms up?" he said. Everyone looked towards the window. Morris, bent over, was pressing buttons and turning knobs on the radio. It was silent for a few seconds, but he stood up and said, "We are good to go, Sarn't."

A static blared which turned heads, and Morris immediately bent down in an attempt to fix it.

"Morris, we got comms or what…?"

"Yup," he said, scrambling to figure out what was going on with the radio, "Just one second."

"Morris, you dog you," a Junior Marine said, chuckling behind him. He grabbed his waist, but Morris pushed him off, still focused on the radio.

A small "tink" was heard but no one thought anything of it.

I moved my eyes from the knobs of the radio to the metal bars that stretched over the window, and I noticed a small hole the size of a quarter.

"What is that…?" I said out loud, loud enough for only a few that stood next to me to hear.

"What are you talking ab-…"

A blast.

And it went black.

Chapter 12
Shattered

Dirt roads and an endless map of farmland that went for miles. Quaint shops lined the streets of a small town called Crimora, a town in Virginia.

"There was only one intersection in the whole town," Danny would say, and laugh to himself as he'd take his first bite of an MRE. "And people got excited for a dollar store! Would ya believe that?!" His mouth was partially full from the entree but still formed a smile through unbrushed teeth.

Danny, although born in Colorado, grew up in Virginia with his mama and brother.

"So," I would start to say, repositioning my gear, "what was it like?" I laid my head on the cement wall and felt its cool surface against the back of my head. It felt sweaty and after a long walk around the city, leaning against a cement wall was bliss.

"What...hanging out in good ol' Crimora?" He started to brush off the sand off of his boots. "Boring as ever, Doc," then he'd continue to say, "but we made the best of it. The best of what we had."

All I could hear was a high-pitched sound. A deafening, constant ring that made its way into my head. Any which way I turned, it was there.

But even in that noise, I could hear something.

I heard a voice, in and out, trying to pierce itself through.

"Doc!!" it said.

"Doc!!"

It sounded muffled, like it was from the other side of a wall. Or with someone's hand over their mouth.

Subconsciously, I wanted to know who it was or if they were hurt.

Then I felt a tapping. A violent tapping.

"DOC. DOC. WAKE UP, DOC!"

Just Glow

I felt my eyes begin to slowly open, fighting a heavy feeling and suddenly felt a quick spray of a warm, odorous mist on my face.

Saliva.

"DOOOOOC," the Marine grabbed me by the collar, "YA GOTTA WAKE UP! MORRIS IS HIT!"

He appeared in a weird slow motion, his mouth moving in such a slowed stare. For a split second, I tried to make out the words. I felt myself squinting at him, trying to decipher what he was saying.

Seeming like it was frame by frame, he grabbed me by the collar and opened his mouth wide.

And without notice, it all returned to normal.

"DOC! DOC! WAKE! UP!"

The room was nothing but a huge cloud of smoke. And frantic yelling. Everyone was moving so fast. In a panic. And the smell of gun powder permeated as I tried to understand what had just happened.

Who am I helping???

I scanning aimlessly, feeling my face tense up.

Another tug on my blouse from the Marine that knelt in front of me and pointed towards the other room, barely visible through the smoke.

"MORRIS, DOC! GO HELP MORRIS!"

Augusto C. Cespedes, Jr.

A wave of pain completely washed over me as I forced myself up to see what was happening to Danny.

I felt my face at an awkward position like I was about to cry, but I held it in.

He was right in front of me.

The thought flashed in my head and burned itself deep. And again.

I stood right behind him. Morris was right in front of me.

I was scared. I felt weak. Helpless. But everything was happening so fast. It was all just so loud.

The smoke cleared once I made my way past the door frame and there he was, lying on the ground, surrounded by the others. A reporter was frantically backing himself up against the wall, his helmet scraping against the stone.

I felt myself breathe in and tried my hardest to keep my composure.

I couldn't see him as my friend. The one who I was just talking to downstairs minutes before.

The one who was my Battle Buddy.

The one who had to spend the night with me against that cement wall and instantly became my friend.

I wanted nothing more than to just uncontrollably yell out and be in a state of panic. But I couldn't. I was his

Just Glow

Corpsman and I had to see him as my patient. My mind flipped like a switch. I took a breath and quickly assessed.

No obvious blood.

Unconscious.

He's pale as a ghost.

"Gotta cut open his blouse," I said, feeling like I had said it too quickly that no one had understood me. But I took the sheers from my pack and started to cut.

Once we exposed his torso, I was expecting blood smeared across his chest but I was wrong. It was clean. Not a drop of blood but only small, darkened holes that scattered his chest, which made me shudder.

"We gotta turn him over, Guys," I ordered. One last assessment. Everyone stopped staring, their hands holding tourniquets.

"He's heavy," one of them said shaking, struggling to turn him over.

No blood, no wounds, No blood, no wounds, No blood, no wounds... the silly phrase rang through my head as I looked at his glazed eyes. It was the phrase that was taught to us in FMSS.

I reached both arms around his torso towards his back, trying to connect my hands and swiped as much of his back as I could, praying there was something. Blood. Anything.

It was clean.

Augusto C. Cespedes, Jr.

I backed up. Helpless.

I looked at his left leg and just a small amount of blood was seen. A Marine was shaking, trying to place a tourniquet around his leg. I could see him, nervous as can be, measuring with his fingers to where to tie the tourniquet.

"Stop, man…" I said, reaching out my hand. I hated to be the one to let him know it was useless. I felt like I wasn't speaking loud enough, the complete shock of it all taking away my breath.

He looked at me confused, but once our eyes met, he understood me. It fell silent except for the exhaled breaths from everyone surrounding Danny.

"Doc," someone said, "what do we do…?"

I thought about my assessment. *No blood, only small holes.*

I thought about Chief holding that helpless recruit.

Danny's smile as he looked from the window.

The moment before the blast.

"There's nothing we can do." I had felt a bead of sweat on the tip of my nose which made me brush my own face with my hand.

On my knees, I inched closer to Danny's face, and put my hand behind his head.

"There you are," Chief would say to the recruit, confidently,

Just Glow

softly. "*Hey…you're gonna be okay…*" *The saliva from his mouth smeared onto her forearms, glistening under the tube lights but she only paid attention to his eyes, staying completely connected.*

I leaned back but was still on my knees and unable to move because of the sudden, intense rush of comfort in the chaos.

Time had stood still, and we could do nothing else but watch.

She caressed his forehead, like she had seen the impact of what her voice and touch had done to him.

My eyes felt heavy and frame by frame, each moment that led to that second flipped through my mind like an indestructible, swirling nightmare.

With all that I had, I held his head as everyone just watched.

It all happened so fast.

The word "why" became the only thing I could see. Could think.

Like floating vessels that took many forms.

Why. WHY. why. WHY. WHY. WHY. WHY. They appeared big, bright then quickly burned, melted and came back again.

Then it all just became a blur.

Augusto C. Cespedes, Jr.

From the door frame, I could hear someone behind me start to loudly speak.

"Medivac is comin', Doc!"

I sat there motionless, thinking about what I saw.

No blood. Unconscious. Pale as a ghost.

"Let's get him outta here, okay?" It was almost whispered to me right in my ear.

My body didn't move. I made everyone else work around me as I sat there.

No blood.

He was unconscious.

Pale. Ghost. I swallowed hard.

They swiftly took him from my view and in one breath, he was gone.

I didn't start to feel the pain in my knees until several minutes later.

Time elapsed. It was nothing but a deafening silence.

"Can we just go back to base?" I could hear rustling and a wave of static from the radio.

"Captain says we need to continue…"

"No way," someone said. We all were shocked. Our first

day out, one has already died, and one severely wounded? We're two men down and he still wants us to continue?

He turned his back and started to walk towards the other room.

"He should come out here and feel this shit," someone else said, "maybe he'd reconsider."

But nothing changed and it was only hours away from Day Two.

Day Two

When we made our way to the next house, the mood changed. An eerie, empty feeling. There were no jokes. No one was laughing. Just that familiar sound of our gear rustling and sliding against the walls.

"Let's settle in," Staff Sergeant said. "Gonna be sometime 'til we hit the road again."

I didn't want to do anything else but go back to base. Rewind it all back. We all did. But a part of me wanted to impulsively raid every house and find the person who killed Danny.

"Mistuh…?"

It was a bit dark in the front of the house, but when I turned around, I noticed there was light coming from the windows of the kitchen.

Augusto C. Cespedes, Jr.

On the floor sat a man, maybe in his mid-50s, who seemed to be the head of the household.

"Please…," he said, gently motioning his hand to the floor, "sit."

I could tell he couldn't speak English well, but he didn't seem to be uncomfortable about it. And I didn't notice his thick accent, or the fact that he only spoke three words, but it was what was in front of him that kept my attention.

He sat behind an enormous array of food.

Large, round silver plates of local food, some looked like things to dip into, others of stew and heaps of rice and naan bread. In the light that pierced from the window, the steam from the rice and bread slowly floated up to the ceiling.

"Are you sure?" I asked but it was only in a whisper because I knew he didn't understand me anyways. So, I tilted my head at an angle and put my right hand on my chest. He just smiled, nodded, and waved me over.

I walked over and sat down.

"Take," he said and handed me a piece of bread. It was steaming and warm against my hands like it was made only a few minutes before.

And I closed my eyes.

The jewelry on her wrist made a jingling sound as she rubbed my back with the palm of her hand. She smiled this radiant smile that

Just Glow

seemed to never go away. Because it was all she could do. That and a few sentences in English.

Grandma Carol, my mom's mother, knew little of the English language.

"She's saying that she loves you," my mom would say across the table. Her hands propped her chin up like a stand letting her elbows rest on the table.

At a younger age, I didn't know any better. I just thought, "she's my grandma who I barely see, but I'll just sit here and see what she'll say to me." I knew she couldn't say much. It was, at first, the common greetings, hi, how are you, how is school and eat. She ALWAYS made sure we ate.

"Pakanan me ing paunakan mu!" or "don't forget to feed your nephew" she'd say to my aunt as the steam from the rice cooker would rise up almost to the ceiling.

She'd say it across the room, and it would echo into the kitchen. Or in passing. While she was sitting on the couch and I would just be waking up, rubbing my eyes.

On her side of the country, cooking food was a special gesture that spoke to an empty stomach. But it was more than just food to feed the body. It was her way of showing love to another soul.

It was the time and energy spent preparing the meal and showing that person that they cared enough to cook for them.

This was Carol.

This was my grandma.

Augusto C. Cespedes, Jr.

Aloha

It took a week to get home. From the dreadful Humvee rides to the C-130 to a commercial plane, we finally landed on the Hawaiian tarmac.

Swaying back and forth, we slowly made our way to the front of the plane.

"Look," someone said, "they're waiting for us."

After eight months of fighting in the desert, it was truly a sight to see.

Crowds cheering. A band playing. And signs that were held up.

"Welcome Home!"

"Thank you, Heroes!"

"God Bless America!"

We all noticed them, but we didn't say anything.

With rifles over our shoulders, our uniforms, for once, were clean.

No blood. No sweat. No dirt.

We felt guilty to see it.

The Room

"Well, Cespedes," my Chief had said to me with his hand on my shoulder. "It's your lucky day."

"Yea? Why's that, Chief?"

"You get a room all to yourself. The nice barracks, actually."

The ones with the heavy metal doors…Hotel-esque vibes.

"Really?" I asked.

"I think you earned it." His hand left my shoulder, and he turned around to his desk, briefly had his back to me and then again faced towards me.

"Here's the key card." He handed me a plastic, white card. "It's a first floor one, too. Room 108."

The last time I was in these rooms was with Conte when we thought we were rooming with each other.

Augusto C. Cespedes, Jr.

A glimpse of his face flashed across my eyes when I saw him bounce himself on the bed, his one hand holding his cellphone talking to his mom.

"You good?"

I felt my eyes shake off the memory.

"Yeah," I said, clearing my throat, "sorry."

I walked through the courtyard and every step seemed to trigger the senses I had felt way before all of this.

Before Iraq.

Before Afghanistan.

The day Conte and I entered those same barracks.

The sound of classic rock or rap music blaring through speakers.

Cleaning supplies from the weekly inspections that hid the smell of cigarettes and cheap cologne.

The slamming of the heavy metal doors.

I placed the card in the slot like at the ATM and the green light flashed.

Click.

I pushed open the door and felt it like it was just yesterday.

Just Glow

The day had quickly turned to night, and I found myself in bed before ten p.m.

Walking across the hardened carpet that was anything but comfortable to the tile floor, I turned off the light and got back into bed.

"Can't believe it," I had said, mumbling. "I'm here."

But it hit me out of nowhere with no warning.

The fast breathing. My eyes widened and stayed open.

I could not catch myself. Like no matter how quick I tried to breathe, my inspirations were being chased by my exhalations.

The light of the moon had hit the floor of the carpet so violently — so quickly that I felt like I'd left the light on. A rich, ghostly white draped over every part of the room, turning it into snow. The moments of leaving the wire for the very first time entered my mind like an unwelcoming demon and took me there. It took me back to Iraq.

How the shops were illuminated under the moonlit sky. The crunching of our boots against the loose gravel as we walked, our heads spinning like swivels.

I wanted to move out of my bed — I did — but I couldn't. I was unable to do anything. The flashback took control of my body.

I was frozen. Completely paralyzed. Like I was given a paralytic drug. But my mind was still intact. I felt like I knew where I was.

Augusto C. Cespedes, Jr.

What the fuck is happening to me…

My body felt like it was being controlled by something else. Something more powerful than I had ever imagined.

Even with my sure sense of clarity, my body still acted out. Stunned. It felt restless, but at the same time, unable to move. I started to back up against the concrete wall like the moonlight was this unforgiving rogue wave and in an attempt to swallow me whole. I could feel my heels digging into the mattress, trying to get away from something.

Stop this… snap out of it…

I had to wait until it was over. Until it ran its course.

Fire Eyes

"Yo!" It was a deep, slurred and bellowed voice. "Docs!"

I stopped looking at the ground and slowly picked my head up.

It was one of our Marines, Lance Corporal Ford. He was one of the Marines that came to the island the same time I did. And by the sound of how he spoke out he had a little too much to drink.

"Th'hell you squids gon'?"

Just Glow

"We were wondering the same thing about you, Lance Corporal."

"Duhn Lanz Corp'ruhl may, Squi'. You ah'ways be uh boo' tuh me."

A boot. Being called a boot in the military was degrading. It was to let you know that you were lower than the others, especially the one who called you a boot.

Doc Po, the other corpsman in the platoon, was more sober than me so he just scoffed it off.

"I know, thanks," he calmly replied. But that only made him talk more.

"Come hitchuh ride with us beh to base," he slurred, waving his arm over that seemed to be in slow motion.

He put his arms around Po and I and started to drag his feet, his rancid body odor of smokeless tobacco and sweat immediately punching my nose.

The other Marines that were with him, ones from our platoon, stuck his arm in the air and flagged down a van that immediately pulled over to the side. It was a white van with a taxi sign that lit up at the roof of the vehicle.

"Let's roll."

When we lined up to pile into the van, Po put his foot on the step and Ford put his hand out and made sure he would sit next to Po. I could see Po scooting over to the window, the pleather cushion squeaking as he bobbed up and down to move.

"Comfy, huh Doc…?"

"Where to?" the driver asked. I could see his eyes looking at us through the rearview mirror.

"K Bay Marine Corps Base," I said. Quickly, please, I thought. I wasn't feeling good about any of this.

"Can I move?" Po asked. He started to get up from his seat when Ford pulled him down.

"Why, Doc? Wuzz wrong? Nodduhgood enough spot? Lez talk."

"I'm good, Bro."

"Not your fucking Bro, Doc."

"Okay. I am okay, Lance Corporal." He started to get up again, but Ford now had his heavily tatted arm over the next cushion in front.

"I'm moving, Ford," Po said.

"Or else what, Doc?"

"Get out of my face."

He didn't move.

"Get out of my face."

Nothing. By this time, no one was speaking. We were either just praying to get back to base or waiting for some-

Just Glow

thing to happen.

"Ford, out of my face."

It was probably the tenth time he said it inside the van. If Po wasn't sober then, he had gained full control over what was happening.

I, on the other hand, felt different.

Too heavy to keep them open, my eyelids, like poorly managed blinds in a deserted window, felt weakened from the alcohol. I just wanted to sleep.

I attempted to glance at my watch — the same one I had went to Iraq with.

Scratches that slid down its face at the same direction.

Heavily worn.

The fabric, now odorous, reeked with a sour, dry sweat.

0030 HRS. It was half past midnight.

"I'm gonna kill you, Corpsman."

Po had an expression of nervousness, but it quickly vanished and tried to play it off.

"What??" he said, laughing it off.

"You heard me, Navy punk."

Augusto C. Cespedes, Jr.

We all thought he was joking, but the tone sounded different. It wasn't the Ford we knew. Not the one from Iraq.

It was lower. Threatening. Sinister.

With full effort, I picked my head up and looked at Ford.

He was sitting up now, blowing out exhaled breaths like a bull and with fire eyes.

"Let me out," Po said, ready to leave the van. He tried to stand up but Ford now attempting to grab Po by his neck.

"Guys, I need help," he said. I could hear the fear in his voice.

Now it was nothing but everyone scuffling, making sure Ford didn't have his hands around Po's neck.

"Ford, chill, man…it's your Doc. From Iraq. What the hell is wrong with you?"

"I want him dead."

"What's going on back der?" the driver asked.

"Nothing, nothing. We're good." I'd said from my seat, with my cupped hand to my mouth so he could hear me.

I kept thinking it was a joke. Like he was just trying to entertain us while we were on our way home. But he didn't stop.

The scuffle got louder and after several attempts, Ford was able to get his hands on Po's upper arms. Po tucked his

Just Glow

neck in and pinned Ford's arms down so he couldn't advance.

Ford wasn't a skinny guy. He was of small stature, definitely shorter than me, and I am 5'6, but damn, the guy packed muscle. None of the Seniors would dare talk down to him because he was likely stronger than them. His upper body was covered with various tattoos, the theme being of automotive, death and destruction.

"Arrgghhhh…" Ford started to grumble like a demon.

"Guys, I need help…" his voice now a bit higher pitched now.

Luckily that was when the driver pulled over.

"Get out! All of you!" We felt the car swerve to the right and abruptly stop.

He then got out, walked around to the sliding door and forced it open.

"Out."

We all moved at once, shuffling out of the van like clowns from a small car.

I fumbled for cash in my wallet, paid the driver and he sped off, leaving us all in a cloud of exhaust fumes at the side of the road.

"Yer mine now, Boot," Ford said. With an unsteady gait, his feet stomped dramatically on the ground like he was a giant towards Po. But Po, still calm and sober, walked backwards.

"Ford, it's me, Doc…"

"Leave him alone, Ford. That's enough," one of the Marines said as he started to open a new pack of cigarettes. His hand smacked the box a few times before removing the wrapper.

But he still kept walking towards him.

There was a flash of blue and red lights that shined across the buildings, and I could hear a siren from the distant.

"Oh shit, we've got comp'nee…" one of the Marines said.

But that didn't stop Ford. It was like he was on a mission to put Po out of his misery.

"Hey Buddy," the cop yelled, "is there an issue here?"

I was about to yell "YES! HELP!" To finally end this nightmare. But someone yelled back, "We're fine! Everything's fine! Just go back to your squad car…"

They seemed to have listened and went back to their car when that statement made him turn back.

"Pardon, Brudduh?"

He fixed his guard belt, made sure it was straight and walked over to all of us.

Just Glow

Shit.

With Ford still on a mission to hurt Po, I could tell he noticed Ford's intentions.

"Hey, Brah, you good?" He pointed to Ford and looked at us. "He good?"

No, he's not.

Both of the cops started to approach Ford, almost surrounding him, and Ford stopped focusing on Po and immediately became in defense mode. He was ready to fight. He put up his hands and spread his feet.

"You dunno who yer mess'n with…" he said, his words starting to become clearer. It was as if the encounter sobered him up to protect himself.

"We just wanna talk…"

"Well, I dun want to talk."

They put their hand up like an entrance gate to a parking garage but Ford, drunk and upset, attempted to lift it up with his forearm. And that caused the scuffle.

"Get the mace, get the mace…" I could hear one of the officers saying, their voice sounding as if it was being trampled on. Ford was tough and he wasn't going to let two officers take him down. Not that easy.

All three of them were on the ground, bloodied, their

clothes ripping from the concrete and we all just stood there. Drunk. Tired. A bit worried.

"Get da fuck on your feet," one of the officers said, pulling Ford up from off the ground. His voice sounded exhausted. Out of breath. But when they finally had Ford in handcuffs, I caught a glimpse of his face. It was beet red, his eyes showed a defeated, saddened rage and his nose was splattered with mucus that shined in the glare of the street lamps.

"You will all pay for this shit," Ford said, violently spitting on the ground.

"Someone call the command," one of the others suggested.

"No, are you kidding me? We'll be forever fucked!" a Junior had said.

I tried to think of something.

"Someone call Staff Sergeant," I said. "Listen, Officers, with all due respect — ..." someone started to say.

"There's nada you can say! He needs to go back to the station, ya? 'Maybe teach 'em a lesson!" the officer shouted. I could see the remnants of saliva that spread on his face from being on the ground.

"You don't understand!" I yelled out.

"Listen, we just got back from Iraq!" someone had finally shouted.

Just Glow

I was expecting them to stop what they were doing and let him go, but they never turned around.

It was silent for a moment with just the distant sounds of their radios giving off spurts of familiar static that reminded me of our patrols, calling in Golf Base to give them our sit rep.

Their car doors slammed and just like that, they were gone.

We sat on the concrete steps of an old, abandoned apartment building, watching the faded, colored lights of the police cars chase each other on the walls of shops as they drove away.

We were speechless. Defeated. Angry. Confused. But there was this unexplainable feeling that hovered over it all.

It was a weird, eerie feeling. I tried to understand it. Pinpoint it.

It was the same eerie feeling when Danny died, watching him being carried away on a litter, lifeless, his arm hanging off the edge.

We knew what each other was thinking but never asked about it. Didn't have to. We simply just knew.

We stared at each other, almost counting each other's breaths, and asked, "what now?"

Augusto C. Cespedes, Jr.

Frocks

At the end of June 2007, I was promoted to an E-4, Third Class Petty Officer. I was a bit surprised, as I wasn't a great test taker. But I was leaving the island in November, so it was nice to know I'd enjoy my last months in Hawaii as an E-4.

Being an E-4 as a Green side Corpsman was nothing short of an ordinary initiation.

"Frocking" is what they called it.

You stood in front of everyone attending your pinning and everyone, eager to watch you get promoted, stood at attention.

You see, as a Corpsman, you wore your camouflaged uniform that bared a pin on each side of your collar. One was the caduceus and the other your rank.

The Senior Chief and the Captain stood beside me and after both of their speeches, Senior Chief said, "Do the good deed, Gentlemen."

I'd never seen it, nor did I know what exactly was coming.

Good deed? Handshake? Can't be.

They formed two lines, one on each side and the guys next to me told me to hold still.

"You won't be needing these for this," the one on the

right said to me. He was a second class petty officer. He lifted up my collar and unfastened the backing to the pin.

My confusion suddenly turned to a nervous fear, and I swallowed the spit that I subconsciously held onto just for that moment.

Then their fists balled up.

Both of them looked at each other, grinned, and I could see one of their faces that had the expression of "better hold on tight, man."

Within a few seconds, they sent their fists flying down the ends of my collar.

Now, the initial pain was like how a blue shell crab would have its claws locked onto your skin, easily slicing its fine pincers through the thick layer of flesh. Honestly, it wasn't as bad as I thought, but the pressure — the PRESSURE — from the falling of fists really made it hard to tolerate. And once it entered my skin, damn.

I looked up out of pain and took a deep breath, tried to keep my composure and saw nothing but a sea of Corpsmen. I'd feel this discomfort ten more times.

"Congratulations, Cespedes," someone would say as they shook my hand after pounding their fist onto the frock, the pin piercing through the uniform right under my collarbone.

"Conte is up there celebratin' with us, ya know…" he said.

Augusto C. Cespedes, Jr.

I felt a heaviness in my face.

I didn't want to cry. I couldn't then.

But with each falling fist that made the pins sink deeper into my skin, the flashbacks kept coming back.

The loud sound of a fist. A clenched hand grinding the pin into my chest.

But I kept my eyes forward. With every bit of effort, I focused my attention on the red pillar of the BAS. The one that Conte would always lean on when he'd tell one of his clever jokes.

Another fist connected.

The day Conte and I had entered the base for the first time.

Another loud sound of a flying fist.

His face, gleaming like an innocent kid as we saw the room we were staying in, sadly thinking we'd be staying together.

Boom. Another one. And another one.

I didn't even care about the pain at this point. My present mind was so locked in on the memory of Conte that he almost gave me this numbness of endurance to take every one of them.

Then stood the last pair that would hit me, and at this point, I could feel a trickle on each side of my chest.

"Well, you definitely earned the new rank, Cespedes,"

Just Glow

Chief had said, who stood next to everyone that had already gone. "Better save that uniform." He laughed with crossed arms.

My mind had wandered somewhere else, but I had luckily come back to respond. "Roger that, Chief," I'd said out of instinct. I turned away and walked towards the tunnel of wind that had always seemed to sweep across the entrance of the BAS.

The words had flashed through my mind as quickly as the first fist that flew down onto my collar bone.

I wish you were here.

Chapter 13
The House on Little Cypress

In 1985, my dad bought our house for 37K at a closed auction. It was in foreclosure at the time.

Located on Little Cypress Lane in Cypress, TX an auction was held in Houston.

"They opened my envelope, and they liked my offer," my dad said.

"How ya wanna pay for it?" they asked.

"Cash," my dad said and bought it as is. He worked as an entry level electrician, having had his experience from the Navy.

The ceiling of the master bedroom and bathroom were heavily water stained. The pipe that ran above the ceiling had frozen and leaked.

"I didn't have money to fix it, so I learned how to do it myself."

Augusto C. Cespedes, Jr.

As a kid, I didn't know any better. I thought, "My dad's got it."

As the years went on, the house that was in shambles started to come together.

The yards were a complete mess, but my parents continuously worked on them every weekend while my sister played in the yard and when it was of season, we'd pick blackberries that were scattered behind our wooden fence. With plastic strainers in our hands, we'd try to see who could get the biggest berry.

"Careful, please!" my mom would yell from the flower bed.

The front yard was probably the main yard that was focused on and in their efforts, it became the talk of the neighborhood, always being nominated for Yard of the Month.

I'll never forget the uniqueness of the house.

The main entrance to the house was not a door but a large opening to a covered walkway that led to the front and kitchen door. And to get to the kitchen door, you had to walk over this wooden bridge that was surrounded with miscellaneous plants. The roof covering that was right over the bridge was made of worn-down sheets of fiberglass. Stained a yellow hue, when the sun was directly beating on it, gave this bright, yellow glow over the bridge.

As a kid, I absolutely loved the bridge. It always brought in small insects, amphibians and even an occasional garter snake, and I was simply fascinated.

Just Glow

I remember sitting out there, scanning the plants so closely just to find a frog or an anole that'd be puffing out its chest.

I would walk over the bridge multiple times just to feel the warmth of the sun, the softened feeling of the bridge's wood panels as I gently walked barefoot over it.

"Mom, do you feel like the bridge reminds you of the doctor's office?" I'd asked, looking directly up at the fiberglass.

"I think the doctor's office is a bit nicer," she would say, chuckling a bit as she swept around the concrete porch.

The doctor's office had the same concept, but yes, I have to admit, it was nicer.

Whenever we entered the medical building of my doctor's office, the first floor was covered with plants, mostly ones with vivid colors of green and walls of glass that reflected its colors even more. And I'd walk through the walkway to get to the stairs and slowly observe it like they were going to change.

"Keep your eyes on the stairs, Jay," my mom reminded me. She was afraid I was going to miss a step and fall.

Eventually, after many years, the bridge and the plants became an unfortunate eyesore, especially when it rained. The fiberglass had let in too much rainwater and practically flooded the porch and the bridge started to rot.

Augusto C. Cespedes, Jr.

"It's gotta go, Jay," my dad had broken the news to me, "it's not in good shape."

It didn't hold in the rainwater as it used to. The wooden panels of the bridge started to become so soft that the nails that held it together began to cause the wood to crumble around it.

I was heartbroken. Speechless. All of those moments were simply going to go away. But I knew it was time.

I knew that it was rotting, and I saw my dad on multiple occasions having to tend to it more because of the rain.

Once the finished porch was completed, it did take the grief away. The tiles were bright, shiny and I could easily see my mom enjoyed it too because she swept it daily. She hung various things on the walls and treated it like an outdoor living room.

"Better than the bridge?" she asked.

"It's very nice, Mom," I had said to her. I didn't lie, but I missed everything that the bridge and plants had offered.

There was life.

There was always something new to find. A bigger frog. An earthworm needing to find its way back into the softened soil. The anole who changed colors so quickly because they were frightened.

Even if the fiberglass was worn and gave the bridge a yellowish look, seeing the plants thrive was a magical thing to see.

Just Glow

The pre-deployment leave before Iraq was the last time I had seen our house on Little Cypress Lane.

"Doc, you've got mail!" someone yelled from across the room. It was January of 2007.

I was sitting on my rack, cleaning my rifle, and he said "8907...Houston? I thought you were from Cypress..."

I stopped rubbing the gun oil on the upper assembly of my M16 and said, "I am..."

I quickly got up and took the envelope from him.

It was an unfamiliar address.

A new address.

"Mom and Dad," it said written on the front.

It was news I didn't know how to take. Not like that.

Hi Jay,

Just sending a letter with pictures of our new house! It's not too far from our old house.

Miss and love you tons!

Love,

Mom and Dad

Augusto C. Cespedes, Jr.

As a kid watching the bridge I had loved to be torn down, it hit hard.

But this... this sunk deep.

"You okay, Doc? You haven't moved from that spot since I gave you the envelope." A Marine looked up from his stack of other envelopes for the others and stared at me.

I cleared my throat. "Yeah, ahem, I'm fine. Fine. Thanks."

The pictures she had sent were nice. Newly furnished rooms with carpets noticeably vacuumed just minutes before the picture had snapped. I had always admired my mom's meticulous way of vacuuming. Each line perfectly spaced out in the length of the vacuum; one shade lighter than the one next to it. And I noticed the new shiny tile floor that made its way to the dining and living room.

I slowly flipped through them with every effort to keep an open mind, but I couldn't help think of the old house and what it had been for me.

Our laundry room housed all our shoes in an overflowing shoe rack. Soccer cleats, summer shoes and river sandals that were stacked on one another. The piles of clothing on the floor that my mom always tried to maintain. The kitchen and its rickety, darkened wooden cabinets. The kitchen table that we had always done our homework on. I had remembered those moments when my dad made me drink all my milk before I left the table, leaving a ring at the top of the glass because I had spent close to an hour at the table just to finish it. The plastic runner that we'd always imagined was a safe place from the "lava" that started yards away in the living room that went into the hallways to the bedrooms.

The core flashbacks of my old house came into a hard focus. Like my mind had walked through a series of glass doors and every single room was of a different memory of the house on Little Cypress Lane. It was what I had longed for all this time, and to see pictures of a new home in a paper envelope was the weirdest feeling. It was confusing. Sad.

I left the pictures in the envelope and put them under the bowls of canned goods I had on the wooden shelf I had made and never opened them again.

Once we made our way back to Hawaii, it wasn't too much time in between until we were granted our post deployment leave.

"My parents are coming here," a Senior Marine would belt out, his hands behind his head as he lay on his bed. "We're living in paradise, baby!" No shirt on, freshly showered with just shower shoes and his green PT shorts, just grateful to be home.

"I'm goin' to North Carolina to see my old lady," someone would say, folding a few pairs of clothes and stacking them next to the duffel bag that was on his bed.

Ahh, home after deployment. It was the best feeling since sliced bread.

It was a weird, unexplainable feeling. For eight months, we did more than we could even imagine. Because whatever we did, it became a routine that we got used to. There was no room to overthink. You were there and you were there to survive.

Endless patrols. Putting ourselves out there on the streets, not knowing if we'd make it back to base. Thinking of home felt like a distant dream. There was always a constant feeling of needing to observe everything. Literally everything. Every open door. Every empty alleyway. Every window. Every crack in the road that wasn't there the day before.

But we never thought of it that way.

Walking into the new house, I immediately noticed the fresh smell of wood. The house echoed because of the endless tile that ran into the kitchen.

After that horrid experience in the room without curtains, I barely slept at night, so I'd stay up all through the night, my eyes fighting sleep until dawn.

Being away on deployment, especially not being around television and then finally coming back home, I found myself watching the shows I had watched before I left my home for the last time, movies I had missed from just being away. Like I was in a time warp or something. But finally, I was home.

Home for 30 days.

"Jay, have you seen this?" my dad would ask me. He pulled out a DVD case and showed me. It was the movie *DejaVu* with Denzel Washington.

I took it from him and said, "Oh, no I haven't." I felt like

Just Glow

I had seen it as a bootleg DVD being sold in a merchant bazaar, but I never saw it.

After being awake all night, I eventually made my way to my new bedroom.

I laid down on the comforter, a stiff, scratchy blanket that had just come out of the packaging.

I could feel how heavy my eyes were and I had no other choice but to close them.

"Hey, did you decide on what you're ordering?" he'd asked.

It was bright in the room like I had been in the movie theater for a few hours and then walking outside on a hot summer afternoon.

But my eyes adjusted quickly then they just suddenly opened.

He had an airy voice. It wasn't too deep, but I could tell it was a young man. He sounded so familiar. It was a comforting tone.

So familiar.

I found myself looking at a wooden table that had smears of what appeared to be sticky — probably honey — and small sprinkles of sugar. Light, soft music was playing over a loudspeaker.

Piano. Brush sticks on a snare. Light floating fingers on the ivory keys that seemed to softly glide just to make the note ring out.

I began to look up.

In the light, there he was.

Augusto C. Cespedes, Jr.

It was Danny.

"It's you," I'd said. I felt like I knew I was dreaming but I didn't seem to care. I was there and that was all that mattered.

"Well?" he asked.

The moment Danny died, there was an immediate void in my heart because he was gone in an instant. In the snap of a finger. The last conversation downstairs with him ran through my mind over and over, him standing at the window. And when he was taken out of the room, a silence like no other silence had taken over. Throughout all the different transitions — leaving Haqlaniyah for the last time, the arrival on the Hawaiian airfield, the flight back home, being in my new bedroom — I needed something, ANYTHING, from him. A sign. Anything to let me know he was there. And I hadn't.

Until this dream.

I felt nervous, but more comforted so I went along with it.

"Uhh...just a black coffee. Nothing fancy, you know that...Danny..." I said to him, making sure it was really him. As I sat across from him, I noticed he was much lighter. The sun seemed to beat down on him, giving a radiant light that placed a heavenly ring around his dark brown hair.

"Well," he had said, putting his hands together smiling, "I'm getting a Fra-..."

"Frappuccino," we both said. There was a slight pause and we both laughed.

It all clicked. It was him. It was really him.

Just Glow

"*How are you?*" *he asked, breaking the awkwardness.*

"*Haha, I'm okay now!*" *I said out of nervousness. I felt giddy. Shocked. I kept looking away and then back at him to make sure I was to stay in the dream.*
Stay there.
It was everything I had waited for. Everything I needed.

But I wasn't okay. I had lied. I missed him terribly and his abrupt death destroyed me. It destroyed all of us.

I knew he had passed away, so I didn't really know what to ask.

"*How…are you?*" *I felt my voice trail off.*

He sat back and crossed his arms, "I'm okay. Still in one piece, right?" Out of all things, he had said that. He was always so clever with his words. Quick comebacks that always made us laugh.

I couldn't help but keep looking at his face. How perfect and untouched it was. It forced me to replay his death in my head over and over again.

And it came to me. The black, peppered spots on his torso were the only injuries he had sustained.

Then the violent flashback.

"*No blood,*" *I remembered saying to myself, turning him over and feeling the gritty dirt and his cold, sweaty uniform.*

But at that moment, I could see that his face was untouched. Perfect.

Augusto C. Cespedes, Jr.

There were so many things I wanted to say to him. So many things to ask him.

"How is it up there?"

"Do you float around?"

"Do you see anyone you know?"

"Does it hurt?"

But time had quickly passed, and he had said those dreadful words I didn't want to hear.

"I've gotta get goin', Doc," he admitted.

"But it's only been a few minutes," I'd said. I could feel my eyes start to become heavy with tears but I forced myself to hold them in so I wouldn't waste my time with him.

"You know I've got things to do..." he started to say, "besides, gonna go see what my Mama's up to," he had said, smiling.

He started to stand up, and that's when I asked.

"Wait, wait..." I'd said, putting my hand out in an attempt to get his attention.

How can I get in contact with you?"

Still smiling, he looked back at me and in the position that he had stood caused the edge of the sun to hover behind him.

"Just glow."

Chapter 14
A Hui Hou

For the faintest second, I felt myself helplessly engulfed in a thick, heavy warp of darkness, like I had been dunked underwater and someone had quickly pulled me out.

"ARGHHH, ARGHHHH, ARGHHH!"

My back, severely arched, felt stiff as I gasped for air. I felt like I had held my breath in for several minutes.

"ARGHHH, ARGHHHH, ARGHHH!"

When I finally came to, I found myself in the bedroom. I caught my breath and remembered the heavy, thickened comforter that was laid out on my bed. Various nautical pieces hung over the spaces of the walls.

And it was again, silent.

I started to hear footsteps approaching the room and someone called out. It was my mom. "Jay, you okay?"

And just like that night, the night at the concert, that

unexplainable touch on my shoulder from someone who was nowhere to be found, I just said, "Yes."

From that moment on, I tried to understand it. Make sense of it, for I had never, ever, EVER heard that phrase in my life.

Just glow??

I tried to think of all of the conversations Danny and I'd ever had, and he never said anything even close to that. He spoke about his hometown, his friends, his Mama, Grandma Johnny or just a few light humored jokes but nothing about that.

And I felt like I couldn't talk to anyone about it either, as it could've been too "far out there" for people.

What did he mean when he said, "Just glow?"

On the plane ride back to Hawaii, I laid my head on the window and started to wonder.

I lost my friends in war and they were so young. The mere fact of it made my eyes heavy. That I was one of the ones that made it back.

I could feel my eyebrows scrunch and my head came off the cold window. *Is that what he meant?* I asked myself.

Did he mean for me to live my life out for them?
It was what felt right to me.

And so, I left it at that.

Just Glow

Over the years, that dream — that magical moment — I constantly thought about. From beginning to end. Its minute details I had never forgotten.

It was the last connection with Danny, and I felt like the more I had replayed it over and over in my head, the less likely I would ever forget it. So, I did. Any chance I could get, I did.

Imagining that burning sun around his head as he stood to look back at me.

His perfect, untouched face.

"Well, Doc? Did you decide on what you're ordering?"

"Close the door," Senior Chief had told HM1, as that familiar gust of wind that blew down the hall of the BAS passed by the office door. I found myself in Senior Chief's office, sitting in his discolored, light brown couch. I had sunk in it and ended up resting my arm on the armrest to almost hold myself up.

"Y'know, it's time to figure out where you're goin' for your next duty station," Senior Chief had said, simultaneously looking at the piece of paper in his right hand and the world map that was plastered on the wall behind his desk. It had various colors of tacks pierced in different areas.

"Any place you had your eye on?" HM1 had blurted out. He spun himself slowly in his desk chair, now facing towards me.

Senior Chief started to study the piece of paper in his hand a little more and sounded off.

Augusto C. Cespedes, Jr.

"Fargo, Scandinavia, Florida, Pennsylvania, California, you can even go to Pearl Harbor…"

I then began to look at the world map. Its edges were frayed and worn like it had been moved several places and holes were easily visible, some bigger than others.

I placed my finger on my chin and said "Well, I've never been to the Northeast. What about New Jersey?"

HM1 spit out whatever he was drinking in a thermos, likely hours old coffee that had gone cold.

"NEW JERSEY?" he'd said as he started to wipe off what he spit his drink on.

"You know what they say about New Jersey, right, Cespedes?"

Nothing came to mind because I knew nothing about any of those states.

"It's the asshole of New York!" They both said, looking at each other and laughing.

I'd noticed my thumb and index finger had gone numb, so I immediately let go of the picture and like a feather drifting to the ground, had fallen to the carpet.

"Jay, please let me know what you want. Gonna clean this out soon, okay?"

"Yea, Mom. No problem," I said, picking up the photograph.

Pre-Deployment leave was such a bittersweet thing. And

Just Glow

only a deploying serviceman would truly understand it. Time with your family was pure bliss but damn it, when the days came to an end, it hurt like absolute hell.

Since my family was in Houston at the time, I always perceived the flight back to Hawaii as my time to reflect. To be whatever-sissy-baby-emotional-wreck I wanted to be but only in silence. I had six hours of feeling the cold atmospheric pressure of the window and the smell of a person's cheap cologne next to me, so I had no other choice but to think. I almost looked at the flight back to the island as a way to put my mind into the mode I needed to be for my job.

The "survival, savage, war, get-it-done" mode.

I took those six hours to leave all my emotions behind and understand that I possibly wouldn't be back. And over and over I ran it through my head until it stuck.

At just 20 years old, it was like I had made peace with myself staring at a foldable table.

I leaned against the barracks wall and watched a few Marines huddling outside of their room. Matt was standing in the field with his mom. The mountains that towered over the H3 highway had a mist over them. I had always admired the mountains that overlooked Kaneohe Bay, its shadows blanketed and careened on the slopes of greens and yellows.

"You take care of y-..."

"Yourself, I know, Mom. I always do," Matt said, smiling as he

finished his mom's sentence. She had her hand on his shoulder and moved it up and down like she was wiping something away.

And that was when it became silent. I found myself looking down but after I didn't hear anything, I looked up and could see they were both just staring at each other.

"I don't want you to go," she said. Her voice sounded shaky, trembling, like she was trying to stay strong for the words to come out clearly for him.

He stood tall, his face appeared stern and said to her, "I don't want to go either but I have to go for- ..."

"Your guys, I know," she said. They both looked at each other with forced smiles. I could hear what she had said and couldn't help but smile because Matt loved his guys.

Since day one, he became one of them.

He leaned into his mom, kissed her forehead, and wrapped his arms around her.

"God, the mountains never looked so amazing."

After a few moments, he looked at her and kissed her cheek.

"Last kiss, Matt," she began to say.

I forced myself to look at the ground so I wouldn't choke up on their interaction.

"Ya," he said, "Last kiss."

I turned away to look at a few 'hop only' birds that stood under the

Just Glow

shade of one of the trees. And the moment that I had looked in the direction of where Matt was with his mom, I saw Matt standing there, alone.

I could only give out a deep sigh and began to walk over to him.

I placed my hand on his shoulder as we both looked out at the greens and yellows of the mountainside.

"You okay, buddy?"

"I always feel like there are never enough times you can say I love you to your mom, ya know?"

I understood what he meant, so I nodded. I was in the "survival, savagery, war, get-it-done" mode at that point, but I still understood. I swallowed hard, hearing and feeling every muscle that it took to get my saliva down into my esophagus.

I could hear his voice cracking, but he continued, "Like you say it, and the moment you say it, you have to say it again because the one you just said wasn't enough. And it just repeats itself."

I thought of myself on the plane, alone. Staring at the folded tray table.

How I had so many things I wish I had done during my time on leave. Making amends. Seeing places in my hometown that I once enjoyed as a kid. Telling people I was sorry for the things that I had done or said.

"There's never enough time, Bro," I said.

"I just wish I could give my mom something to know that I'd be okay."

Augusto C. Cespedes, Jr.

The moment came into my mind, the one where he said "last kiss" to his Mama, and it caused a deep, lasting tone in my ear, like the old church bell over a small town on an early Sunday morning. Deep. Low. Echoing and rippling through the streets.

"Right?" he asked.

I faced towards the closet and stared into what was in it.

Everything was in there. A complete standstill. A comforting feeling knowing it wasn't going anywhere.

At one point, I'd thought, "if I'd just throw this in there," whether it was anything pertaining to the military, high school, or my past relationships, that it wouldn't go anywhere.

It would just stay in the closet.

And I had kept all of my keepsakes in the closet. The silly little love notes from high school, the journals from photography class that were filled with random quotes that I had loved from the songs we all sang. I locked it in the closet.

Close the door. Walk away. For YEARS.

To me, it was comforting to know that my most memorable things were just behind that door. My closet. It was a simple wooden door that separated me from it all but it worked. And what hung on a white plastic hanger was Matt's med pack.

Just Glow

"*Cespedes!*" *A shout from the belly.*

Anyone who called out your name like that and you didn't immediately recognize their voice, your head turned to acknowledge them. Didn't matter what you're doing.

"Please report to my office after your company's formation," HM1 ordered, his voice now quieter after he'd seen me look him into his eyes.

"Should I be worried?" I asked.

He just laughed and said, "After formation, Cespedes."

When we were dismissed, I ran back to the BAS, curious and a bit nervous as to what he was going to tell me.

I closed the door behind me with my hands at my back still holding onto the doorknob.

"Nothing to worry about, I promise," HM1 started to say as he knew I wanted to get right down to the reason.

There laid on his desk was a black medical pack, one that was strapped to the upper leg. High speed, incredible material quality and could carry a good amount of supplies.

He lifted it up.

"It was Conte's," he began to say. "We know you guys were close, so…" he moved his hand towards me, "We thought you should have it."

I was speechless. The thought of Conte never coming back crushed me. I'd never hear his "Heeeeyyyy buddyyyy!!!" or his contagious laugh ever again. Or how his eyes bulged out when he got excited over the smallest, most random things. His unique, comedic facial expressions, even in the worst of situations.

There was a sudden, dark curtain that drew itself around me and I could only see the med pack. I focused so heavily on it.

Weathered.

Worn.

I could easily see that it's been through the wringer. Its different swirls of dust had layered the fabric.

"I ...don't know what to say...," I admitted.

"He would want you to have it," HM1 said.

On the plane ride to New Jersey, I'd have a conversation with myself and speak out like I was talking to them. It was comforting.

Gonna live out my life for you.

Going to experience this life for you.

And it would only give me encouragement to keep going. Whatever I was doing.

There was nothing — I mean NOTHING — that meant more to me than to experience life for them.

It crushed my heart to know they died so young.

Just Glow

Nineteen years young. Heath and Danny.

Matt, not much older, at 22.

And the more that I thought about that, the more I grew angry.

They didn't even get to legally have a beer.

They'll never see another holiday again. Never will be able to raise a family.

But me....ME. I was given another chance to live.

I turned the knob of the door, pulled it towards me and found myself staring at Matt's med pack. The same tattered, dusty med pack that was given to me in the office.

Something…anything… echoed in my head.

Something.

Anything.

The echo of Matt's voice.

And for the very first time, I grabbed the med pack.

Chapter 15
In Reverie

I sat in the front seat of my car and mindlessly watched the wiper blades wave in succession on the windshield. And like little mice, squeaked from the lack of raindrops that touched the glass.

The clock on the dashboard glowed 1907.

I couldn't believe I was actually doing it.

Meeting her.

The last time I had seen Conte's mom was when I stood at the barracks wall.

"Last kiss, Ma," echoed in my head.

My phone lit up saying 'New Message' that splashed on the screen. I touched it and saw that it was her.

"Are you here?" it said.

My thumbs started to move to type.

Augusto C. Cespedes, Jr.

"Yes, I'm in my car."

I looked at the passenger seat, and it was surreal to me. All of it.

The flight to Hawaii.

Afghanistan, the elevation and its unforgiving heat.

Iraq. The patrols. The boys that didn't get to come back.

The blast.

The dream. And now this.

Matt's med pack laid on the seat cushion with its straps nestled neatly under itself.

I got out of my car and started to walk, placing the med pack in my left arm, cradling it.

Several people had walked out of the hotel entrance and my eyes scanned for her.

I remembered she had glasses, a little shorter than me and a smile like Matt's.

But it was then when she walked out of the building that I felt myself holding my breath, almost letting go of Matt's med pack.

My memory of the mountains that overlooked Kaneohe rushed itself into clear view. And even in the bustling of the

Just Glow

city's streets, I felt a familiar gust of wind that smacked my face.

But I still took a step forward.

"That was you!?" Conte's voice rang in my head, *"I was outside of my room in my boxers!"*

But the memory started to fade.

I took a few more steps.

"Mom," he'd said with the biggest smile on his face, *"this is incredible! They put us in the nice barracks!"* The sound of his voice went in and out like a frequency of a radio wave, but I felt the pure joy in his voice. It then quickly faded, his voice trailing off like a slow, passing train.

And a few more.

But I could only feel my face hold back. I swallowed hard, hearing a strong, vibrating wave rattle the canals of my ears.

Then it stopped.

"We'll be okay, Doc," Heath said, looking straight at me with the straw still at his mouth.

Then it just kept happening. Fast forwarding.

"No blood no wounds, no blood no wounds."

Then Danny's face. His eyes rolled in the back of his head as I held him one last time.

Augusto C. Cespedes, Jr.

"You're okay, Buddy…you're okay…" I had said, trying to stay calm. I could feel my ears were still ringing.

"Doc! Doc! What do we do?!!"

"Nothing," I remember saying, "there's nothing we can do."

I kept walking, keeping my face straight.

The grips of the straps felt indented into my arm.

I stopped focusing on the cracks of the sidewalk and our eyes met in unison.

I felt myself slightly squint and I could see Matt's eyes in her stare. The expression that he had made when he had to be serious.

"You both are being separated today, ya hear me?! Better get used to it!" Chief dragged us both by our collars over the lawn that led to the BAS. It was the moment I glanced over to him as he kept his eyes forward that I could see that he wasn't smiling.

"Hi," we both said. I wanted to laugh a bit but I just couldn't.

I instinctively lifted the med pack and raised it to be in between us.

"You have no idea how much this means to me," she started to say. Her eyes became heavy and started to glisten.

"Thank you," she said.

Just Glow

It felt like the longest pause as we just stood there.

I didn't say anything. I felt like I didn't have to say anything.

But I touched her hand and smiled.

I lifted my eyes from staring at my dust painted boots.

He took his eyes off of the window, their shade of baby blue now in my direction.

"You and me."

In that very moment in time, I felt an emotion that I couldn't express. Words I couldn't spill out from my mouth but unforgivingly, the memories of it all devoured me like a rogue wave.

Sitting with Heath on that worn out booth seat at the restaurant for the last time, gladly listening to his innocent slurping of cola through a straw.

Watching Conte from the passenger seat as he drove his car with that contagious smile he always had, trying so hard to catch a glimpse of the waterfalls that towered over the H3 while it rained.

An overwhelming feeling of the saddest joy finally waved its hand over me.

I knew.

Chapter 16
Knowing

"You knew…?" they asked.

Something had cut through the dead of silence.

Her voice was soft. A woman. Gentle. Not too stern but one I could listen to.

I instantly felt the cold, hard, plastic chair press against my thighs that made my feet numb. My eyes seemed to roll forward to the sound of a pen scratching paper.

"You're doing pretty well," she said, glancing at her watch, "going on almost two hours now."

I could only stare blankly at the poorly grouted floor. My mouth felt dry, parched, like I'd been talking nonstop.

"I am?" I asked. It didn't seem like it was a long time, but I felt relieved, as if I had gotten something heavy off my chest.

Augusto C. Cespedes, Jr.

"I've learned so much about you," she started to say, "why you joined the Navy and all that you've been through. I cannot even begin to imagine what you're feeling, but I want you to know that I am so proud of you for sharing so much."

I was so hesitant in speaking to someone I didn't know, let alone even sitting in the same room.

I slowly brought my eyes up and remembered the metallic name plate that sat at the edge of the desk in front of me.

THERAPIST.

I didn't feel fear or an uneasiness. It wasn't awkward. In fact, I didn't want to run out of the room. I felt as if the more I closed my eyes, I only wanted to talk more.

"So, tell me," she started to say, "what are your plans on moving forward from this?"

From where I was sitting, I could see through the window that there were only a few minutes of sun before dusk.

And I noticed it.

It was a bright, pink sky with clouds that looked like they were spread across a painted canvas.

The most colorful one I had seen in a very long time.

I must have been the last one for the day. I had to have been.

Just Glow

I turned my eyes towards her and asked, "When can I come back?"

Epilogue

I must have said it a thousand times.

Could've been the perfect squad picture.

I would stare so hard at the photo and look at our faces like they were somehow going to change.

But no. Still blurry.

Still the same as all of the other times.

And over and over again, when I told myself that you weren't there, that you were the one who took the picture, the guilt of surviving the blast consumed me.

Danny, you stood right in front of me.

...How things would've been different if you just stepped away.

But it was a day when we spent an evening on the beach that I realized it.

Augusto C. Cespedes, Jr.

It was when the sun lowered itself onto the horizon, casting an unforgettable glow.

A glow that only a clear, cloudless sky could bring.

Radiant but soft colors that blended so perfectly that I just couldn't take my eyes off of.

And there it was. The moon.

It shimmered alone in the distance.

A tiny, beautiful pearl that was to carry the glow into the long hours of the night.

You took the picture.

You stood there. All alone in the courtyard.

You aligned the camera.

You captured the moment that would last forever.

We will always see ourselves through your eyes.

I felt this powerful wave of emotion sweep over me as I took it all in.

Just Glow

Augusto C. Cespedes, Jr.

PVT Heath D. Warner, KIA 11.22.2006

Just Glow

HN (FMF) Matthew G. Conte, KIA 2.01.2007

Augusto C. Cespedes, Jr.

LCPL Daniel T. Morris, KIA 2.14.2007

Just Glow

Danny's Silhouette, Iraq 2006

Acknowledgments

I would like to express my deepest gratitude to all who have supported me throughout the writing of this memoir.

To my wife and best friend Lindsay who has been there for me and believed in me from the very beginning. I love you with all of me (times infinity).

To my beautiful daughters, you motivate me every day to become a better man and father. I cannot wait for you to read this when you both are older.

To Mom and Dad, who worked and loved hard to give Steph and I an incredible life with the childhood memories I'll never forget. I can't thank you enough.

To my NJ parents, thank you for taking me in from Day One as the "6th Plate." I will never forget the kindness and love you showed from the beginning when meeting your daughter. Even to this day.

Thank you to the parents, family and friends of Heath, Matt and Danny for not only sharing your deepest emotions and memories with me through the years but your friendship that I will always cherish.

Thank you to the ones who I met at the start of this journey. The ones who've spoken out about their unforgettable memories, fears and unending love for the ones they've lost. Your stories helped me shape the memoir in ways I never thought possible. You all know who you are.

Thank you to Apara, Lisa and Gary who saw the potential in me and my writing. I will always cherish your inspiring words, support, kindness and friendship.

Heath, Matt and Danny, thank you for your friendship and undying spirit in my life. I truly felt your personalities in every word that I wrote and every time I saw the time 8:08. Although they were some of, if not, the hardest times of my life, they will always be the best ones because they were with you.

Lastly, I want to thank God for not only giving me the ability to write but also to remember.

www.ingramcontent.com/pod-product-compliance
Lightning Source LLC
Chambersburg PA
CBHW051534230426
43669CB00015B/2591